STUDIES IN FRENCH LITERATURE

XX

ROMAIN ROLLAND
ONE AGAINST ALL

A biography

by

WILLIAM THOMAS STARR

Northwestern University

1971

MOUTON

THE HAGUE · PARIS

LIBRARY OF CONGRESS CATALOG CARD NUMBER: 71-134548

Printed in The Netherlands by Mouton & Co., Printers, The Hague.

To

Larry and Jeff

and

my Wife.

*Without her encouragement, assistance, and intuition
this book would never have been written.*

FOREWORD

This biography is meant to be the portrait of a man and a writer as seen in his writings, in his correspondence, and the observations of others. We have frequently allowed Romain Rolland to speak for himself, having taken only the liberty of putting the texts into English. However, heeding Rolland's warning, we have not hesitated to correct the author's vision, or his perspective as he has portrayed himself in his letters; at such times we have had recourse to his works of fiction, his plays and novels, where, he assured his reader, any author unwittingly discloses his true self, since he is not then writing for some one particular person whose sensitivities and quirks must be partially spared.

Since his life and writings are so inextricably intertwined, we have not separated them. While moving in a roughly chronological sequence we have, as a glance at the table of contents will show, picked out what we feel to be the guiding lines, attitudes, problems or activities of the various periods of his life. In some cases, notably the chapters on his interest in the Orient and on his religion, this method has necessitated some departure from a strict chronological approach, for these interests and attitudes extend over long periods of his life, beginning in his youth. In general the movement is from the roots or the beginning, to the end of his life. But Rolland's life, like a tree, bears large branches which extend from the main trunk, each of which must be explored before one proceeds to the top.

Finally, as Rolland pointed out in a letter to a friend, one generally reads a book not to find out what is in it but to find oneself in it. Applying the converse one may perhaps say that one writes books not merely for the subject ostensibly treated but in order to find oneself; thus, Rolland; thus, the writer of the present biography; thus, the reader.

I wish to acknowledge with deep gratitude the various sources of help and inspiration upon which I drew in writing this biography. I am especially indebted to Mme. Marie Romain Rolland, who has so generously placed Rolland's correspondence and papers at the disposition of scholars and students; to Professor Emeritus Don L. Demorest of the Ohio State University for his critical reading of the manuscript and his invaluable criticisms and suggestions; to the Northwestern University Graduate School for travel and research funds which made it possible for me to consult Rolland's papers, correspondence, and unpublished writings; and finally, to my wife and to my colleagues of the Department of Romance Languages of Northwestern University, who have, wittingly or unwittingly, given me the encouragement — and time — necessary to complete the undertaking.

CONTENTS

I

A LONELY YOUTH (1866-1886)

Romain Edme Paul Emile Rolland — future writer, musicologist and pamphleteer more familiarly known as Romain Rolland — was born in a prosperous, middle-class, small-town family, on January 29, 1866, in a quiet house overlooking the Canal du Nivernais, in Clamecy, on the Yonne River.

Clamecy, set amidst the forested hills of western Burgundy, some one hundred kilometers west of Dijon and the Cote d'or wine district, is now a rather quiet town, but from there in the sixteenth century the first lumber and firewood rafts were floated to Paris on the Yonne and Seine rivers. Until faster modes of transportation and changes in fuel and building materials put an end to this trade, it was a thriving provincial city. One of Rolland's forebears was among the first to begin the profitable business. Rolland described the atmosphere of Clamecy as it was in his childhood: "A house on the bank of a canal. The silence of slow, empty days... The odor of a Venetian lagoon... A thin sickly child living alone without comrades, dreams and looks forward to life."[1] The quiet, tranquil, almost stagnant atmosphere of the provincial town; the omnipresence of a river — the Rhine, the Seine or another — penetrate most of Rolland's creative works. It is particularly important in *Jean-Christophe,* and is revealed again in the name of the heroine of *L'Ame enchantée,* Annette Rivière.

The temperament bequeathed to this 'thin, sickly child', lonely and dreaming, was a mixed one; the family, with some exceptions, was not such as to lead one to expect a descendant of the character

---

[1] "Music and Life", translated by Dr. Kalidas Nag in *Visva Bharata Quarterly,* III (April, 1925), 64-66.

of Rolland to appear. His father's family were hearty people who enjoyed life to the full; they were practical men, generally connected with the law. Emile Rolland, his father, died at the age of ninety-five, having kept the joy of life until the very end. He had never lost the warmth of his voice, the laughter in his blue eyes, his ceaseless activity, his affection for others, for his neighbors, for the German-speaking Swiss among whom he spent most of his summers in later years — although he stubbornly refused to learn a word of German (*Beckenried* he pronounced 'Bec-Henri'). The son seems to have taken after his mother and her family. Although the Courot family also knew how to enjoy and to love life, their attitude was serious and they were never able to forget the frail, transient nature of human kind. Strongly influenced by Jansenism and its severe demands on the individual conscience, they were more given to introspection than the Rollands.

As a boy, Romain went to school in the 'collège' at Clamecy, in the 'classe de rhétorique', from 1873 to 1880. The 'collège', like his home, became a sort of prison, another of the protecting but sometimes stifling shelters from which he vaguely yearned for escape. He found it to some extent in Jules Verne, Gustave Aimard, and in Corneille's theater (*Compagnons de Route* [Paris, 1961], p. 60), as well as in his own first youthful attempts at creative writing — a tragedy : "Les Noces d'Attila", some novels, in which he probably imitated his favorite authors : "Le capitaine Hermont" (1877), "Histoire d'un voyage à l'Ile du Volcan" (1878), "Les Aventuriers de la Floride" (1879). These attempts, however, were unsatisfactory; thus after 1882, at the age of twenty, he turned to his "Journal".

The death of Romain's younger sister during the summer of 1871, after part of the season had been spent at the seashore in a vain attempt to restore her health, left a lasting impression on the five-year-old boy (*Le Voyage intérieur* [Paris, 1942], pp. 25-27). His mother grieved over the loss of the three-year-old child until the end of her life (letter of Romain Rolland to Paul Seippel, June 28, 1919), and seems to have allowed the tragedy to color her relationships with her son, whom she surrounded with a stifling physical and emotional solicitude.

His mother's position in the family was the dominant one. Rolland speaks almost solely of his mother when telling of the important influences on his childhood. Not until he was past middle-age does he speak of his father, nor could he properly appreciate him before that time. One of the few times he mentions his father is in a letter to his mother, dated September, and written between 1886 and 1889; he tells of a long walk the two of them took together not far from Montreux. Rolland's attitude appears to be reflected in his writings, in which fathers generally play a secondary rôle. Christophe's father in the novel *Jean-Christophe* died when the child was about twelve. Aërt, in the play of that name, was an orphan. In *L'Ame enchantée,* Marc Rivière's father plays only the part of the fecundating male, and is repudiated first by his wife, Annette, and then by Marc.

A frail and sensitive child, Rolland suffered greatly throughout his childhood from a rather morbid fear of death. His own hostilities and the sudden disappearance of his sister must have opened the way for such a preoccupation, which filled his days and nights with dread, especially during his frequent illnesses (see *Le Voyage intérieur,* p. 19). He later wrote about his fear to Sofia Bertolini Guerrieri-Gonzaga (Sept. 20, 1901) (*Chère Sofia. Choix de lettres de Romain Rolland à Sofia Bertolini Guerrieri-Gonzaga.* [Paris, 1959], I, p. 25-26). "J'étais souffrant; je me sentais constamment — jusqu'à onze ou douze ans comme maintenu par un fil au-dessus de la mort; et je n'ai jamais perdu tout à fait ce sentiment..." The fear was intensified by his tendency to dream — dreams of terror and anguish, dreams of tenderness and hope, and, very early, dreams of glory, heroism, and literary fame (*Souvenirs de jeunesse* [Paris-Lausanne-Bâle, 1947], p. 11). Such dreams represent fantasizing which may result, when motivitation is lacking and the emotions remain unchanneled, in non-creative inactivity. In Rolland they seem to have resulted in creative activity, though at the expense of reality. Some of these fears and dreams he later embodied in Christophe (*Jean-Christophe* [Paris, 1950]). In these years of physical weakness and dread it was music, in his opinion, which helped him through his terrors.[2]

[2] See his account in a letter to Anna Maria Curtius, published in German

Undoubtedly music substituted another area of fantasy for the childish imaginings and dreams of death and glory.

His physical weakness, besides the possible inherited tendency, was due, Rolland thought, to the negligence of a servant who left him as a year-old baby exposed too long to the cold of a winter day (*Le Voyage intérieur*, p. 18). He was in fact plagued throughout his life by a weakness of the bronchial passages. He was constantly threatened with tuberculosis, and suffered more than one period of active infection. Robert Kemp, who studied under Rolland, has left an interesting description of him (*Les Nouvelles littéraires*, Feb. 22, 1951).

Je reverrai, à jamais imprimé dans ma mémoire, le maître d'histoire de la musique, en Sorbonne, qui exerçait sur mes contemporains et moi son charme maladif. Nous nous inquiétions de cette maigreur, accentuée par une redingote à l'ancienne mode, de cette voix râpeuse et de ce souffle court qui nous trompaient sur la durée de sa vie, et quand on l'approchait, de cette haleine glacée qui nous envoyait à la fois l'odeur de pomme mûre des diabétiques et celle de l'amande amère; de cette toux sèche qui coupait ses tentatives de rire, de ce front trop pâle, et des mains trop rouges qui se promenaient comme des crabes cuits sur le clavier.

The cough may well have an emotional basis as well as a more purely physical one. All of Rolland's creations strangle when they laugh — as is the case with Christophe and Schultz; Schultz it is true is old, but Christophe when he visited the old man was in his prime as a young robust person. Physical or psychical as the reasons may have been, Rolland found life uncertain, both when a young man and even in his early youth. One of the compulsions that shaped his efforts was the desire to finish a piece of work before death should overtake him.

---

translation, "Romain Rolland und die deutsche Musik", *Neue Zeitschrift für Musik*, XV (1926), 13-15; the original French text is in *Souvenirs d'enfance* (Paris, Delayance, 1927), and is difficult to find. For evaluations of Rolland's work in music, musical history and musical criticism see the following: J.W. Klein, in *Music and Letters*, XXV (January, 1944), 13-22, and J.W. Klein, in *Musical Opinion*, LXVII (July-August, 1944), 313, 346-347; H.W. Beckwith, "The Formation of the Esthetic of Romain Rolland" (Doctoral Dissertation, New York University, 1936); Alain, in *Europe*, X (1926), pp. 272-278.

In spite of physical and emotional handicaps, Rolland finished his studies at the 'collège' of Clamecy in the normal time. The family then decided that the youth needed the greater educational opportunities of Paris. But his mother would not permit him to go alone. The whole family, even his grandfather, had to move to the city, at a considerable sacrifice. From a relatively prominent and respected position in Clamecy and the surrounding region, they entered an obscure situation in the great city. His father, who had in Clamecy a privileged position in municipal affairs and the most prosperous law office in the district, sold his practice and accepted a subaltern post in the Crédit foncier bank in Paris. Both father and grandfather, accustomed to the easy-going life and open spaces of a small town, accepted the cramped confines of a city apartment, at the unreasonable demand of Mme Rolland, ostensibly for the sake of keeping the family intact. It was also Mme Rolland's insistence that kept Romain persevering in his studies for a career not of his choice and not to his liking.

In the fall of 1880 he entered the Lycée St.-Louis as a boarding student. He wrote frequently to his mother in spite of the Thursday and Sunday holidays which he spent at home. On January 1, 1882, he wrote that he had placed third in physics in the examinations of the preceding month. The following November, 1882, he entered the Lycée Louis-le-Grand as a day student in 'rhétorique', to prepare for the competitive examination for entrance to the Ecole normale.[3]

This period of his life was one of the most difficult of all for him. The city and its masses stifled him; the proximity of so many people was repugnant to him. The crowds, the indifference and seeming immorality of city dwellers, the noise, the brutality of city life (different from the brutality of country or small-town life) oppressed him and filled him with fear, dread, and anguish. Accustomed to the pleasant countryside (in which he was inclined to discover the reflections of his own emotions), he was denied this relief in Paris. Scarcely a day passed without his sighing for the Burgundian countryside (letter to Malwida von Meysenbug,

---

[3] See Jean Bonnerot, *Romain Rolland, sa vie, son œuvre* (Paris, 1921), p. 12.

Feb. 26, 1894, in *Choix de lettres à Malwida von Meysenbug* [Paris, 1948], p. 111).

Rolland transcribed many of his experiences of these years in his description of Christophe's arrival and first months in Paris. The world that Christophe (and Rolland) had been taught to believe in apparently did not exist in the metropolis. The resulting crisis in his inflexible adolescent soul was great, and the religious and moral shocks experienced by Christophe — and by Rolland who was equally uncompromising — reflect Rolland's first years in Paris (letter to Stefan Zweig, Jan. 10, 1920). Rolland came, in fact, very near to suicide because of the anguish which filled his soul. In *Le Voyage intérieur* (pp. 129-130) he says that he had inhaled the vapors of the abyss between 1881 and 1883. The result was a temptation to self-destruction, as he bent over the handrail of the sixth-floor apartment, no. 31, rue Monge. Among the causes, besides the sudden and complete change in his way of living, were undoubtedly the usual difficulties of adolescence, greater perhaps in the case of an intelligent, sensitive, and lonely boy, dreamy and self-centered. Rolland thirty years later called it an inorganic period when everything crumbles and nothing is created, when doubt is rampant and aspiration everywhere, when the soul, overwhelmed by dream and desire ('le rêve et la sève'), is open to chance or to Fate.[4] At the same time he was led to doubt of his religion.

Although reared in a Roman Catholic family — his father however a non-believer — Rolland began in Paris to feel his faith slipping. In the light of later years, he felt that he had never really believed in God, even before Paris, but the religious nature of his personality has always been strong. The atmosphere of the Paris of his day was one of religious nihilism, and because it destroyed his faith it almost destroyed the young man (*Le Voyage intérieur,* p. 129). His doubt was soon followed by a rupture with formal Catholicism. The break caused his mother considerable grief, and even offended his father, who thought that religion was

[4] "Shakespeare", *Compagnons de route* (Paris, 1936), pp. 25-34; first published in German translation, "Dem genius Shakespeares. Autobiographische Erinnerungen", *Genius,* I (1921), 101-106.

desirable and perhaps necessary for children. But the young man was too sincere and too aggressive not to make an open break, although it caused pain to himself and to others, especially his mother.

Music was again his solace, the strength and the means for living through this and other periods; it was also a bond that united the mother and the son (*Le Voyage intérieur,* p. 133). It was then, he said, that Beethoven came to take him by the hand. He was a child (in his own words) of fifteen or sixteen years of age, without a friend or guide, in the midst of the city crowds. Beethoven was the air he needed, the Nature he missed, and the window opening onto infinite space, the contact between himself and Existence.[5] His musical experiences in 1883 were profound, and closely associated with the religious crisis of those years. He had gorged himself on Berlioz, Beethoven, and Wagner during the years 1882 to 1884. His account of how he heard Wagnerian fragments in the Pasdeloup concerts is remarkably similar to Christophe's experiences in the Paris concert halls. Wagner rapidly became the center of the musical experience of Rolland, whose stubborn will and youthful idealism caused him to fight against the prevailing spiritual and moral apathy and indifference of the metropolis.[6] Music is, however, an art that can encourage isolation or partial, even complete, withdrawal. It is significant that this art was so important in Rolland's formative years and remained so throughout his life.

In these years, an experience that was to bear its full fruits only later, although its immediate effect was intense, was his first trip to the mountains. In 1882 he spent some time with his mother and his sister, at Allevard, near Grenoble. In September, at the end of their stay, Mme Rolland took them to Lausanne. It was the first time Rolland had crossed the French border. His first contact with the Alps, at the age of sixteen, secretly shook and exalted him (*Le Voyage intérieur,* p. 35), although because of his

---

[5] Rolland, *Beethoven: Les Grandes époques créatrices,* IV: *La Cathédrale interrompue,* 1: *La Neuvième symphonie* (Paris, 1943), p. 18.
[6] For these accounts, see *Souvenirs de Jeunesse* (Lausanne, 1947), pp. 17-18; "Carnets de Romain Rolland (1886-1889)", *La Nef,* III (January 1946), 3-23.

inexperience he was unable to decipher the emotions within him.
Along with music, mountains were the most profound and powerful revelation of his youth. There were moments, he admitted,
when he not only loved mountains but became the mountain.
Writing much later about the emotions aroused in him by the
Alps, he described in very erotic terms the revelation that also
came to him as he stood on the terrace at Voltaire's Ferney, near
Lake Geneva: "Why did the revelation come to me here, and not
elsewhere ? I do not know. But it was a veil which was rent
asunder. The spirit, violated virgin opening in an embrace, felt
the male rapture of nature rush in. And for the first time, the
spirit conceived" (*Le Voyage intérieur,* p. 31). In notes written
at the time, he expressed the same emotion. "Je défaille sous
l'étreinte [des montagnes]... Si j'avais été seul, je me serais jeté
par terre, j'aurais mordu les pierres... J'étais possédé par la nature,
comme une femme violée...". (*Souvenirs de jeunesse* [Lausanne,
1947], "Notes de journal de 1889", p. 14 (dated September, 1889)).
The terms are not merely erotic; they reveal certain less prominent
aspects of Rolland's character. It is noteworthy that he thinks of
himself — or feels himself — in a female rôle : his spirit is the
violated virgin; he becomes possessed by a nature that is male.
Although doubtless in part the uncertainty of adolescence, this
view of himself was to remain as part of his temperament. In his
Mémoires (Paris, 1956; "Introduction", 1939), he refers to himself as 'l'araignée', in the midst of its web, and as 'l'arachne',
lurking by the remnants of its web. The spider, in or out of a web,
is a frequent female symbol.

In spite of the crises of adolescence and his unsocial temperament, Rolland did participate in some of the important events of
his day. In 1882 he attended Gambetta's funeral.[7] On May 15,
1884, he was present at a festival in the Trocadéro, where Saint-
Saëns directed the première presentation of his "Hymne à Victor
Hugo". Hugo himself came to the concert, and Rolland took part
in the ovation accorded to the poet (*Mémoires* [Paris, 1956],

[7] "Journal inédit de Romain Rolland", *Revue de Paris,* June, 1950, pp. 12-18.
Gambetta was an ardent Republican, member of the 'Défense nationale'
government during the Franco-Prussian War, 1870-1871.

p. 161), whose funeral ceremonies Rolland attended the following year; Hugo's death, he noted, left a gap in his gallery of living French writers.[8] He was deeply impressed by the Hugo who sang of the French Revolution and of the barricades of 1830, the author of *Quatre-vingt-treize,* which Rolland saw on the stage in 1882. To this play, and to Hugo, he attributed the idea of his own later dramas of the Revolution (*Compagnons de route,* p. 176). Perhaps his greatest interest during these years, however, was Shakespeare. He kept a collection of notes about Hamlet that he called the best and most intense of his youthful writings (*Ibid.,* p. 181). What few of these notes have been published (*Souvenirs de jeunesse,* pp. 20 ff, and *Mémoires,* pp. 29-31) reveal an interesting and lesser known aspect of Rolland's character — an intense desire to act. His need for action arose from a semi-voluntary reaction to his spiritual and moral conditions, to his own tastes, and to his physical condition. He gave the name of Napoleon to Fortinbras, who appeared just in time to pick up the falling crown. Hamlet, he wrote, charged Horatio to give Fortinbras his dying voice, and Shakespeare handed over to the man of action the succession, rights, and powers, of the man of thought who had never been able or willing to exercise these rights and powers. Fruitless speculation led Hamlet to annihilation after a life of melancholia and disgust. "The sole man worthy of the name is the one who acts", Rolland wrote. His conclusion is that the fatalist, who fails to act, is a sick man; Hamlet is sick, and "I am ill". It is immoral willingly to remain mediocre, he wrote, in a tone that reveals his generally uncompromising nature. Whoever wilfully withdraws from the struggle, he continued, is a coward who should be punished by law, for he is a criminal towards himself; this is the greatest crime of all (*Souvenirs de jeunesse,* pp. 19-21; the selections from his "Journal" are dated May 23, 1884). This strictness was an integral part of his personality. In 1884, he said, he did not act; he was passive ("j'ai été agi") (*Mémoires,* p. 22). Towards the end of his life the same inflexible attitudes continue to appear.

---

[8] "Journal inédit de Romain Rolland"; "Le Vieux Orphée", *Compagnons de route* (Paris, 1936), p. 181, "Journal inédit de Romain Rolland", *Revue de Paris* (June, 1950), pp. 12-18.

In the preface (dated February, 1939) of his *Mémoires* he wrote that it would be unfortunate and criminal not to do all he was capable of. Fortunately, this rigorous demand for heroism at all times is limited. It may produce great men — or perhaps great men produce it — but it could be, as it was for Rolland, an extremely uncomfortable ethic. Such intolerance, bordering on the fanatic, seems to indicate that he was reacting violently to personal and family problems. This attitude, which closely resembles overweening ambition, may have arisen from well-concealed feelings of inferiority, unintentionally aroused in him at home by the severely high standards and difficult demands of his mother and by a certain mocking indifference on his father's part, an indifference which appears in the picture of Colas in the novel *Colas Breugnon* [Paris, 1919], written in 1913-1914, and of the Stadhouder in *Aërt* [Paris, 1895]. Whatever the cause, this deliberate incurring of trouble and setting of inordinate demands on himself in order to prove his superiority in his own eyes is the attitude which would carry him through the difficult years of *Jean-Christophe,* of the First World War, and of the no less difficult period between the two World Wars, in fact through most of his life.

Unfortunately for the young man on whose shoulders, at his mother's insistence, lay the future of his family, or on whose shoulders he felt lay the future of his family — one is unsure why he felt this burden; his father was still providing for the family — devotion to Shakespeare consumed so much time and energy that he failed twice in the examination for the Ecole normale supérieure, which he was to enter for a university career, according to his mother's plan. In 1886 he succeeded on the third trial, being tenth on the list of twenty-four successful candidates, July 17.[9]

The Rolland of these early years already contains the essence of the man who will attract such controversial attention during the World War I. Of a musical, dreamy, and solitary nature, an

[9] H.W. Beckwith, "The Formation of the Esthetic of Romain Rolland" (Doctoral Dissertation, New York University), 1936, p. 16; Jean Bonnerot, *Romain Rolland, sa vie, son œuvre,* pp. 12-13; Stefan Zweig, *Romain Rolland, l'homme et l'œuvre* (Paris, 1930). Zweig's biography, which first appeared in 1920 (English translation in 1921) is one of the best up to the date of its publication.

intransigent character, demanding more from himself than from others, strongly motivated psychologically to attempt to create his own view of the world, psychologically perhaps uncertain of his rôle as male or female, the young man who was ready to enter the Ecole normale supérieure in the fall of 1886 was an egocentric, almost romantic rebel, fantasizing his own rôle in life, introspective and tending towards hypochondria. Death, music, mountainous country, solitude, Shakespeare and Beethoven, what motifs and sources of inspiration and emulation could be more similar to the Romantics of 1830?

II

THE ECOLE NORMALE (1886-1889)

Rolland entered the Ecole normale in the fall of 1886 to prepare for a teaching career. Successful candidates received bed and board at the expense of the state. In return they contracted a ten-year teaching engagement which then took the place of obligatory military service.[1] First-year students, 'les conscrits' ('draftees'), studied together in groups in small rooms, called 'turnes'. Rolland's comrades were Georges Dumas, future psychologist; Dalmeyda, philosopher; Levrault, and Renel. When André Suarès (who was to be a second-rate writer and critic), dark and with long black hair, arrived from Marseille, he was accepted only by Rolland, Dumas, and Dalmeyda. The friendship that began then was to result in a long and interesting correspondence.[2]

Rolland chose the study of history and geography. It was a deliberate choice, and was to have an important influence on his writings. The professors, Guiraud and Monod were, he believed, better than Ollé-Laprune and Brochard, who taught philosophy. The spirit that animated the teaching of history was the most liberal of all. Rolland felt that training as a historian was the best basis on which to build his life. He was afraid of becoming bogged down if he devoted himself solely to abstract thinking (how far he avoided that path may be seen on almost any page of his prose). He could apply his philosophical faculties and his literary sense

---

[1] See *Le Cloître de la rue d'Ulm. Journal de Romain Rolland à l'École normale (1886-1889)* (Paris, 1951), pp. 15, 121-122. See also Maurice Martin du Gard, *Caractères et confidences* (Paris, 1936), p. 213.

[2] Rolland's letters to Suarès, extending over many years, still remain to be published. A selection of Suarès' letters has already appeared: *Cette âme ardente. Choix de lettres de André Suarès à Romain Rolland* (Paris, 1954).

to the study of history. Finally, specialization in history would give him the opportunity to travel on missions (*Le Cloître de la rue d'Ulm* [Paris, 1952], pp. 124-125). Work in this discipline made of Rolland a scholar trained in the scrupulous study and analysis of texts, with great respect for the use of rigorous scientific methods in the quest for truth. His apparently innate desire to write made him seize upon history as a medium of expression. In February, 1888, he wrote in his Journal (*Le Cloître,* p. 189) that he wished to write a realistic and psychological history, a history of souls. It would be a long work, for, he said, he could comprehend souls only in the course of their evolution. Even as a young man he had a profound feeling for the continual process of change that is life, and this attitude was very important in his creative works. We see it in his novels, *Jean-Christophe* and *L'Ame enchantée* especially, in which he traces the development of a musician (Christophe) and a woman (Annette Rivière), and in his cycle of dramas of the French Revolution.

His professors at the school also included Brunetière, the controversial critic and historian of French literature; Vidal de la Blache, the geographer; Chuquet, the Catholic philosopher; and the hellenists, Tournier and Weil. Rolland was very critical of his professors. None of them, he later assured Paul Seippel, had any intellectual influence on him; Gabriel Monod alone made his personality felt. He admired Vidal de la Blache, who had made a new science of geography. Rolland frequently denied the intellectual influence of others, preferring to believe that such influences were moral, ethical, or spiritual; he made the same statement many years later about Tolstoy. This need to deny the intellectual influence of teachers or friends, no matter how much he admired them, is a curious trait. It seems to be related to his exaggerated need for self-assertion and independence; he needed to escape from his mother's domination and to form his own character and life, as well as to compensate for a feeling of insecurity.

The 'conscrits' participated in a 'monôme', a traditional student demonstration that was noisy and irksome to the police. After the 'monôme', Rolland and his comrades hesitantly assembled in the court of the rambling building of the rue d'Ulm, fearful of the hazing, the 'canular', — not a physical ordeal, but a trial of wits — which lay ahead (Rolland later started a protest against this tradition). It frequently degenerated into obscene speeches or 'verses' that disgusted Rolland, who was little accustomed to the more rough and tumble student life. It terminated in a ludicrous ceremony called the 'canularium'; each 'conscrit' stood on a pedestal while a satiric poem about him was read aloud. Allusions were made to flaws in character and physique; mental and moral peculiarities were satirized. Rolland, tall, thin, and pale, was made to stand with the fattest of the new students, and the verses in their honor turned on Don Quixote and Sancho Panza — not a bad characterization of one whose temperament contained an extraordinarily large dose of Quixotism. The particular targets for the rhyming wit were his cult of Wagner, his somber appearance, and his idealism. One of the exercises of student wit was to formulate euphuistic judgments of fellow students in which the principal terms, two nouns and two adjectives, were symmetrical and antithetical. Rolland was described as follows : "Rolland : — le Bouddhâ musical d'une mysticité révolutionnaire" (*Le Cloître,* p. 18). Here indeed are the essential elements of Rollands personality, permutations and combinations of which add to his complexity and to his friends' perplexity. He was a mystic and a revolutionary, a musician and a metaphysician, a meditative but unorthodox philosopher, an intolerant opponent of intolerance, and a contemplative man of action.

Enthusiastic devotion to two thoroughly different writers marked this period of his life : Tolstoy and Renan. Translations of Tolstoy appeared frequently between 1885 and 1895. In his *Vie de Tolstoï* (4th ed., Paris, 1913, p. 1), Rolland says that the great soul of Russia was the purest of the lights that illuminated his generation. His first act as a 'normalien' was to have his section buy the French translations of the works of Tolstoy and Dostoevski. Each student found something significant in them. What appealed particularly to Rolland ? Tolstoy, he wrote, was a kindred spirit because of his ardent life, his youthful heart, his ironical disillusionment, his pitiless clairvoyance, his concern with death, his dreams of fraternal love and peace, his castigation of the lies of society, his realism, his mysticism, his closeness to nature, his sense of the invisible forces of the world, and his rapture in the face of Infinity (*Vie de Tolstoï*, p. 3). Many of the qualities he found in Tolstoy are important in the character of the author of *Jean-Christophe*, especially his ardor for life, his concern with death, his mounting disgust at the lies of society, his feelings about nature, his mysticism.

Of Tolstoy's writings, it was *War and Peace* that left the deepest mark. In his "Journal" under the date mid-September, 1887, he wrote that *War and Peace* and *Crime and Punishment* were the greatest of Russian novels. In these novels he found qualities congenial to his own temperament. He had begun the reading with some antipathy, but little by little the souls of Tolstoy's creations invaded and dazzled the aspiring writer. The very number of important characters appealed to him, but even more the fact that they were not seen solely in moments of crisis, but at all times, under all lights, in all stages of their development (*Mémoires* [Paris, 1956], p. 177; *Compagnons de route* [Paris, 1936], p. 185). *War and Peace* made him think of the immensity of life; he described it as 'l'océan des âmes, aux millions de pensées', and he felt himself to have become the Spirit of God moving over the waters.[3] The epic quality of the novel undoubtedly had an important effect on Rolland.[4]

Rolland was, however, frequently in disagreement with Tolstoy's ideas. He could not follow Tolstoy's condemnation of Beethoven and Wagner, who were for Rolland towers of strength, and whose vertiginous revelations had saved him from self-destruction. In Tolstoy alone of all living artists, he found the same power as in the two musicians, but although he drew strength from the Russian, he considered his judgments on art invalid because Tolstoy was an intuitive genius, and not primarily a critical artist. The only judgments by Tolstoy that Rolland accepted were those condemning the artistic charlatans of the Parisian market place.[5]

[3] Rolland's "Journal", in "Tolstoï et Georges Eliot", *Les Nouvelles littéraires* (Feb. 7, 1946), p. 1.
[4] See *infra* p. 135-136.
[5] Letter of Romain Rolland to H.W. Beckwith, published by Beckwith in "The Formation of the Esthetic of Romain Roland" (Dissertation, New York University, 1936), 286 pp.; letter dated Oct. 15, 1933, p. 29.

A reflection of Tolstoy's influence is found in a letter to J.-R. Bloch (published in *Europe* [May, 1948], 15-16) dated Aug. 10, 1911, and written shortly after the publication of his *Vie de Tolstoï*. For Tolstoy, Rolland wrote, belief is not a faith, but a wish; virtue is not perfection, but the ascent towards perfection, the movement of a continual effort. His heroism is a principle of action offering an inexhaustible field of activity to human energy (see also Rolland's *Vie de Tolstoï*, pp. 80-95). Here is Rolland's personality itself; he has said many times that to believe is to act, that faith is action, a striving towards perfection, an ascent toward the summit.

But Tolstoy was not a guide for Rolland; he was an inspiration. "His tormented genius has always been incapable of finding a practical way out", wrote Rolland in a letter to Dilip Kumar Roy in March, 1922 (published in Alex Aronson, *Europe looks at India* [Hind Kitab Publishers, 1946], p. 184). Rolland later would accuse Tolstoy, when under the sway of his passions, of unconscious deceptions.[6]

The young student of 1886-1887 was perturbed by the conflicting ideas of Tolstoy, but impressed by his creative works. Uncertain about his own still immature ideas, struggling for his own development, Rolland wrote, on April 16, 1887, to the Russian, who replied some time later in a letter of thirty-odd pages, in which he tried to answer the young man's questions and to explain his own ideas. Tolstoy's serious kindness so impressed him that he determined to answer all letters addressed to him. In all, Rolland wrote seven letters to the Russian, over a period of twenty years: April 16, and Oct. 7, 1887, Jan. 24, and Jan. 29, 1897, July 21, and Aug. 23, 1901, and Aug. 27, 1906. In one he sent the proofs of his first published work, *Saint-Louis*; with the last one he sent his *Vie de Michel-Ange,* and some affectionately reproachful com-

---

[6] "Tout de même, que Tolstoï était de mauvaise foi, quand une de ses passions l'emportait". See also a letter to Malwida von Meysenbug, Feb., 1898; *Choix de lettres à Malwida von Meysenbug* (Paris, 1948); and letter to Mme. Louise Cruppi, Dec. 2, 1915; Louise Cruppi was a close friend of Rolland's and the wife of the future senator from the Haute Garonne, Jean Cruppi.

ments about various judgments and ideas on art expressed by Tolstoy.[7]

The other writer in whom Rolland was then interested was Ernest Renan, philologist, theologian, and author of a controversial *Vie de Jésus* (Paris, 1863). Rolland proposed to his comrades, only half in earnest, that each of them write to some great man of the day. Without further ado he himself wrote to Renan, believing rather naïvely that he knew his works thoroughly. Rolland expounded what he believed to be Renan's philosophy as expressed in *L'Abbesse de Jouarre* and *Le Prêtre de Némi*.[8] In an account of his visit to the illustrious sage ("Paroles de Renan à un adolescent", *Compagnons de route,* and also in *Le Cloître de la rue d'Ulm,* pp. 21-27), he says he called on Renan in his apartment at the Collège de France, December 26, 1886.[9] During the visit, which lasted over an hour, Rolland did not hesitate to question his host in detail. Renan answered willingly, if rather ironically and sometimes mockingly. After the visit, Rolland concluded that he would have to add the word 'perhaps' to his formulation of Renan's thought. It was, he said, an optimism which was not without melancholy, and seasoned with scepticism. From Renan he took the phrase "la route en lacets qui monte", which he later gave to a wartime article. In June, 1888, he described his own ambitions in a way that seems to reveal the influence of Renan. He intended to write a great realistic history of the Wars of Reli-

---

[7]   Some of the letters have been published and discussed. But the correct dates have not always been given — information from Moscow is rather difficult to get — and the correct dates, taken from copies of the letters made in the Tolstoy museum in Moscow, differ from those given by Wilson, *The Pre-War Biographies of Romain Rolland* (Oxford, 1939), pp. 72-76. Even Rolland, in a letter to J.-R. Bloch (Jan. 20, 1935), is in error, since he himself kept no copies; after thirty years a lapse of memory is pardonable.

[8]   Letter to his mother (Dec. 21, 1886), in *Le Cloître,* pp. 324-325. The letter was also published by Henriette Psichari, in *Renan d'après lui-même* (Paris, 1937), pp. 147-149.

[9]   See also "Ernest Renan vu par Romain Rolland (lettre à Serge Radine)", *Journal de Genève* (Jan. 25-26, 1947), literary supplement; letter to his mother (June 18, 1890), in *Printemps romain* (Paris, 1954), p. 319; and "Le grain de vie", *Mercure de France* (June 1, 1947), pp. 201-213 (extracts from his 'Journal', dated September, 1890, where he explains the influence of Renan on his own dramas).

gion and to provide in it an example of what history can be. He wanted to recreate the past in its integral, living reality by utilizing both artistic intuition and textual criticism (*Le Cloître,* p. 237). The philological study of texts and the use of intuitive creation closely resemble Renan's methods. Rolland's interests, like Renan's, were broad and varied. His knowledge in the field of philosophy was considerable; he studied the pre-Socratic philosophers as well as the Cartesian and Spinozan philosophies. He was also greatly interested in biology (letter to Stefan Zweig, June 10, 1920). Later, in 1913, he expressed a desire to study metaphysics and mathematics, although he was dubious about his ability to extend his knowledge of mathematics very far.

Although retiring in nature, Rolland participated occasionally in the political life of the time. He observed closely and uneasily the spreading Boulangist movement. On April 19, 1888, he spent the afternoon watching the pro-Boulanger demonstration. He noted that all true Republicans, and they were few, were tense. The following Monday, April 23, Rolland helped circulate protests against Boulanger among the students. On July 13 he heard speeches by the President and members of his government in the courtyard of the Louvre. On July 14, although the examination for the *licence* was only three days away, he went to see the military review at Longchamps. In November of the same year he wrote that he was studying the sixteenth century in France, and that he recognized analogous pogroms in his present surroundings. Suarès and he were playing their small rôle in this immense drama by sending out letters signed by student groups, addressed especially to president Floquet, to support and encourage his vacillating opposition to the Boulangist movement.[10]

The election of Boulanger, Jan. 27, 1889, was a severe blow

[10] This account of Rolland's participation and interest in the political movements of the day is taken from "Carnets (1886-1889)", *La Nef* (Jan., 1946), pp. 3-23. General Boulanger (1837-1891) gained widespread popularity by some genuine reforms in the army and by other less meritorious means, thereby becoming accepted as the man to avenge the defeat of 1870-1871. In 1889 the possibility of a *coup d'état* under his leadership seemed great; hence Rolland's fears, especially since Bonapartists had attached themselves to Boulanger's faction. After escaping arrest in 1889, the general committed suicide in 1891.

for Republicans. Rolland spent the next day at the sessions of the lower house in the Palais Bourbon. His discouragement was complete; he believed that the Republic was lost. Until this election he had had confidence in the Republic and in the people. Now he feared that the shameful stain of Boulangism would spread from Paris to all of France (*Le Cloître*, p. 300). He concluded that he would no longer be able to live there or in any country which denies liberty. This great need for liberty was one of the basic traits of his character. It developed perhaps both from tradition, from his relations with his mother, and from his reaction to the family situation; it was especially strong during his student years in Paris, when he was trying to establish himself.

He was an ardent Republican, not an ardent Frenchman, and not a super-patriot; in fact he said at this time that there is only one true fatherland: Love. Political fatherlands he regarded as the fruit of pride and hate. France alone in Europe was the incarnation of the Republic, and the thought of the death of the French Republic stopped the breath in his throat.[11] Until the end of his life, he continued to consider France the bastion of liberty, but not without bitterly criticizing some of the errors and flaws he saw in the society and the government.

In the summer of 1888, during a stay in Switzerland, Rolland made the acquaintance of Isidore de Breuilpont, an elderly musical enthusiast whose knowledge of music, especially of Beethoven's, was great, and whose enthusiasm was even greater.[12] The Breton gentleman taught him to see in the music of the great classic masters a 'discourse' which has its own unity, logic, and laws (*Mémoires*, pp. 153-160). The Marquis opened up new vistas of interpretation for the young musician, who took regular lessons from him after returning to Paris. In piano music, M. de Breuilpont preferred Handel to Bach, and one cannot but see in his preference part of the reason for the special cult Rolland devoted

[11] "Le patriotisme est la religion des âmes médiocres... C'est un devoir imposé par la fatalité douloureuse d'un monde encore barbare. On est contraint de le faire; il serait stupide de le faire volontiers" (*Le Cloître*, p. 300).
[12] M. Isidore de Breuilpont lived in the Morbihan of Brittany; one of his great-grandfathers was the *fermier-général* La Pouplinière who was Rameau's patron and who brought to France the creator of the symphony, Stamitz.

to Handel. Both men appreciated Bach, especially his fugues; both felt that his music was a philosophy, but that Handel was an incomparable artist. This preference may be revealing of Rolland's character and artistic temperament. One writer speculated that Bach's perfection of form seemed to Rolland to indicate detachment from the world and a lack of interest in contemporary life, and that Rolland reacted to this detachment and gave only lip service to the great master. It is true, on the other hand that Rolland signals for comment and praise many very unimportant musicians, chiefly because, it seems, their work reflected certain events in their lives or certain characteristics which he considered important. However, during his stay in Rome, he found the music of Bach increasingly meaningful. He played a great deal of the music of J. S. Bach in the salon of Donna Laura Minghetti, and of Mlle von Meysenbug. He wrote to his mother, Feb. 1-2, 1890, that he was limiting his music to those artists who correspond exactly to the particular quality and needs of his own soul, and he names Mozart, Gluck, Rameau, and Bach; later, on June 9, 1890, he wrote that he did not know any Italian artist, except Michelangelo, as well and profoundly as he knew Bach.[13]

The Marquis agreed with Rolland's piano teacher (Joséphine Martin) that Rolland's style and technique in playing Mozart were superior and that he had exactly the right intelligence for it. While Rolland admits that his interpretation of Beethoven differed from that of de Breuilpont, who had given him a deeper insight into the works of Beethoven, it was largely the Marquis' lessons and conversations that determined Rolland's interpretation in the works he later devoted to that musician.

In July, 1889, Rolland took the examination for the 'agrégation', success in which admits the candidate to the professorate. He was pleased to be able to write to his mother about the favorable result, but he was unenthusiastic about a university career. He was simply doing his duty as imposed by her, meeting a responsibility

[13] Wm. H. Beckwith, "The Formation of the Esthetic of Romain Rolland" (Dissertation, New York University, 1936), pp. 195-196. *Printemps Romain (Choix de lettres de Romain Rolland à sa mère (1889-1890))* (Paris, 1954), pp. 145, 307.

which lay heavily on his shoulders. However, he seemed to have had no very clear notion of what other career or profession he would prefer.[14]

He also wrote to his mother, who had proposed that he take a year off after completing the work at the school, that he did not wish to increase his burden of debt to his family. He was grimly determined to fulfill his obligation to his parents, and then to follow his own bent. He was also bound by the ten-year engagement contracted upon entering the Ecole normale. These two conditions had to be satisfied before he could live his own life. Three years in the school, seven years in teaching; not one day longer. During this time, he said, he would write his great realistic history: The Wars of Religion. At the age of thirty (1895-1896), he would abandon the university and history, and would publish his first novel. "If I do not succeed", he wrote in his typical unbending way, "it will be because I lack the ability; if I succeed, I must be able to die at thirty-five, having given the measure of my ability" (Le Cloître, pp. 236-237). It is surprising how nearly he maintained the time he set for himself, falling only some ten years behind schedule, a reasonably good performance, considering the demands and unforeseen difficulties of life.[15] His determination to leave his unchosen profession was merely a question of timing. He stated flatly in 1888 that it was impossible for him to remain a professor. If he had no responsibilities — but he felt that he had, towards his mother — he would leave this career immediately (Le Cloître, p. 260).

His years at the Ecole normale were difficult for him. Looking back on them in 1901 (letter to his friend Louis Gillet, June 14, 1901; Correspondance de Louis Gillet et Romain Rolland [Paris,

---

[14] "Comme je te l'ai promis, je suis content, mais rien de plus. Mon année n'est pas *tout à fait* perdue; oh! elle l'est bien tout de même; mais enfin, elle a un petit dédommagement. Voilà tout! Je ne considère pas du tout cela, — je t'en prie, répète-le à g[randpère], — comme le couronnement de mes études, etc., etc. Je méprise absolument l'agrégation; j'ai promis de le dire, et je le dis. Maintenant que je l'ai, j'affirme mon mépris pour le professorat. C'est une somme de 3 400 ou 3 500 francs; ce n'est rien de plus pour moi" (unpublished letter to his mother, August, 1889).

[15] *Jean-Christophe* was published between 1904 and 1912.

1949], pp. 145-146) he says that he spent despairing nights in his bed at the Ecole normale. They had continued the sad years of his residence in the lycées, when he was almost without friends, hope, or confidence in himself. He wondered how he had been able to live through these periods. The first year of the Ecole normale, as is to be expected, was the most difficult; it resulted in a crisis, which he dates April 11, 1887. The reason for the date is that he then completed a private statement of his own personal philosophy (*Mémoires,* p. 47), which he called his "Credo quia verum", the first formulation of his beliefs and attitudes toward life (first published in the Appendix to *Le Cloître*). Five days later he wrote his first letter to Tolstoy, seeking guidance and comfort.

The training he received at the school made of him a competent and exacting historian. By combining his creative intuition with his ability in music, he was soon in a very favorable position for his future work as a musicologist. The first chair of musicology at the Sorbonne was in fact created for him after he completed his doctorate in 1895. The influence of Renan and Tolstoy undoubtedly contributed to the direction of his future writings. Tolstoy and music were largely responsible for *Jean-Christophe* and perhaps *L'Ame enchantée* (1922-1933); Renan and his interest in history for such plays as *Aërt* (1898), the plays of the cycle of the French Revolution (which occupied most of his life), and probably such a propaganda novel as *Clerambault* (1919). Perhaps, however, the most important factor in his future writings was his sojourn in Italy after the completion of the Ecole normale.

III

ITALY (1889-1891)

After his success in the competitive examination for the 'agrégation', Rolland was uncertain as to his next step. Ordinarily the
students in the Ecole normale remain three years. There was little
question of the possibility of a fourth year at the school. The
alternative was to accept a teaching position in a lycée, probably
a provincial one. This he was loath to do; teaching was not his
primary interest, and in spite of his sighs for the countryside, he
had little love for provincial towns. At this juncture sheer good
fortune aided him. He received a fellowship for study and research
in Rome at the Ecole française d'Archéologie et d'Histoire. The
fellowship had been offered to two of his comrades who had
placed higher in the examination (Rolland was the eighth on the
list). Their refusal had opened the way for one of the most important events in Rolland's life: his two years in Italy.[1] After
some discussion, principally with his mother, who was violently
opposed to her son's leaving, Rolland accepted. He knew he was
causing her grief, but he was driven by his own rigid character
to fulfill his destiny in his own way. His mother's insatiable desire
to have her son near her, to be everything for him, to spare him
all the petty annoyances of daily living was the cause of her
opposition, which he had to overcome in order to live to some
extent his own life. Probable echoes of Rolland's mother and her

---

[1] *Le Cloître de la Rue d'Ulm. Journal de Romain Rolland à l'École normale*
(Paris, 1952), pp. 272, 313-314, 342-349. See also W.H. Beckwith, "The Formation of the Esthetic of Romain Rolland" (Dissertation, New York University,
1936), p. 32; Paul Seippel, *Romain Rolland, l'homme et l'œuvre* (Paris, 1913),
p. 30; Jean Bonnerot, *Romain Rolland, sa vie, son œuvre* (Paris, 1921), pp.
18-20.

demands on him, her stifling control, are heard in the relations of Christophe to his mother, Louisa, in the relations of Annette Rivière and her son Marc, and in the play *St.-Louis,* where the mother of Louis IX interferes in her son's marriage.

In Rome he was given a room in the Palazzo Farnese, which housed the Ecole française. Directed by Auguste Geoffroy, the school was not an institution like our colleges, but simply a small group of students engaged in study and research under the nominal guidance of the director. They were semi-official representatives of the French government, and as such were expected to appear at official functions. Only four rooms were available in the Palazzo Farnese, but since the occupant of one was engaged in excavating in Algeria, Rolland took the room normally occupied by the candidate of the first choice.

He began work in the Papal Archives on a subject proposed by Gabriel Monod, who had talked with Geoffroy about the new fellow, and had proposed as a plan of research a study of the relations between the Holy See and Francis the First of France, during the pontificates of Hadrian VI and Clement VII (letter to his father, Nov. 12). Rolland accepted the plan without joy (no plan would have pleased him) and was soon occupied in reading the documents concerning the papal nuncio Salviati. He worked conscientiously, but without enthusiasm; the task seemed useless and dry, because without significance. Nothing is more futile, he felt, than to attempt to resurrect a tiny segment of the past, which we are now unable to comprehend in its entirety, especially since the powerful and pressing interests in the life of our own time, or of philosophy, or of art, are truly important and significant. Why should the state pay all his expenses for three years in a school in Paris and another year at Rome, merely to discover what the papal nuncio said in 1527? As he wrote in a letter to his mother (unpublished, Dec. 7, 1889), he found this a superfluous luxury, while many of his compatriots suffered from hunger and lack of necessities. This letter reveals a Rolland whose social conscience was already well developed. This is the Rolland who was to take a definite, if controversial, stand during World War I and during the period between the two wars. It is the Rolland who felt himself personally responsible towards his fellowmen and towards society. However, he placed art — for him, the plenitude of life — at the summit of man's activities. The differences between Rolland and Tolstoy are here apparent; both felt the responsibility of the artist to men, but Tolstoy did not place art above all other human activities. Filled with the desire to create, to sublimate his emotions in literary and artistic works, Rolland was dismayed by dry intellectual research, although he admitted that his mind, if not his emotional life, profited from it (letter to Malwida von Meysenbug, Dec. 18, 1893; *Choix de lettres à Malwida von Meysenbug* [Paris, 1948], pp. 96-98). Such research could never be worth a single sincere word from a loving heart. Only the responsibilities he felt towards his parents (towards his mother), whether rightly or not, enabled him to surmount the hours of dull labor involved. Furthermore, he said, after having learned so much he had no taste for any profession. Unable to be an artist, he refused to be a critic, and he would not, could not be a professor (*Printemps romain* [Paris, 1954], pp. 118-120). His dislike of the professorate is the basis of his analysis of Olivier Jeannin's dislike for this profession, in which he expresses his own feelings (*Jean-Christophe,* éd. déf. [Paris, 1950], p. 992):

Dans cet affaissement moral où il avait faim de silence, sa tâche de professeur lui était devenue intolérable. Il n'avait aucun goût pour ce métier, où il faut s'étaler, dire tout haut sa pensée, où l'on n'est jamais seul. Le professorat de lycée exige, pour avoir quelque noblesse, une vocation d'apostolat, qu'Olivier ne possédait point, et le professorat de Facultés impose avec le public un contact perpétuel, qui est douloureux aux âmes éprises de solitude... Deux ou trois fois, il avait dû parler en public : il en avait éprouvé une humiliation singulière. Cette exhibition sur une estrade lui était odieuse... surtout cette parole du haut de la chaire déforme la pensée...

(See also his letter to Mme E. Marchand, Dec. 12, 1907; *infra,* p. 99, n. 2).

Rolland did not lead a secluded life in Rome, despite his temperament and his research. He was frequently forced to various expedients to save some time for himself in the evenings. Besides

the *soirées,* more or less obligatory, of the director and his wife,
there were others at the Villa Medici, the residence of Prix de
Rome students and of art and music students of the Académie de
France. The director of this institution, Hébert, was an amateur
violinist, often in need of an accompanist. Rolland's reputation
as a pianist in the French colony soon made him Hébert's rather
unwilling accompanist. The elderly Malwida von Meysenbug,
German by birth, who had settled in Rome, was another of his
acquaintances. He first visited her in Rome on Dec. 13, 1889; the
acquaintanceship was to ripen into a rich friendship.[2]

He had met her briefly at the Monod's home, in Versailles; but
at the moment of their first visit in Rome, he was unsure of her
name, which he spelled variously Meysenberg and Meysingen
(*Printemps romain,* pp. 93-103, 110, letters from Dec. 14, 1889 to
Jan. 7, 1890). She was he soon wrote, charming, and by March,
1890, he declared that he had a very sincere affection for her, and
that she did him the honor of having great confidence in him and
of speaking frankly with him (*Ibid.,* p. 225). Soon he began to
refer to her simply as Malwida; the familiarity that existed between
her son and this seventy-three-year-old woman irritated and
probably frightened Mme Rolland, who inquired sharply who
'Malwida' was, and why he called her so. To which he replied
that it was her given name — but thereafter in all his letters to
his mother he referred to her as Mlle de Meysenbug.

If the serenity and calm, the profound and ardent interest in
music of the elderly Malwida, her sincerity and generous interest
in others, affected the young Rolland whose visits to her soon

[2] For an account of the first visit, see an unpublished letter to his mother,
Dec. 13-14, 1889, and a letter from Malwida to her foster daughter Olga Monod,
Dec. 13, in *Im Amfang war die Liebe. Briefe an Ihre Pflegetochter von Malwida
von Meysenbug* (Munich, 1926), pp. 214-215. Malwida von Meysenbug was
born in Kassel, 1816, and died at Rome in 1903. Of a family of Hugenots who
fled from France at the time of the Revocation of the Edict of Nantes, she was
reared in an ultra-conservative atmosphere to which she reacted by drawing
close to German revolutionary circles. Forced to leave Berlin in 1852, she went
to London, where she participated in the life of political exiles; she knew
Mazzini and Alexander Herzen, the Russian revolutionist. From 1870 on she
lived in Rome, and counted among her many friends Wagner and Nietzsche.
See her *Memoiren einer Idealistin* (1876) and *Lebensabend einer Idealistin*
(1898).

were almost daily, her impressions of the young man were not less vivid. From the first visit he paid to her she found pleasure in his company; he was, she wrote, the most clean-cut of all the young Frenchmen she had yet known.[3]

Malwida also saw him as an over-serious, earnest, and unusual young man. "I take him out", she wrote, "into social gatherings as much as I can, because it is necessary for him; otherwise he becomes too serious and earnest and too much absorbed in an ideal world of music, which causes him to dislike life".[4] May 12, 1890, she spoke of him as her 'neuer hiesiger Sohn' (her current new son).[5]

A note of warm affection can be detected in her words about him, but for some time Rolland's friendship with her remained, for him, on a rather intellectual plane. He wrote to his mother that if anyone ought to complain about his preferences, it would be Mlle de Meysenbug, for their friendship had a purely intellectual character, and he tried to calm his mother's irritation (she feared the influence any woman might have on her son) (*Retour au Palais Farnèse. Choix de lettres de Romain Rolland à sa mère (1890-1891)* [Paris, 1956], p. 38; letter dated Oct. 28-29, 1890). This pattern is not unusual in his life. A large part of his correspondence consists of letters to women, with whom he felt spiritual or intellectual sympathy, but who were either married, older, or otherwise safely barred from a more emotional union. As for Malwida's influence on him, he denies that she had any intellectual effect. It was by the radiance of her soul, calm, pure, serene, always young, that she had a calming effect on him. After his departure from Rome, he maintained a steady and voluminous correspondence with her until her death in 1903. Some of Malwida's traits and temperament will form the character and personality of Schulz and the blind girl, Modesta, in the novel, *Jean-Christophe*.

---

[3] *In Anfang war die Liebe. Briefe an Ihre Pflegetochter von Malwida von Meysenbug* (Munich, 1926), pp. 214-215. Letter to Olga Monod (Dec. 13, 1889), and pp. 218-219.
[4] *Ibid.*, pp. 218-219.
[5] *Ibid.*, pp. 220-221; letter dated May 12, 1890.

Malwida soon discovered in her visitor a masterly interpreter of Bach, Beethoven, Mozart, and Wagner, and he often played for her. Character traits which would be found later in Christophe began now to appear. He detested dilettante audiences, and to amateur artists or musicians he preferred listeners who were frankly and completely ignorant of art. One reason for this attitude was that in his scale of values, art was a religion to which its followers must be entirely devoted (*Printemps,* pp. 240-243; letter dated March 9-10, 1890). Music was for him an inviolable world, and only true artists, or the pure and simple, were admissible to this sacred precinct. Fortunately for the world, this attitude is a peculiarity of Rolland's, and not a musician's temperament. He particularly disliked compliments for his playing and discussions of the music. Like Christophe, he occasionally took malicious pleasure in perplexing his hearers, especially if he had had to suffer from them in any way. When Geoffroy announced that Rolland would play some noisy, wild, incomprehensible music from Wagner, Rolland vexed him by playing a soft, sweet and limpid air from *Tannhaüser* — and laughed to himself (*Printemps,* p. 231; letter of March 4-5, 1890).

Rolland had been one of the early enthusiasts of Wagner's music, which he did not always understand; all was mysterious to him: the new sonorities, the rhythms, the subjects, but he was entranced by the composer's superhuman passions and strength. These qualities, he said, are always a joy, whether in themselves joyful or painful. He thought this strong and passionate music was necessary for the youth of his generation, who were enfeebled by inaction and living in an urban and excessively intellectual civilization far from nature, and for all strong, true life. We can, he hoped, drink in strength and courage from the most sincere, heroic and generous manifestations of the era.[6] Wagner was the greatest man, not merely of music or the drama, but of all humanity (letter, Feb. 1-2, 1890; *Printemps,* pp. 144-145). Wagner is the creator of a world of illusion more living than the world of reality, a robust genius; those who would penetrate his thinking and

[6] Rolland, "Le Centenaire de Richard Wagner. Initiation wagnérienne", *Annales politiques et littéraires* (May 18, 1913), pp. 441-442.

works must be vigorous of body and soul, for otherwise soul and body succumb. His creations are strengthening for the strong, but not "for little girls like me", he added pessimistically.

By 1892, however, cracks began to appear in Rolland's cult of the creator of the Ring. Wagner's art had an irresistible power but it created illusion as the sole reality, and life itself then became illusion. It was perhaps the example of Suarès, who wanted to live entirely in a dream world, that was partly the cause of Rolland's mistrust. He wrote to Malwida that he was becoming an enemy of Wagner precisely because of his own love for life, which Wagner's dream tended to cause him to neglect (May 19, 1892; *Choix de lettres à Malwida von Meysenbug* [Paris, 1948]). His innate tendency was to fly to illusion, to an ideal that existed only in the artist's mind; but with his stubborn rational idea of what life should be, of what the artist's duty was, he fought against the tendency. Philosophically he loved life, the life of the universe; emotionally, he was tempted to flee from it into the realms of pure meditation.

He judged Wagner's works, with some exceptions, thoroughly unfit for the people. What, he asked, can the people find in the decadent complications of the metaphysics of Walhalla, the unhealthy desire of Tristan, or the mystical torments of the knights of the Grail? This is the art of an *élite* infected with neo-Christian and neo-Buddhist subtleties; it should not be allowed to poison the people. However, in an article on the centenary of Wagner's birth, 1913, he granted the decadent aspects of the music, even the modern hysterical neuroses of Wagner, but insisted that he was a great musician in the line of the classic composers, a necessary heir of Beethoven's epic breadth, passionate metaphysics, and Napoleonic phrases. In his great moments he is as fine as Beethoven, but these moments are best heard in concerts; he remarked that Wagner's operas were most beautiful when the singers stopped. Nevertheless he admired Wagner's vitality, will, mysticism, and even the profound sensuality that was part of his mysticism.[7]

[7] See Lucien Price, "Romain Rolland Converses", *Atlantic* (Dec. 1935), pp. 718-726. See also Rolland, "*Tristan*", *Les Nouvelles littéraires* (Feb. 1, 1936), p. 7.

Each composer had a particular appeal for him. Wagner was enchanting; Beethoven's exaggerations were sometimes shocking. He often preferred the music of Gluck, Bach, Rameau, and Mozart.[8] Handel was one of his great admirations. "I nourish myself on Handel", he wrote to his mother, Dec. 21, 1890. "It is like rare roast beef. It is healthy, robust, and fortifying. There are powerful passions, and a will equal to the passions. I would have dreamed of such a musician for the early nineteenth century. He would be Napoleon's man". Besides the eighteenth-century composers and Beethoven, the composer Berlioz aroused his enthusiasm (letter, Dec. 26-27, 1889; *Printemps,* p. 94). He changed his opinion about Berlioz later, although the essay in *Musiciens d'aujourd'hui* (which appeared first in the *Revue de Paris,* March 1, 15, 1904) reveals a continuing interest in the romantic composer. He expressed some adverse judgments to André Suarès (June 15, 1892). There are, he said, only two sincere sentiments in Berlioz: Nature and Nothingness; the best part of his art is classic and is the direct continuation of Gluck and Mozart, through Beethoven, Schumann, and Wagner.[9] Rolland also knew Richard Strauss and his music; indeed, he helped the German composer in the preparation of the text of *Salomé* (*Correspondance de Richard Strauss*

---

[8] "Moi, je me Mozartise tous les jours davantage; ah! et puis Bach, dont je fais une énorme consommation... Rien ne m'est doux à l'âme comme quelques pages de Mozart, de Gluck, et de Bach. Si tu ajoutes Rameau, tu vois que Suarès avait raison quand il me disait: 'Oh! toi, tu as un cœur du XVIIIe S.[iècle] en Allemagne'. Je suis de son avis sur moi-même. Wagner est Dieu, c'est sûr; mais il m'épuise; et les violences de Beethoven, et son exagération de langage parfois, me choquent" (Letter to Madeleine, "Vendredi matin", Nov. or Dec., 1899).

[9] "Deux ou trois morceaux sont beaux à pleurer. Le reste est bête — aussi à pleurer. — Je ne sache rien d'aussi énervant. — Je suis bien revenu de mon parti pris pour Berlioz;... Impossible de résister au divin septuor de la mer et la nuit. Il y a deux seuls sentiments sincères chez Berlioz; mais personne ne les a (en musique) ressentis si profondément: c'est le sent.[iment] de la Nature, et celui du Néant. Et puis, ce qui est curieux chez ce romantique, c'est que la meilleure partie de son art est du plus pur classique, et la continuation directe, (par dessus la tête de Beethoven, Schumann et Wagner), de Gluck et Mozart... j'ai déjà remarqué... tout ce qu'il y a d'italien, de foncièrement italien, dans cette âme bouleversée, désorientée, assotie par le romantisme pseudo-germanique" (Letter to André Suarès, June 15, 1892).

et de Romain Rolland [Paris, 1951]). His *Musiciens d'aujourd'hui* (Paris, 1908) testifies to his interest in contemporary music.

Malwida, well known in Rome, introduced Rolland into the salons of the Guerrieri-Gonzaga family and of Donna Laura Minghetti.[10] The two daughters of the former family immediately captured his fancy, the one blond and delicate, the other dark and ardent. Sofia, whom he seems to have been most attracted to, maintained a regular correspondence with him from 1901 until her death in 1932. In an undated letter several years after the events, André Suarès wrote from Rome, in 1895, that he had been in the Guerrieri-Gonzaga home, and that 'la petite Sofia' was very pretty, even a bit coquettish, with beautiful eyes which she knew how to use. In reply Rolland wrote: "So you have seen the one who harmed me so much, consciously, and did me so much good, unwittingly? Her eyes are beautiful? It is their light which made me what I am. She is not aware of this".[11] Although Rolland affirms that he had told no one about his 'roman de Rome', and that 'she' would never know what an important influence she had been in his life and writings — and he certainly said nothing of his feelings at the time to the young lady — he later told Sofia that he had written the play "Orsino" under her influence (letter to Sofia Bertolini, Dec. 6, 1901; *Chère Sofia. Choix de lettres de Romain Rolland à Sofia Guerrieri-Gonzaga* [Paris, 1959], p. 44). The pretty brunette was one of the reasons for his visits to the salon of the Marchioness — where he also spent some less agreeable moments. "I was somewhat monopolized by the Marchioness", he wrote to his mother on March 20-21, 1890 (*Printemps*, p. 251), "who is very argumentative, and who forced me to discuss art, politics, etc., although I do not like to argue. My ideas are too set". Doubtless he would have preferred to speak of other things with the

[10] Letter to Stefan Zweig (June 10, 1920); see also *Mémoires* (Paris, 1956), pp. 100-101.
[11] Letter to André Suarès (May, 1895). "Ta lettre a remué de vieux et chers souvenirs. Tu l'as donc vue, celle qui me fit tant de mal et de bien? — le mal volontairement, le bien à son insu. — Ses yeux ont essayé de leur pouvoir sur toi? Voilà donc la lumière qui fit de moi tout ce que je suis devenu. Elle ne s'en doute guère".

daughter. The note of irritation is more understandable in the light of the latter's pretty dark eyes.

If Rome benefited him in no other way, it did him the service of softening ever so slightly the shell he interposed between himself and the world. Under the Italian sun he relaxed enough to recognize partially one of the great needs of his life — love. It is part of his character that has not been generally recognized for its full importance. Love, 'amour-passion', in his mind was the essence of life. Unfortunately in his life, 'amour-passion' was for the most part 'amour-spirituel', unconsummated. Other emotions or passions were more frequent and more vital in him. In a letter to his mother, May-June, 1890 (*Printemps,* p. 347), he wrote that he always had to have a passion in his heart — love, anger, or pride. An empty heart, an unloving and unloved soul, a person in whom love for the world and for fellowmen was absent were abominations. Various of his creations bear this stigma; they are portrayed in a style that reveals his dislike. We find such characters as Mme de Kerich and Hassler in *Jean-Christophe,* Salisbury and Lia in the plays *St.-Louis* and *Aërt.* During the moments when his heart was empty, he complained of the lack of meaning in his life. He wrote to his mother, Jan. 14, 1890 (*Printemps,* p. 119), in answer to her anxious warnings that he should keep his heart whole and not allow himself to be caught by any pretty girl, assuring her that unfortunately his heart was whole; he was interested in nothing, and he was always alone, as he had been since childhood.

His mother's worries and anxieties did nothing to improve his confidence in himself or in his relationships with young women. She was perpetually fearful that her son might transfer his affections to another woman. She continually worried about Malwida's influence, fearing, it seems, that Rolland might be converted to Protestantism (he had already lost his Catholic faith). Her fear was probably less fear of Protestantism than fear of losing her son. His mother's influence affected adversely Rolland's relations with young women, and such failures are echoed in the character Christophe's life. The Breton maid who nursed him when he was sick in Paris fell in love with him — but her love was primarily a maternal sentiment, and Christophe, pleased to be so treated, never became aware of her feelings (*Jean-Christophe*, p. 814-815). When he was about to join Antoinette in Paris, street traffic and the crowds on the sidewalk separated them; he failed to find her, and both were carried away from each other — in spite of the fact that Christophe was large and robust, and Antoinette had only to stand still (*op. cit.*, p. 805, 917). The closest thing to a real, permanent, sexual and spiritual love affair is that between Christophe and Françoise Oudon. After they were separated by various circumstances, love increased, but so did a feeling of relief : "Jamais ils ne s'étaient aimés autant qu'en se séparant. Et après qu'elle fut partie, il revint à l'art, son vieux compagnon. O paix du ciel étoilé" (*op. cit.*, p. 1183) — not a very durable union ! In spite of the handicaps in his own ability to love, Rolland gained confidence in himself as his attempts at creative writing satisfied him more fully.[12] From February to the end of June, 1891, he travelled extensively throughout the peninsula.[13] He met Malwida in Venice on July 15 (*Ein Briefwechsel, 1890-1891. Romain Rolland und Malwida von Meysenbug,* transl. by A. Lubbe and Berta Schleicher [Stuttgart, 1923], p. 256), and they went together to Bayreuth for the presentation of *Tristan, Parzifal,* and *Tannhaüser.* Malwida declared that she especially enjoyed seeing Venice with Rolland, whose deep feeling for art and nature greatly increased her own pleasure. At Bayreuth, because of his friendship with Malwida, he was presented to the Wagner family, with whom he lunched at the Villa Wahnfried. Present at the table was a musician whom he did not then know, and whose acquaintance he made eight years later, the composer Richard Strauss. Strauss

[12] "Il me reste à te dire quelques mots, non plus de ma vie intellectuelle, mais de celle de mon cœur. — Chère maman, le sentiment de l'an passé est le même aujourd'hui; mais je ne suis plus tout à fait le même, moi. J'ai pris conscience de ma force, et quand je souffre, je me raidis dans mon orgueil. Je sais que je suis digne d'elle, et que si elle ne le sent point, le tort en est à elle, et non à moi" (Letter to his mother, Dec. 7, 1890).

[13] See for the remarks about the trips, the places, and the dates, *Ein Brief-wechsel,* pp. 214-230, 233-243, 256; and letters to Malwida (Feb. 5, 7, 10, 13-14, 17-18, 1891); *Retour au Palais Farnèse* (Paris, 1956), pp. 192-231, letters to his mother (Feb. 2 to 25, 1891).

was to have a decided echo in *Jean-Christophe,* for he is, in part, the model for Hassler and for Christophe himself.[14]

These two years were among the most important of Rolland's life. His recognition of the need for love, for 'amour-passion', was possible perhaps only in the warm atmosphere of Italy. It was a need that had surely existed before his trip, but he had been unable to recognize it. Rich in enduring friendships and emotions. and with vital new experiences, these years opened a vein of creation. The first works, plays, grew directly from his interest in Italy and the Renaissance. The choice of subject was unfortunate, for it was not until Rolland began to write about his own times or the French Revolution that he began to show his stature as a creative writer. But although his first attempts were in an erroneous direction, within them can already be discerned certain themes and motifs that were to become important in his mature works.

[14] "Souvenirs sur Richard Strauss, par Romain Rolland", *Les Œuvres libres,* 253 (1948), 3-18.

IV

EARLY PLAYS (1888-1893)

The Italy of the Renaissance inspired Rolland to write for the stage, despite such obstacles as research and preparation of a thesis, but these were not his first creative attempts. In March, 1890, he wrote to Malwida that he was writing a novel. He had, in fact, already written one novel before his trip to Italy, "Amour d'enfants", in October, 1888. It was, he said, in the style of Thackeray, who was then delighting his spare moments. Jules Lemaître had skimmed it, made some false but amiable comments, and dismissed the author. Rolland destroyed the manuscript, but claimed that some of the material appeared fifteen years later in the love affair between Christophe and Minna (*Ein Briefwechsel. 1890-1891. Romain Rolland und Malwida von Meysenbug* [Stuttgart, 1923], p. 50, and *Mémoires* [Paris, 1956], p. 69).

Inspired by the vigorous and ardent life of the Italian Renaissance, Rolland turned his attention from the documents in the archives to his world of fantasy, and in August, 1890, began to work seriously on his projected plays (letter to his mother, Dec. 30, 1890; *Retour au Palais Farnèse* [Paris, 1956], pp. 134-138). The first was a drama in four scenes about the condottiere, Orsino. The second was a sort of Greek tragedy about Empedocles. He undertook both of them in order, he said, to assuage his thirst for sunlight and the far-away love by recreating both (*Le Voyage intérieur* [Paris, 1942], p. 216; text probably of 1926). He wrote the second act in Paris in September, the third and fourth acts in Rome during November and early December, and the first act shortly before December 30 (letter to his mother, Dec. 30, 1890; *Retour,* p. 137). Thus the first act was written last, and he felt that this was a grave error; it was written painfully and was inferior to the others.

Suarès, to whom he showed parts of "Orsino" and of "Empédocle", was surprised at this kind of writing from Rolland's pen, and he himself was not much less astonished. Hardly were these finished when two other subjects filled his mind; scenes for other plays formed there without his conscious participation. One of them was about the Baglioni family of Perugia; the other about a tyrant like Malatesta.

During the same summer he had written parts of a short poetic love novel. Suarès had been displeased by what he had read of it, and Rolland was hurt, for artistic and other reasons. He believed that he was attracted and best suited to the drama and not to the novel (letter to his mother, Dec. 30, 1890; *Retour,* p. 137). His statement reminds us to proceed with caution, for a man may be very mistaken about his own abilities. His good faith is not in question, but deeply rooted emotions affected his perspective. Rolland later remarked that circumstances had turned him aside from various paths he wanted to follow: music and the theater. He regarded himself as a 'musicien manqué'. In a conversation with Lucien Price many years later, Rolland said that he was a thwarted composer who thought in music first, but wrote in words because he was unable to write in music (Lucien Price, "Romain Rolland Converses", *Atlantic* [Dec., 1935], 718-726). We may regard him as a 'dramaturge manqué' also — a glorious failure after sincere and highly ideal efforts.

"Orsino" was never published. Although it pleased him at the time, Rolland judged both the play and his own ability immature. In a letter to Malwida in January, 1891, he declared that the last scene alone pleased him, and that the only pleasure he had taken in the play was in the writing of it (*Briefwechsel,* p. 211). Because Rolland felt that it was far too different from the current stage productions to be accepted without explanation, he drew up an "Examen" (letter to his mother, Dec. 30, 1890; *Retour,* pp. 134-138). The differences did not deter or dismay him; he was sure of his strength and originality in various parts of the play — just as he was well aware of the weaknesses of such parts as the first act. His letter contains the very essence of the man : his independence and disregard for material success; his consequent indifference to opinion, public or private (except perhaps for that of such people as his mother, Malwida, or Suarès — but even these he refused to allow to sway his convictions in art or in politics); and his almost absolute refusal to work for the success of his writings. His sole criterion was his 'triomphe intérieur'. He always insisted on absolute sincerity, and the satisfaction of his own conscience was his touchstone.

One of the notes for the "Examen" is particularly meaningful for our knowledge of Rolland the writer. One rule of dramatic composition, he wrote, is to prepare separately, in the first act, two or more passions or forces, which are then developed as fully as possible. They are brought together in the last act. There, according to the nature of the forces, the most powerful dramatic or comic effects will be obtained by their opposition, or by the harmony of their combination. It is a musical rule: the passions are stated, developed, and then combine, meet or repel each other, like musical motifs which keep their independence and yet fuse in the powerful harmony of the whole, as all lives meet in universal life.[1] This 'rule of composition' stresses the relationship between the aesthetics of music and drama. It is, of course, not surprising in the enthusiastic young musician and musicologist. But it is significant also for the mature writer, for the author of *Jean-Christophe* and of *L'Ame enchantée*.

The subject of the almost complete "Orsino" is the intrigue surrounding a powerful condottiere of fifteenth-century Italy, Orsino, and his love affair with Catherine, sister of the Duke of Florence. The intrigue develops stormily and melodramatically.

---

[1] "Poser *séparément,* dans les premiers actes, deux ou plusieurs passions, ou forces vivantes, et leur donner le plus libre développement. — Au dernier acte, les mettre en présence. — Suivant la nature de ces forces et de leurs différences, jailliront spontanément de cette simple opposition, ou de l'harmonie formée par leur rencontre, les plus puissants effets dramatiques ou comiques. — C'est une règle musicale. — Les passions se rencontrent, se combinent, ou se repoussent, comme des motifs musicaux, qui gardent leur forte indépendance, et se fondent pourtant dans la puissante harmonie de l'ensemble. — Comme font toutes les vies dans la Vie universelle."

Through battle, storm, and trickery they pursue each other and others, until Catherine, moved by rightful jealousy, serves poisoned wine which both drink. Rolland changed the ending (note to Act IV); in the original version, Orsino became aware of his approaching death and found ultimate fulfillment, because only the richness of their love was left after his egotism had been stripped away.[2] Orsino recognizes the fullness of love only in the face of death; both death and love then are an ecstasy, clearly related to each other in a romantic mysticism. The original version was more in harmony with Rolland's romanticism and his idealized love than with the character of Orsino. In the scene as finally written, Catherine dies first, and Orsino, raging at the loss of his love, in the midst of preparations for the attack on Florence, is unaware that he is dying. Orsino has the same great capacity for life (although he has no scruples), that we find later in Rolland's principal creations — Christophe, Annette, and the characters of the heroic biographies and of the dramas of the French Revolution.

Rolland's notes of Dec. 8, 1891, reveal his almost complete disregard for any but his own feelings and ideas — his mixture of egotism and altruism, his intuition and his iconoclasm; they also disclose the intimate relationship that exists between himself and his characters, a relationship one finds important when considering his later works. One of the joys of the dramatic art as he sees it is that one can express all of one's thoughts without being completely understood by everybody. In reply to a question put to him by Malwida, Rolland said that he had himself in mind when he created Pompeo, duke of Florence;[3] he meant, in part,

[2] "Acte IV. La mort. Les deux égoïsmes disparaissent absorbés en un égoïsme supérieur. Car à peine l'a-t-elle tué qu'elle se désole de l'avoir arraché à la joie de vivre. Et lui, tout au contraire, l'en remercie: car seulement alors, il connaît la plénitude de l'amour, forme supérieur de la Vie."

[3] "Oui... [Malwida] est Italienne, à peu près autant que je suis Russe. Rien ne prévaut contre la force du sang. Quand elle vit Orsino, elle me dit: 'C'est à Cesare Borgia que vous avez pensé, n'est-ce pas?' Un tel mot suffit. Ses clairs yeux profonds ne *virent* jamsis l'aubergiste qui la servait, ni le contadino qui lui parlait. — Elle me dit encore: 'A qui avez-vous pensé en faisant Pompeo?' — Je lui dis 'A moi' — 'Non,' fit-elle, 'soyez sérieux; avouez que vous avez pensé à Luigi Guerrieri... Jamais de la vie, je vous assure que c'est à moi' " (Letter to André Suarès, postmark June 20, 1892).

his intense desire for a life of action. The dominating impression of the play is one of force, unchecked ambition, and individual egotism. It was this aspect of the Renaissance man that attracted Rolland, although he later came to see that strength for the sake of strength is bad. Strength can be used or abused, and the choice lies in the hands and mind of the possessor. Force, he wrote, is the primary condition of all greatness and of all goodness, but it is a means, not an end. Hence his attitude towards the Italian Renaissance changed to one of some dislike (letter to Mme Bertolini, Jan. 8, 1902; *Chère Sofia. Choix de lettres de Romain Rolland à Sofia Bertolini Guerrieri-Gonzaga* [Paris, 1959], p. 48).

The other play, dating from 1890, "Empédocle", was inspired by his enthusiasm for the Sicilian philosopher. Rolland was well prepared for the task. He knew the philosopher; he knew Greek tragedies; in fact, he claimed to know by heart all of *Oedipus Rex* in Greek.[4] It is also probable that Renan's philosophic dramas were a source of his inspiration. The play, less a drama than a poem, is a mixture of enthusiasm, irony, and scorn (see Rolland's notes, Aug., 1890); the subject is that of a man, master of his world, who has been able to understand reality and to manipulate appearances. The contrast between the philosopher Empedocles and the ruler Hieron is one of the themes in this poem, in which Rolland seems to debate a dichotomy in his own feelings. Empedocles has a philosopher's view of man; he looks to the remote results of an action, while ironically scorning the crowd. A bit like his character Rolland admitted to a furious hatred for individuals, yet claimed (and justified the claim by his actions) to love man. In fact, however, he experienced some difficulty in really understanding — much less liking — other people. He confessed (letter to Malwida, Sept. 11, 1890; *Choix de lettres*, p. 29) that his ability to observe others was hampered by several factors: his concentration on his own inner life, the struggles of his idealistic nature, the restraint under which he had lived (mother, family, self), and indeed the disdain, amounting at times to disgust, which he felt when in contact with most people. Need it be said that

---

4 See his notes on these dramas, published in "Le Grain de vie", *Mercure de France* (June 1, 1947), pp. 201-213.

the last of these factors is not a cause, but a result of other and deeper elements underlying the other traits?[5]

In the play Hieron is a politician who acts solely for the immediate result, but whose actions are generally effective. Both he and Empedocles are disillusioned about life and men. Hieron, however, clings to life, power, and wealth, while Empedocles, convinced of the vanity and futility of everything, seeking union with the great Being that is the essence of all existence, throws himself into Aetna's crater.[6]

Carried along by his enthusiasm, Rolland was soon writing another play, "Les Baglioni" (1891). According to Malwida, he spent Twelfth Night, 1892, with Mounet-Sully, the French tragic actor, who had been greatly pleased when he read "Les Baglioni". The actor had found this play superior to "Orsino", more effective and better theater, and had prophesied a great future on the stage for the young author.[7]

---

[5] In his Journal for 1898 (*Mémoires* [Paris, 1956], p. 239), he confessed that he had no confidence in anybody, man or woman. The peace and unity of his life were in God alone. Physically and spiritually he was unable to work closely with other people. This was true even in music, as he admitted in a letter to Mme Cruppi dated Wednesday, Dec. 7, 1911. "Il faut que je vous dise aussi une des raisons pour lesquelles nous n'avons jamais fait de musique ensemble... c'est un vice de ma nature, je n'ai jamais pu faire de musique avec personne, même avec ceux que j'aime le mieux, et dont j'aime le sentiment musical. Je suis un indépendant, jusqu'à un degré maladif. Jamais je ne pourrais faire partie d'un orchestre ou d'une société de quatuor. Dès que je suis 'plus d'un' à jouer, je ne sens plus rien. Tout au plus si j'entends".

[6] The form of the fragments dates from April, 1909, when he copied the plays for preservation. In his notes of that date he says that this copy is a summary choice after the elimination of the worst. Much remains to be eliminated. Their value is documentary rather than artistic (Notes, April, 1909). In 1918, Rolland reviewed the poem "Empédocle" and his notes, while preparing the plaquette *Empédocle d'Agrigente et l'Age de la haine* (Geneva, Cahiers du Carmel, 1918), which shows a close resemblance to the poem of 1890. For a good discussion of Rolland and the philosophy of Empedocles, see H.L. Götzfried, *Romain Rolland, das Weltbild im Spiegel seiner Werke* (Stuttgart, 1931); and also his German translation of Rolland's *Empédocle*, especially the introduction (*Empedokles von Agrigent* [Erlangen, 1947]). The plays of which he had typescripts made are: "Jeanne de Piennes" (131 pp.), "Savonarole" (81 pp.), "Le Siège de Mantoue" (175, 4 pp.), and "Orsino" (120 pp.). "Savonarole" was published in *Europe* (Jan.-Feb., 1955), 78-129.

[7] Malwida von Meysenbug, letter to Olga Monod (Jan. 8, 1892), in *Im Anfang war die Liebe. Briefe an ihre Pflegetochter von Malwida von Meysenbug* (Munich,

Closely associated with this play is another drama, "Arcangelo", which did not survive as long as "Les Baglioni". Rolland mentions both plays in a letter to Malwida, indicating that he had outlined the action of "Arcangelo" before April 20, 1892. The play concerned a fifteenth-century tyrant; the second principal character was a kind of Michelangelo, incidents of whose life had been deeply moving for the author (letter to Malwida, April 20, 1892; *Choix de lettres,* p. 73). In his notes on another unpublished drama, "Le Siège de Mantoue" (1892-1893), he remarked that the principal character was Arcangelo de Malatesta, who became Cratès in his "Caligula", another unpublished drama written in Rome in 1891 and 1892.[8] Raphael in "Caligula" became Olivier in the "Siège de Mantoue". Rolland wrote to Malwida (April 20, 1892), that the plan for "Caligula" was complete; he called it a play mad in subject and style, written to bring relief to its creator, not to be played. Worst of all, it was neither a love play nor a drama of political implication, and there were no feminine rôles. The theme could be "all is a dream". "Caligula", which he did not include among the plays worthy of attention when he reread his early efforts, must have been abandoned early in 1893 (letter to Malwida, March, 1893). While writing this play he was busy on still another, "Niobé", which progressed so far as to be submitted to Mounet-Sully, who read it before Rolland (*Journal des années de guerre* 1914-1919 [Paris, 1952], p. 682).

"Le Siège de Mantoue", which was in part composed of the débris of "Arcangelo", was finished in June, 1894 (letter to Malwida, Jan., 8, 1894; *Choix de lettres,* p. 108, and in his notes to the play, where he dates its completion June 3, 1894). The

1926), pp. 249-250. In his *Journal des années de guerre* (Paris, 1952), p. 682, March, 1916, Rolland commented on the death of the actor, the only great tragedian he had known. Mounet had received his early efforts at dramatic writing with an enthusiasm as naive as was Rolland's confidence in the world of art. The actor had supported, passionately but unsuccessfully, Rolland's first plays. The latter had spent many pleasant evenings in the apartment of Mounet-Sully, near the Panthéon.

8   In a letter to Stefan Zweig (Jan. 2, 1919), he dated the composition of "Caligula" 1891-1892; in his *Mémoires* (Paris, 1956), pp. 209-210, much of which was written from his papers in 1926 and 1939, he dates its composition 1892-1893. Arcangelo he says in his notes is a masque of Michelangelo.

action occurs about 1630, in a purely imaginary Mantua. It is dedicated to "Ariane et Sofia", presumably the Guerrieri-Gonzaga sisters. Rolland outlined the principal themes of the play in his notes; the symbolic meaning is the intense agitation of life when death approaches; it is the collapse of modern civilization undermined by its own members and overthrown by the pressure of attacking barbarians. There are two actions — one portrays and develops the character of a man, Claudio, the protagonist; the other is the love, poetic and tragic, of Olivier the artist and Ariane, daughter of the Marquis Ranuce. The background action is the defense of the city against the Imperial forces. The nobility wish to negotiate; the townspeople prepare to defend the city by military action. All the elements of tragedy are then present : the military force that threatens from without; the dissension within the city, opposing Claudio and Ranuce; and the love triangle, consisting of Sofia who loves Olivier, who loves Ariane, who hesitates long before admitting her true feelings for Olivier. The clash of opposing forces and the intrigue move against a background of selfish preoccupation. Claudio is the only one who rises above the egotistic atmosphere.

The theme of life, all-pervading and all-powerful, intensely active up to the very moment of its metamorphosis in death, is consonant with one of the basic drives of Rolland's personality. He did not know of later developments in photo-micrography as applied to bacteriology, but filmed research results show an intense agitation, at an increased tempo, of microscopic life in water as evaporation reduces the volume. It is most intense immediately before final (but not permanent) immobility in waterless surroundings. This intense activity before impending doom is characteristic of his dramas of the Revolution, especially *Le Triomphe de la raison* and *Robespierre.*

Other themes and characters of this drama will recur in later works. Persée, Ariane's brother, whose intuition of the thoughts and emotions of others is sharpened by the chronic illness that has undermined him, is obviously related in physique and temperament to Aërt in the play by that name, to Olivier in *Jean-Christophe,* and to Marc in *L'Ame enchantée,* as well as to Rolland himself. The uncompromising character of Claudio, a victim to his ideals and to duty, is also a step on the road towards the character of Aërt. Another theme that will reappear is that of the calm, self-centered love of Olivier and Ariane, who, in the midst of fighting and confusion, see and know only their love and their hopes. This is the theme of the idyll *Pierre et Luce* (1920), which is set in Paris during the First World War. The theme of the collapse of modern civilization we shall find at intervals throughout the years before 1914 in Rolland's letters and writings (*Jean-Christophe* [Paris, 1950], p. 698). In his *Péguy* (Paris, 1944, I, p. 103, n. 21), he wrote that even before 1892 he had perceived the chasm into which European civilization would inevitably fall. It is also the theme of some of his dramas of the Revolution (*Pâques fleuries,* for example), and of the later volumes of *L'Ame enchantée* (one of which is entitled *La Mort d'un monde*). The composition of the play is approximately contemporary with that of *Saint-Louis,* the first of his plays to be presented to the public. But its origin is more closely connected with the play *Aërt* (1895-1896). In his notes about "Le Siège de Mantoue", Rolland pointed out this filiation. Claudio is Jean de Witt, and this Dutch hero is the inspiration of *Aërt* ; Ariane is, he says, "la jeune Gonzaga" (Sofia).

None of the plays which he left in typescript have more than documentary value. The characters in "Orsino" are flat; the action it is true is rapid, but melodramatic. On the other hand, there are fewer monotonous passages in which the author exposes his own ideas or feelings — not an infrequent failing in Rolland's attempts at writing for the stage. We have analyzed "Le Siège de Mantoue" at some length because it is significant in view of Rolland's later works. "Orsino" remains unique among his works, whereas "Le Siège de Mantoue" leads primarily to later efforts. His thinking by 1930 will lead him to conceive a new hope, a new society, a socialist society, to replace the dying one. This hope was only beginning to glimmer in 1894-1895. Unlike his later works, these early plays brought with them no great breath of hope, and aside from their technical weaknesses, this is perhaps the main reason he did not publish them in later years (*Mémoires,* pp. 209-210).

In the plays are echoes of his readings (for example Pasolini, *Caterina Sforza*; Villari, *Savonarola*); it is in part these bookish sources that account for the lack of the breath of life. Despite his training as a historian, his attempt to write such plays was doomed to failure because of his own nature. Not until he wrote of men and society in his own day was he successful in his creative writings. Christophe was to be a purer and more effective embodiment of Life, Love, and Action than any character in these youthful efforts. They are significant for the biographer, however, because they reveal themes and characters that become important in his more mature writings.

It was important for Rolland to write the plays, abortive though they may be. Two of them aroused real interest, as a result of which Rolland's ego undoubtedly received some necessary encouragement. He needed some form of recognition especially at this time, for in 1892 he had fallen in love. But his confidence in his relations with women of his age was small, and his relationships with them uncertain. Praise from Mounet-Sully was extremely beneficient to the budding writer and the awkward lover.

V

THE SORBONNE AND THE STAGE (1891-1900)

Rolland returned to Paris in 1891, where he continued research and writing. The question of his future was increasingly worrisome during this period. He was certain of his ability to write, but from all sides he met opposition to his plan to abandon his academic career, except from Malwida, Mounet-Sully, and Suarès. Geoffroy said he was convinced that art was the only activity truly befitting Rolland, but carefully pointed out the difficulties involved (letter of Rolland to his mother, June 25, 1891; *Retour au Palais Farnèse* [Paris, 1956], p. 312). His professors were especially desirous of keeping a promising candidate in a university career, and were — probably sincerely — certain of his eventual failure as an artist. What they read of him in 1892 failed to change their opinion. Gabriel Monod, more than anyone else except the historian Lavisse, tried to keep Rolland in the university. The latter explained in some detail various aspects of his character not easily perceptible to others, in an attempt to justify his desire to make creation rather than research the center of his life. He pointed out what we have already seen; his sickly, lonely childhood; the deaths and other shocks which had caused him to withdraw into himself; the dreams too numerous and too advanced; the obsession with death. Then the two years in Rome, which were a rebirth, after which he faced life with confidence; but life punished him harshly, and he again withdrew, into art.

Enfin je me délivrai du doute, et je me créai ma foi. Alors je commençai à vivre. Mes deux années de Rome furent une renaissance; je m'ouvris à la vie avec une confiance enfantine; la réalité se chargea de m'en punir durement. Je me retrouvai seul, et me repliai en moi. Le peu

que j'avais vu de la vie m'avait montré qu'elle n'avait pas grand'chose
de commun avec moi; l'Art m'offrait son asile, et je m'y refugiai.[1]

But art, like music, was for him a means of withdrawing from real
life into an artificial, substitute life.

The problems, economic and emotional, of this time, were difficult to solve; this difficulty was increased and arguments for his
need of a stable situation were strengthened by his engagement.
The small encouragement he had received concerning his writing,
his increasing success, had helped give him the confidence to
propose marriage to Clotilde Bréal, daughter of the distinguished
philologist Michel Bréal. Soon, before the end of the summer,
1892, the engagement was announced and the marriage set for
October 31 (Mémoires, [Paris, 1956], p. 137). The temporary
solution was for Rolland to continue his work for the doctorate.
He had decided on a field of investigation for his theses: the
origins of the opera. For this work it was necessary to spend a
year or more in Italy. His wife was to bring a dowry to the marriage, and since her family was well off it was unlikely that the
young couple would be plagued by serious financial problems.
However, Rolland did not relish a situation in which he might
again be dominated by a woman. He was therefore pleased by
an offer of an official mission in Italy, but irritated by the inadequate remuneration it carried — six hundred francs. He would,
however, be attached to the Direction des Beaux Arts, and museum
doors would be open to him (letter to André Suarès, Sept. 20,
1892). It certainly would be helpful too in his efforts to shake off
his mother's domination.

On October 31, 1892, the marriage was celebrated at the 'mairie'
(not the church) of the Place Saint-Sulpice. Rolland appears to
have entered into marriage with great reservations; it did not seem
to be a completely satisfying and absorbing event. In fact, the week
before the ceremony, he wrote to Malwida that he needed her
friendship at that time especially; without her he would feel alone,
and Suarès was not to be present. Apparently his bride was not

[1]   Letter to Gabriel Monod (unpublished, June 8, 1892).

sufficient (*Choix de lettres à Malwida von Meysenbug* [Paris, 1948], p. 83; Oct. 24, 1892). Again, we must remember that he was very much alone and grappling with some severe problems. In spite of his mother's earnest wishes, Rolland insisted on a civil wedding only; since his bride was of a Jewish family, this was also her wish. We are tempted to see in this dispute with his mother and his consequent guilt feelings one of the causes, and one of the symptoms of other causes, of the divorce nine years later. Although the marriage was apparently one of love, it lasted only these few years. In a letter to Suarès on October 31, shortly after the ceremony, he told his friend about the difficulty that had arisen as a result of the decision to have only the civil ceremony. His mother had come to the wedding for the sole reason that Clotilde had made a scene the day before when she learned that Mme Rolland did not intend to be present at the ceremony. Although he would have been more unhappy had his mother not attended, and although it was Clotilde who was responsible for her presence, Rolland wrote that he was unable to forgive his wife completely. A remarkably bad start for a happy marriage! Perhaps some of the wrongs were on his wife's side, but certainly far from all.[2] If he felt anger at his mother's unreasonable attitude (and he could not fail to), further guilt feelings were doubtless aroused by his suppression of the anger. Certainly guilt feelings plagued him for years afterwards. In 1917, for example, Rolland wrote that he and his bride had acted as they saw fit; his mother had forgiven and forgotten the suffering he had caused her (he did not yet realize the suffering she had caused him), but he had not forgotten. He still reproached himself, in 1917, for his 'uncompromising'

---

[2] Letter to André Suarès (Oct. 31, 1892). "Ma mère est venue au mariage. Depuis la lettre d'hier, — le soir, Clotilde est venue toute bouleversée, avec des pleurs et un emportement de passion qui a décidé, forcé ma mère à promettre de venir. Cette scène m'a été très pénible, et je ne te cache pas que je ne puis la pardonner tout à fait à Clotilde. Maintenant ma mère est si supérieure à tous deux! et ma dette envers elle s'est accrue de tout le sacrifice cruel qu'elle nous offre aujourd'hui. Pour la 1ère fois de ma vie, je regrette qq. chose de mon passé. Si j'étais à recommencer, *j'exigerais* le mariage religieux. — *Mais ma mère, en une heure, hier, a plus fait dans mon cœur pour la religion* que toutes les cérémonies auxquelles je me fusse soumis" (Italics are Rolland's). His mother had, in his mind, made a still greater sacrifice by attending the wedding.

attitude in 1892 (letter of July 12, 1917; *Journal des années de guerre* [Paris, 1952], p. 1256). Perhaps the feelings of guilt were not so much because of the kind of wedding as because of the wedding itself. By refusing to attend the wedding his mother had symbolically rejected his bride in an effort to keep her son to herself. Rolland's emotions were then compounded. The fact that it was a lay ceremony would seem to be merely a pretext; the real reason is to be sought far deeper. He apparently never questioned his belief that he had caused his mother suffering, and was never aware that she had caused both him and his bride equal suffering. His mother's domination was strong. Rolland had had to fight stubbornly to complete the separation when she opposed his going to Rome. Later, his mother opposed and apparently prevented his second marriage, in 1920. In his *Voyage intérieur* (Paris, 1942), p. 134, he insists that he could not have remained in Paris, that he could not have avoided inflicting pain. The healthy duty of living, he argues, is stronger and perhaps more sacred than filial piety. Nevertheless, he had at different times sacrificed first the one and then the other.

Rolland and his bride left immediately for a villa belonging to an uncle of Clotilde's, near Vintimille. They were scarcely installed when Rolland wrote to Suarès urging him to come and stay with them in the villa (letters to André Suarès, Oct. 31, Nov. 6, 7, 1892). Again one wonders, although the evidence is small for a positive judgment, if Rolland were not ill-advised to urge his friend, morose, 'fantasque', and undoubtedly difficult for others besides Rolland to get along with, to stay with them at a time likely to be relatively complicated for two persons, without the presence of a third.

Be that as it may, the young couple spent several years in Italy and Switzerland, and summers in Normandy. But it was not a simple period for them; their happiness may have been great, but Rolland felt the pattern of his life had been so disrupted that he found it difficult to regain full intellectual and emotional equilibrium. Twenty years later he looked back upon the years of his marriage as one of the two periods of crises in his life: 1883-1888, and 1895-1902. In 1895 he had been married a scant three years.[3]

[3] Letter to Paul Seippel, Genevan journalist and critic and friend of Rolland's

In his *Mémoires* (Paris, 1956; text of 1939, p. 188), which he prepared from his notes and 'journal intime' in 1939, he speaks with
considerable emotion about his marriage and his wife:

Les peuples heureux n'ont pas d'histoire, dit la sagesse des nations.
Ah! la menteuse! C'est la plus belle histoire du monde ...Je couve la
mienne, 'l'Ile Fortunée', — 1892 — l'heureuse année d'amour partagé.
Elle a beau s'être enfuie. Elle fut, nous l'avons eue. Je la berce dans
mon cœur, avec piété reconnaissante. Qu'importe les tristesses qui l'ont
suivi !... C'est assez que ma bouche ait touché la bouche du bonheur...
Béni soit-il ! Et bénie soit celle qui fut sa bouche!

How little happiness he really expected or felt he deserved from
life! In fact, when we compare his scattered remarks in the *Mémoires* about his bride, his marriage, we find that the story of the
love, marriage, and divorce of Olivier Jeannin and Jacqueline is
a very thinly disguised transposition of his own love, engagement,
marriage and divorce.

Besides working on his theses in the winter of 1893-1894, he
was also teaching the history of painting and music at the Lycée
Henri IV. He gave lectures on Mantegna, Signorelli, and Leonardo
da Vinci in December, and on the history of music in February,
1892. He liked neither his audiences, nor the research for the
course, nor the lectures. He was fatigued because of the physical
effort and his work for his theses. The intellectual tension was
maintained at the cost of his emotional and physical life, and the
minute and erudite labor excluded all sentiments (letters to Malwida, Dec. 4, 12, 1893; *Choix de lettres à Malwida,* p. 91-96; letter
to Suarès, Nov. 13, 1893).

In September, 1894, he was appointed to teach ethics at the
Ecole J.-B. Say (Ecole primaire supérieure at Auteuil). In October
he was giving courses on the history of art in three Parisian lycées,
and he had agreed to lecture some months later, at the Sorbonne,
on the origins of the Italian opera.[4] In February, 1895, he began

(Feb. 10, 1913); see also the letter to Louis Gillet (July 29, 1903), where he
says that this was the state he was in some ten years previously, i.e., 1893;
Correspondance entre Louis Gillet et Romain Rolland [Paris, 1949], p. 219.
[4] Letters to Malwida von Meysenbug (Oct. 2, 10, 16, 1894); *Choix de lettres,*
pp. 122-126.

a course on the history of art at the Lycée Louis-le-Grand, while correcting proofs of his theses (letter to André Suarès, n.d., but probably mid-February, 1895). The burden of these various courses for a man of his temperament was great. Physically it was difficult because it necessitated long trips through Paris. Spiritually it was frustrating. One reason for his dislike of teaching was that he felt all teachers to be secretly actors, and not very good ones. Although he wanted to write for the stage, he had a profound distrust, almost a puritan dislike, for actors and especially actresses. Their profession is to pretend to have emotions they do not feel; they live in sentimental falsehood. A profession which requires one never to be himself is surely shameful, he wrote.[5]

Because of a lack of sympathy for his subjects, teaching at the J.-B. Say school was especially irksome for Rolland. He wrote to Malwida (Oct. 2, 1894, *Choix de lettres,* p. 123), that he disliked talking about moral and ethical questions without a faith on which to base them, for without faith such questions as Duty, Good, and Conscience seemed but empty shells. What he would prefer to teach would be faith in the Hero, in the Divinity. But his course was a lay course, and he was unable to talk about the Divine or the Immortal. He must perforce teach the superiority of the government of the Republic, the excellence of the Army, of capital, of the contemporary social order, "of everything necessary to lead the lamb to the slaughter". Nevertheless there was some profit even in such a course, he admitted. Life is forged by difficulties, and his task caused him to review all — and not merely some — of the principles he had been taught to live by. None of them stood the test. Social questions too began increasingly to occupy his attention partly as a result of this examination. "My life will not end before I take part in action", he wrote to Suarès (May [no day given], 1895). This was a first step on the road to "Au-dessus de la mêlée" in 1914, and to "A la Russie libre et libératrice", in 1917. Just as he had undergone a religious crisis ten or fifteen years before, so now began a social crisis that

---

[5] Letter to Mme Sofia Bertolini (Feb. 7, 1904), in *Chère Sofia. Choix de lettres de Romain Rolland à Sofia Bertolini Guerrieri-Gonzaga,* I [Paris, 1959], pp. 162-163.

was to last most of the rest of his life, well into the period between the wars, when he came to some definite conclusions based on the social principles he believed necessary.

Rolland upheld his theses before a European jury in June 19, 1895. The gruelling ordeal came off extremely well, he wrote to Malwida, June 20, 1895 (*Choix de lettres*, p. 140). Rolland's was the first dissertation on music to be presented before the Sorbonne, and he intended it in part as a protest against the disdain in which that art had always been held by the university.[6]

In the fall of 1895, he was named lecturer on the history of art at the Ecole normale supérieure. His lectures were dull, he said, because he had to begin the course with Gallo-Roman, Merowingian, and Carolingian art (letter to Malwida, Dec. 2, 1895; *Choix de lettres*, p. 151; *Mémoires*, 1956, p. 227). In spite of his research and his courses, he had not given up what lay closest to his heart, his creative writing. After "Le Siège de Mantoue", he completed *Saint-Louis* in 1893-1894, the first of his attempts that was to be published, although later (*Revue de Paris*, March 1, 15; April 1, 1897). *Saint-Louis* was followed by "Jeanne de Piennes", 1894-1895, which was never published. The next works were the three-act play *Aërt* (1895-1896), first staged in 1898, and "Savonarola" (1896), never completed.

The drama of "Jeanne de Piennes", laid in the first half of the sixteenth century when the rival houses of Guise and Montmorency were engaged in a struggle for power, is based on a historical event. François de Montmorency (son of the Connétable Anne de Montmorency) is secretly engaged to Jeanne de Piennes, of a less noble but eminently worthy family. François is told by his father that he must marry Mme de Castro, the king's bastard daughter. The secret engagement is revealed against the wishes of the weak-willed young man, and the father summons Jeanne to him. The scene between the two strongest characters in the play, one intensely virile, the other feminine despite her strength and energy, is a fine and dramatic one, and recalls Michelet's *Jeanne d'Arc*.

The case is brought before the ecclesiastical court, where Jeanne

[6] See A.F. Sanborne, "Romain Rolland", *Century*, Aug., 1913, pp. 512-518. See also his *Mémoires* (Paris, 1956), pp. 221-222.

is convicted of beguiling the young man into defying his father's wishes. She is sentenced to the Couvent des Filles-Dieu, a virtual prison for prostitutes. The sentence satisfies the High Constable by removing one bar to the projected marriage, and the Cardinal hopes that it will sully the name of Montmorency. Jeanne, duped by the High Constable, and by the weakness of François, is forced to read aloud the letter from François renouncing the engagement.

Rolland wrote two endings for the play. In the one intended for the German stage, Jeanne confides to a young noble, Robortet, who was attracted by her beauty and character, that she still loves François. Robortet asks for her hand, but she is proudly and bitterly resigned and determined to live so as to harm no one — and she cannot love Robortet. The ending for the French stage occurs after the marriage of François and Mme de Castro. François, still hesitant and pusillanimous, still in love with Jeanne, is almost detested by his father who calls him a booby. The play ends with the triumphal entry of the King and Queen, and Robortet's reflection: "Magnificent. — All the enormous power of the kingdom of France to crush an unfortunate girl". The scene for the German stage is of a more intimate character. The ending for the French stage is exterior and fits more readily into the action. The endings are not variants of the same scene, but two different moments of the action, and they could well follow one another.

In 1895, Rolland discussed with Malwida a possible drama about Savonarola (Dec. 2, 1895; *Choix de lettres,* p. 151), and actually began to write it early in the following year. His notes on the play (dated Jan. 8, 16, 18, and Feb. 19, 1896), reveal as much about Rolland as about the play. Concerning the character of Savonarola and the motives for his actions, Rolland wrote that the Italian reformer suffered from his inability to improve and to save men. Savonarola was convinced that he would succeed in his task, but he exhausted himself and was finally vanquished. He was in despair until the moment when, near death, he understood that man's rôle is not to escape suffering and evil nor to protect others, but to struggle against suffering and evil. The struggle is the duty and happiness of man on earth, whatever the results.[7] This tensely combative, puritanical attitude, which persisted throughout Rolland's life, probably had its origins in his childhood and especially in his relationship with his mother; it certainly affected his relations with others, and even his creative writing. He wrote in his notes that the principal subject was to be the death of Savonarola. An increasing melancholy had led him so to conceive of the play, for he was tired of life. His real interest was in sharing the sufferings of men who have loved, alone and despairing, and who have been revolted by the world's injustice, men like Savonarola and Beethoven. This need to share men's pains was one of the motives for his heroic biographies, written some years later.

But the death of Savonarola is only the outward aspect of the true drama, which is in the soul of the reformer. Rolland wished to concentrate the drama in the protagonist's soul, the seat of so many conflicting emotions: horror of the surrounding world, bitter solitude, imperious and passionate desire for action, sudden changes from absolute faith to gnawing doubt, spiritual isolation at the height of his triumph, opposition to his own family, distrust of his body and his soul, inner tortures of uncertainty about the truth of his vision. Rolland was attracted to the Italian priest not only by the dramatic story of his inner struggles, but also by the very similarity of Savonarola to himself. His solitude, his growing desire for action, the weakness of a body which hampers an imperious soul, uncertainty (at times) of the truth of his own vision, characterize Rolland also, perhaps more than he realized.

In considering whether he should put on the stage the interrogation of Savonarola under torture, he concluded that it was permissible and necessary: "My subject", he wrote, "is the revelation of a soul betrayed by its body, — the worst of all suffering! A will and a heroic faith dwelling in flesh too weak, which betrays them. But why show this suffering? To encourage those who suffer" (unpublished notes about scene XIII, Jan. 18, 1896).

[7] Notes on Savonarola, Jan. 16, 18, 1896. See Rolland, "Savonarole (théâtre 1896)", *Europe* (Jan.-Feb., 1955), 78-129, where all the notes and the entire fragment can be read. The play consists of a few completed scenes and outlines and notes for others.

A hint arises of the dilemma he faced later concerning the "Vies des hommes illustres". Their purpose was to bring aid, comfort, and invigorating strength, but the value of showing suffering in order to comfort those who suffer may justifiably be questioned.

"Savonarola" was preceded by *Saint-Louis,* written in Paris, 1893-1894. It is based on the last crusade of 1270 led by St.-Louis, who died before reaching Jerusalem. The poem — for it is more a dramatic poem than a drama — is the exaltation of an ardent faith and the exaltation of death in the service of a divine cause, and hence of the first steps towards a life of beatitude (see *Le Périple* [Paris, 1946], p. 48 [text of 1924]). It is also an expression of Rolland's great need for faith, his hatred of doubt (perhaps because of an innate tendency to doubt, or because of the insecurity of his emotions) (see *Correspondance entre Gillet et Rolland,* pp. 126-127).

Louis is lovingly portrayed, not as a saint only, but as a man of joys and sorrows who suffers periods of doubt and uncertainty. He hesitates once, in the last act shortly before his death, when he wonders if he would not have been a better monk than king because he has partially failed the people of France — The simple souls of his people need a hearth for their flame to glow in; they suffer when this beautiful fire of love subsides or dies for lack of fuel (*Les Tragédies de la foi* [Paris, 1913], pp. 103-104). In these words there is contained one of Rolland's purposes: to furnish matter for the flame of love, for idealism, courage, strength, and faith.

The play embodies another theme characteristic of many of Rolland's heroes; Louis is the very type of the 'vaincu vainqueur', the man who, defeated in the immediate situation, is yet the ultimate victor.[8] The word 'frustration' has been used in describing Rolland's creations (Wilson, *The Pre-War Biographies of Romain Rolland and Their Place in his Work and the Period* [New York, 1939], p. 127). However this attitude does not seem to be one of frustration. The characters who fall, such as Louis IX, are not

---

[8] The reverse of the medal also appears in some of Rolland's works: the 'vainqueur vaincu', the victor whose victory eventually leads to a defeat — a personal defeat — which finally outweighs the victory of the moment.

frustrated. They act full of confidence regardless of the results. Nor can Rolland be called frustrated. His purpose is to act in accordance with faith regardless of the outcome. The French lords under Louis cannot understand why this man, so weak, so near death, apparently defeated, can yet wield so much power. They cannot understand that he wields power because he acts in absolute sincerity, moved by love and compassion, guided by justice and tolerance. He is a true Christian dedicated to the service of a higher cause. Such a man offers no weak spots through which an enemy can attack him. He has unintentionally acquired an extraordinary power because he submits completely to his cause. His inspiration enables him to understand all men. He explains to Rosalie that everything that exists has its being in God; in order to understand others, it is necessary only to love Him. This is essentially Rolland's belief; one must merely substitute the words 'universal being' for God.

Other persons in the play are more or less typical of Rolland's creative works and reveal various traits of their creator. Rosalie de Brèves, utterly selfish, is incapable of feeling love for her husband. Eventually her actions aid Manfred in his plot and cause the death of her husband. Too late she realizes her selfishness and her sin, and yearns for death to complete her expiation and release. The mediocre person, egotistical, unable to love, is particularly repugnant to Rolland (cf. *supra,* p. 42). There are, on the other hand, characters whom Rolland is very fond of, and whom he generally portrays vividly. Bérangère, the pure and delicately beautiful daughter of Quentin the blacksmith, is touching in her simple, unquestioning faith and candor. Etienne de Coucy, not much more than an adolescent, is a simple, sincere youth as candid and pure as Bérangère, and as full of faith. The two young people fall in love. The freshness and purity of their love is gently presented, and brings to mind the poetic *Pierre et Luce,* which Rolland was to write during the First World War. Their love forms an effective contrast to the sensual, adulterous love of Rosalie de Brèves and Gaultier de Salisbury. Quentin, man of the people and robustly courageous in maintaining his own opinions, showing an obvious tendency to revolt against injustice, is also a character who reappears in Rolland's works; there are for example, Haubourdin in *Le Triomphe de la raison,* Christophe himself, Annette Rivière, and especially Marc.

Another theme found in *Saint-Louis* is that of the relations of mother and son. The first hint of the dominant mother figure occurs when Queen Marguerite tells Rosalie of the difficulties she and Louis encountered in their marriage because of his jealous mother, Blanche de Castille, who had interfered almost to the point of preventing the physical consummation of the marriage. It is significant that Rolland makes this theme the subject of an entire scene (Act. III, sc. 1). The unusually close, perhaps unhealthily close, relationship between Rolland and his mother comes to mind.

The religious exaltation that Rolland glorifies in the play is expressed by him also in a letter to Tolstoy, in 1897, where he wrote that the French peasant no longer has a God; his life is empty; God must be reborn in him, and he must again taste the ardor of dedication and self-sacrifice in a higher cause.[9] Sacrifice (of self, not of others — the difference is important), the free giving of oneself to a higher cause, a joy in this devotion and sacrifice which can cause the accomplishment of great deeds, these conditions Rolland found in the period of the French Revolution. Before the end of his life he was to write a cycle of eight plays about the Revolution. Marc Rivière in *L'Ame enchantée* sacrifices himself in a cause — no longer a religious one, but for the sake of a better society. In the years after the war of 1914, Rolland's inclinations to place social questions at the heart of his creative works and to make such questions the center of his action replace almost completely the pantheism and individualism which are still the most important sources of inspiration in *Jean-Christophe*. One who is capable of sacrificing himself usefully to aid in the solution of complex social problems is of necessity a strong personality; this type, frequently portrayed in Rolland's writings, is at the core of his works.

Saint-Louis met with only slight success at the time of publica-

---

[9]   Cited by Dvořak, *Das Ethische und das Aesthetische bei Romain Rolland* [Münster, 1933], p. 25.

tion. Rolland wrote to André Suarès that its failure had shaken his confidence in himself to the point that he was undecided about his future; he was unsure whether to devote himself to a university career, or to use this position merely as a means of obtaining sufficient independence to devote more time to creative writing. His very convictions and standards of artistic judgments were upset, and he felt the necessity of revising all his values. Worst of all, he felt himself entirely alone with no understanding person to turn to, and this in spite of an intelligent wife. It seems to be because he had, as he says in his *Mémoires* (pp. 257-260), made himself a promise not to succeed, believing that, or telling himself that the creative artist is more endangered than aided by success — and he quoted from Goethe to support his contention. Furthermore, again in his *Mémoires* (p. 260) we see that his motto could well have been his 'Beata solitudo, Sola beautitudo...'.

At the same time another heroic soul was arousing his interest. The idea of a drama about Mazzini soon became the project for another heroic biography. In Mazzini's letters to Mme d'Agoult Rolland perceived the greatness of soul he sought, the generosity, and the need to sacrifice oneself to others (letter to Malwida, March 18, 1896; *Choix de lettres à Malwida,* p. 173). He continued to collect materials about the Italian patriot for some time; in 1907 he again mentioned the project to Mme E. Marchand (Oct. 17, letter). He did not definitely renounce the plan until 1912, when he felt that it was bootless to throw oil on the troubled waters of Italian chauvinism (letter to Mme E. Marchand, Dec. 12, 1912). This was, however, not the only reason for his decision. *Jean-Christophe* absorbed his energies during the years from 1904 to 1910, and he created around himself the moral and spiritual atmosphere necessary for this important work. The biographies of Michelangelo and Tolstoy coincided with the development of the novel; a life of Mazzini at this time, however, was not in harmony with his faith and ideas.[10] Moreover Rolland had already

---

[10] "Il s'est trouvé que Michel-Ange et Tolstoy s'accordaient avec le développement actuel de Christophe; c'est pourquoi j'ai écrit ces biographies. Et pour la même raison, je n'écrirai peut-être jamais le *Mazzini*... ni le *François Millet,* (bien qu'il soit déjà esquissé en anglais), — parce qu'ils ne s'accordent plus

in 1902 begun to feel some doubts about the opportuneness of this heroic biography because of the political situation.

He spent the summer of 1896 in England and Germany. At Berchtesgaden he began to write *Aërt,* his first play to be presented to the public. It was played in Paris at the Théâtre de l'Œuvre on May 3, 1898. His original intention had been to write a cycle of three dramas in which the cause of peace would emerge triumphant. As he wrote, however, his vision of the protagonist and of the theme of the drama changed. As it now stands it is rather the encomium of a just war (when peace would be degrading) and national exaltation (*Souvenirs de jeunesse* [Lausanne, 1947], p. 215). On November 5, 1896, he wrote to Malwida that he was also busy with a long novel and a suite or cycle of dramas, the first of which he hoped to finish the same year. Both works embodied a part of what he had been seeking in the past four years, namely the union of modern thinking with his former conception of art — which he called 'Roman' because he had first received in Rome the inspiration for his literary career. The novel is the story of a genius (Jean-Christophe), and the drama, the struggle of a prince against the world (Aërt). Their subjects were similar but expressed in different spheres — one in action, the other in thought. One takes place in Germany, the other in an imaginary Holland.

Actually, *Aërt* had been begun four years before. In a letter to Malwida, April 20, 1892 (*Choix de lettres,* p. 74), after discussing the dramas he was engaged in writing ("Les Baglioni" and "Caligula"), he wrote that he had as a counterweight to these the completed plan of another drama, a drama of Duty, of Sacrifice to the Divine, of Belief in the Fatherland, a drama of revolt in seventeenth-century Holland. The last scene of *Aërt* in its present state is the crushing of the revolt, Aërt's betrayal by his friends — in order to save his life — and his suicide. It would appear that the idea of the sacrifice of self — first by utter devotion and then by suicide when all else fails — of a pure and idealistic youth who

---

avec mon atmosphère morale d'aujourd'hui" (letter to Paul Seippel, Feb. 10, 1913). See also letters to Mme Bertolini (Jan. 27, 1902); *Chère Sofia*, I; p. 55 (March 21, 1910); *Chère Sofia*, II [Paris, 1960], p. 62; to Malwida (March 18, 1896); *Choix de lettres*, pp. 173-174; and to Mme E. Marchand (Dec. 12, 1912).

is willing to give up everything for his fatherland, was the embryo of the play. We cannot, however, be entirely sure of this, for the original idea was somewhat different from its final form. Rolland conceived of the play as a trilogy, and the first version consisted of five acts instead of three, as in the final version (letter to Mme Cruppi, Feb. 21, 1914).

The Stadhouder, governing with the tacit support of Spain, finds it expedient to keep Aërt, youngest son of the former governor of Holland (now fifteen or sixteen years of age), under his control to avoid attempts of exiled supporters of the overthrown government to excite subversive action. He had done all possible to corrupt Aërt in order to turn him aside from any dreams of national resurgence. Aërt is essentially too pure and too sincere, and is inspired by too much faith in his country to be touched by these crude means. However, he falls in love with the Stadhouder's daughter, and naïvely confides to her the plans for the revolt organized by the exiles. Lia, very much — although ambiguously — in love with Aërt and wishing to save his life, turns to his trusted friend Dirck. Lia and Dirck, motivated by a complex of scruples and feelings (friendship, love, fear, prudence, filial devotion, weakness, and courage) reveal the projected landing of the rebels. The governor drowns the movement in the blood of its participants. Lia inadvertently discloses her action to Aërt, who, despairing and unable longer to live without trusted friends, fidelity, and liberty in a corrupted world, commits suicide by throwing himself from his window.

The play is thus a glorification of sacrifice to a higher cause, one's country and family, and appears to admit war as a necessary evil in some circumstances. For Aërt, war was better than injustice and slavery in a nation corrupted by defeat. For Maître Trojanus, Aërt's tutor, peace at any price was the greatest good. Maître Trojanus is the very type of false intellectual that Rolland attacked on every occasion. Trojanus assured the Stadhouder that the history texts he was using were thoroughly impartial: "Ils sont de notre parti". Aërt tells Lia that most of the people who desire peace are motivated less by love of peace than by fear of action. (Rolland adopted the sentence from Spinoza's *Tractatus politicus*:

"Peace is not the absence of war, but the virtue which arises from the strength of the soul". [V, § iv]). When Lia and Dirck thwart the conspiracy for the welfare of Aërt, they reveal their almost complete lack of comprehension of his true character. How could they know ? Lia's love for him, after she had for political reasons, married an elderly Spanish grandee, is a rather turgid mixture of sensual, fraternal, and maternal love. It is more egocentric than generous, despite her expressed wishes for Aërt's safety. Dirck is too weak, self-centered and skeptical, too fond of pleasure and good company, too prone to compromise, to understand Aërt's purity, sincerity, and intransigence. Aërt, who embodies some of Rolland's character, is the strongest of the three; he refuses to accept a reality contrary to his own wishes. He is horrified at the idea of consenting to defeat, horrified at cowardly resignation. My will, he proclaims, will forge my life, or will break it (*Les Tragédies de la foi,* p. 173). Aërt's will had been formed by moral solitude in spite of the efforts of the Stadhouder. The tragedy of the play lies in the fact that Aërt is betrayed by Lia and Dirck at the moment when, because of his love for them, his motives have become truly unselfish and purified, even to the point of relinquishing his hatred for his country's enemy. The purifying or catalytic agents, having accomplished their work unwittingly, consciously undo their beneficial effects because they have understood neither Aërt nor their own importance in his life. Such lack of comprehension, even between lovers and close friends, although common enough in literature, is significant in Rolland's works. The rarity and beauty of true friendship is a frequent theme in his writings. The portrayal of a maternal or semi-maternal affection which we have seen in *Saint-Louis* is developed in *Aërt*. The scene in the garden, in which Lia allows her love to be known, reveals a distinct mingling of eroticism and motherly feelings. Lia wants Aërt to call her 'maman', and he agrees, his face hidden against her breast (p. 152).

Aërt was close to Rolland's heart, as he later admitted to Mme Cruppi.[11] The play reflects a period of Rolland's life not when

---

[11] Letter to Mme Louise Cruppi (May 25, 1913).

he was Aërt's age, but a later time. Aërt's state of mind is very much like Rolland's as an adolescent, but the latter's mental anguish, reflected in the play, was not caused merely by the threat of war, by the Dreyfus case, or by the adverse atmosphere of the times; the cause is to be found in the beginnings of the failure of his marriage. A certain distrust and dislike of women appears in his portrayal of Lia — although she had to be, for dramatic reasons, the type she is. If he had made her the heroine, Aërt would no longer be pitied; he would be understood and truly loved, but not pitied. Rolland wished Aërt to be alone, the only pure and heroic person in a corrupt ambience, whose friends are no less dangerous to him than his enemies (letter to Malwida, July 25, 1898; *Choix de lettres,* p. 237-238). One may conjecture nevertheless that his domestic difficulties were not without effect in his portrayal of a very attractive woman.

Aërt represents another part of Rolland's works; he is the first outline of Christophe, a Christophe in whom Olivier dominates. Like Olivier and Rolland, Aërt is not physically strong; he is inclined to introspection, and his idealism is sometimes as far removed from reality as Olivier's and Christophe's. He has an unusually keen sense of justice, but is frequently blind to the realities of the world around him — as was Christophe (not Olivier). Lia said to him: "Let's try to make it (the world) less ugly"; Aërt replied: "Let us try to make it more just" (p. 155). It is a reply that could come from the lips of Christophe, and which Rolland also found in the spirit of Savonarola (*Europe* [Jan.-Feb., 1955], 102). Unlike Christophe, Aërt hesitates to act.[12]

Aërt is also the result and the embodiment of another conviction that lay close to his creator's heart: one's need for spiritual isolation. It is an important part of the character of Christophe, of Marc, and of others. The line can thus be drawn from Aërt through Olivier and Christophe to Marc. We find in Marc the same proud confidence in himself and distrust of others as in Aërt

---

[12] "Avez-vous jamais lu mon petit Aërt? ... C'est un premier Christophe, où l'Olivier domine, un Christophe vaincu, mais immaculé... l'édition publiée, à très peu d'exemplaires n'a jamais contenu que trois actes sur cinq de la première version" (Letter to Mme Louise Cruppi, Feb. 21, 1914).

(p. 148). To be sure, Aërt had more cause than his later descendents to be suspicious of those around him.

Aërt, Christophe, Marc all assume complete responsibility for the social action they believe in. Aërt refuses to desist from the plot that will rid his country of the hated occupant. He feels personally responsible for his country and his people. His actions are for them, not for himself. Like Rolland, he was forced on by his conscience to act, even though action perturbed him (see A. R. Lévy, *L'Idéalisme de Romain Rolland* [Paris, 1942], p. 239). Christophe and Marc, with equal sincerity and intransigence, take upon their shoulders the righting of wrongs, literary, musical, or social; they refuse to remain inactive or to disclaim the responsibility for their acts.

Rolland saw Aërt played successfully in Brussels, where it was presented several times in March, 1914 (letter to J.-R. Bloch, Feb. 28, 1914; letter to Alphonse de Châteaubriant, March 1, 1914). More recently, in 1948 and 1954, it has been played successfully at the Théâtre de Poche by André Cellier and his troupe. In general the enthusiasm put into the play by the author and his interpreters, the generosity of the inspiration, the flavor of grandeur and of candid purity have aroused sympathetic responses. In France in the years shortly after the German occupation, the subject was a very living one.

In the summer of 1897, Rolland and his wife went to Bussang (in the Vosges) to attend plays at Maurice Pottecher's "Théâtre du peuple" (letter to Suarès, Aug. 11, 1897). The idea of a People's Theater was beginning seriously to occupy Rolland's thoughts because of his belief in the responsibility of art and the artist to the people. The first indications of this interest appear in his notes of 1892 (which he included in his *Mémoires*, pp. 139-144) under the heading "Préface de mon théâtre":

1. L'Art pour l'art (l'art autonome. "L'Art se suffit à soi")
2. L'Art du Peuple
3. L'Art d'action.
    a Drame national
    b Drame héroïque
4. L'Art du rêve (c'est l'art même)

a Drame olympien
b Drame symbolique

In such a theater he also saw a possible means of more direct action. His ideas were to crystallize in 1903 in *Le Théâtre du peuple. Essai d'esthétique d'un théâtre nouveau* (Paris, 1903), a work that ran through several editions. The importance of his wish to write for the theater can hardly be overemphasized, for he remained a rather thwarted dramatist all his life; his belief in the social responsibility of the artist was the cause of some political pamphleteering, both in and out of his novels and plays.

The years after Rolland's marriage were increasingly difficult for the couple. Differences in temperament were considerable. His wife's rationalist education stopped short of his world of mystic intuitions and aspirations — which Rolland himself admits would have been difficult to define. She was accustomed to brilliant society life, but such a life did not interest her husband. Clotilde was willing to spend several quiet and laborious years, providing the result would be either a brilliant stage career or a less brilliant but eminently satisfactory university career (*Mémoires,* p. 221). When it became apparent that neither would be the result, her dissatisfaction was great, and not unreasonable. Determined to live as he saw fit, proudly independent, Rolland found considerable difficulty in achieving any measure of financial independence. He complained bitterly in a letter to André Suarès, July 9, 1896, that for seven years he had been working to the limit of his endurance, and had not yet succeeded in earning the minimum necessary for a household. He had earned less than two thousand francs in three years, and was living almost solely on his wife's dowry. He could not even console himself with satisfactory progress in lieu of financial success. He felt that his mission was to influence the young people of his day, but that his works were not reaching them. He thought that helping the youth was an important activity of any young artist, and that auch an aim was of greater consequence than mere success (letter to Malwida, Oct. 13, 1896; *Choix*). The international uncertainty, the dissensions within the Third Republic, the cheapness and vulgarity, or worse the shallowness, of contemporary writers exercized a depressing effect on him. He was irritated by the triflings of writers who in a time of bloody tragedies more poignant than ever remained, in his opinion, unaware that they could act in a beneficent and glorious manner more important than their poor creative efforts (letter to Malwida, Dec. 3, 1896; *Choix de lettres,* p. 188).

One of the causes of this depression may have been the Dreyfus case. Towards the end of 1897 there occur in his letters to Malwida occasional discussions of the famous case. Those around him were greatly impassioned, he wrote; Clotilde and her father were completely convinced of Dreyfus' innocence, but Rolland, despite his urge to action, refused to support the pro-Dreyfus party because he was not sure that he shared its convictions; evidence for or against Dreyfus was too uncertain, he thought. And he saw that there was as much fanaticism in the pro-Dreyfus groups as among the anti-semitic, anti-Dreyfus circles. There was blindness on both sides. He feared the result, for if Dreyfus were convicted again religious and social hatreds would be doubled; if he were acquitted, it would be the 'Panama' of the Army.[13] Interestingly enough, Rolland saw in the army, given the state of anarchy then prevalent, an element of order and even — for many — an ideal (retarded as it may have been for men like him) (letters to Malwida, Nov. 3, 28, Dec. 7, 1897; *Choix*).

He wrote to Malwida that he attended the Senate session (Dec. 7, letter; *Choix,* p. 216); and to Mme Halévy he later wrote (April 17 and May 1, 1910), that he would some day tell what he had observed during this famous case, and why he had never been entirely with the pro-Dreyfus forces (although certainly never with the anti-Dreyfusists). It was a promise he never fulfilled; this seems to be as much as he wrote of 'The Case'. When he wrote that every great crisis reveals previously ignored depths of one's nature, he revealed the basis of his stand 'au-dessus de la mêlée' (during the First World War). For some, he wrote, justice must

---

[13] A financial crash and scandal of the eighties that ruined a great many well-to-do speculators and even some poorer French families.

be preserved; for others, the national tradition; for me, he said, it is Reason.[14] The fact was that in order to save 'la raison' he had to remain neutral, or at least free from the passions of both sides. His refusal to enroll in either party earned him the disapproval of both sides. He wrote to Mme Bertolini on August 16, 1906, that the victim of the judicial error (or crime) was not even very interesting, except because of his misfortune; he had some affection only for Picquart, who was a hero, and who is the hero of several of his works (*Chère Sofia,* p. 268). In 1903 he wrote in the preface to his *Beethoven* (Paris, 1903, p. vi) that they had just seen two of the purest flames, Justice and Liberty — Colonel Picquart and the Boers. They had not succeeded in dissipating the shadows, but they had shown the route in a clearer light. Part of his reaction to the case was the play *Les Loups,* written early in 1898, signed with the pseudonym Saint-Just, and with the title *Morituri*; it was presented at the Théâtre de l'Œuvre in May, 1898. Contrary to his usual procedure he wrote it in a week, March 20 to 26, without the usual period of slow maturation (some works matured over a period of twenty-five years) (Rolland, *Les Léonides* [Paris, 1928], p. 9).

After the reading before Lugné-Poë (who played the rôle of Teulier), Rolland rewrote the play in one day (March 29), in order to protect the two ideals that are opposed to each other (*Souvenirs de jeunesse,* p. 230). The sudden appearance of *Les Loups* and the rapidity of its composition reveal the deep feelings the events had inspired in the author. His refusal to take sides, his need to remain above the conflict, may be the result not of strength and determination but of weakness and insecurity. Trained in scientific historical research, surely he could have found proof enough on one side or the other to take a more positive stand. Rolland himself almost forty years later, while rereading his notes and his 'journal intime' for that period, did not understand the reasons for his attitude. Gabriel Monod, who published his denunciation of the judiciary error (*Le Temps,* Nov. 6, 1897), told Rolland about

---

[14]   Letters cited by Cécile Delhorbe, *L'Affaire Dreyfus et les écrivains français* (Paris, 1932), pp. 302-303.

his torments and uncertainty; the younger man was indignant that no great French writer had come forward — but neither had a lesser one. In 1939 he comments: "Mais le plus étrange était que, lorsque cette mêlée serait déchaînée, moi qui l'appelais je m'en retirerais et que je ne m'inscrirais pas parmi les compagnons de ce Zola, dont le courage cependant me saisissait d'admiration et dont le rôle dangereux me faisait envie..." (*Mémoires*, p. 283-284). His reasons seem to have been, as one gathers from various remarks in his writings: the difficulty of knowing where the truth lay; the 'monstrueux amas d'insanités et d'injustices', on both sides; the many defenders of Dreyfus who were unconcerned with other social problems; the infamous character of some of the pro-Dreyfusists; the folly, frenzy and fanaticism of both sides. These do not seem to be good reasons. Later he was able to take a firm position on the question of many a victim of injustice in parts of the world far from his own. Perhaps it was easier for him to be positive when he was not in any way involved. To defend the rights of a Cuban poet and to condemn a Cuban dictator (Machado) was perhaps simpler in Paris than in Havana. There was obvious insecurity in Rolland's character, and much of his tenseness and combative attitude may have stemmed from his overcompensation for this part of his temperament.

As the pro-Dreyfus movement lost its original idealism and became a tool in the hands of political speculators, he withdrew even farther from the controversy. He was to allege the same reasons for a long silence in 1915 (*Journal des années de guerre*, pp. 614-615). He had seen, he wrote, what he had noted many times in the history of modern nations: noble idealistic movements that end ignominiously because the people who are its instruments are still immature. He perceived the corruption of what had originally been a movement of intense faith and idealism, and he refused to lend his support to it.

There was no doubt in his own mind about the public reception of *Les Loups* ; he wanted to defend the ideas there debated, and he knew that to do so would create a scandal (letter to Malwida, April 30, 1898; *Choix de lettres*, p. 238). In fact, the presentation was almost the scene of a battle. Colonel Picquart was present with Edmond Rostand, and at certain of Teulier's speeches the public turned towards Picquart to acclaim their hero.[15]

The scene of *Les Loups* is Mayence, where the Republican army is under the command of Quesnel — commissar of the Convention — Teulier, Verrat, and d'Oyron. The academician Teulier is a fanatic for justice and truth. Verrat, man of the people, wishes to save his country, even at the cost of truth and justice. The two are temporarily united in their hatred and suspicion of d'Oyron, ex-aristocrat, who has nevertheless given proof of his devotion to the Republic. But he is suspect because of his origins. The opportunity to rid themselves of the *ci-devant* occurs when a letter from the Prussian command is found in the possession of a German peasant. The letter, addressed to d'Oyron, is an unlikely message; employers of spies do not jeopardize their men by writing letters of gratitude. After a short debate the officers condemn d'Oyron to death. Before the sentence is executed, Teulier learns that Verrat had discovered and destroyed evidence of d'Oyron's innocence. Adhering strictly to truth and justice, Teulier demands a new trial. The German peasant, on whose words the fate of the accused man depends, is found hanging dead in his cell. It is no wonder if the similarity to the Dreyfus case obscured any other intentions Rolland may have had. The audience identified Quesnel with General Billot, Verrat with Esterhazy, Teulier with Colonel Picquart, d'Oyron with Dreyfus, the German peasant with Colonel Henry, the letter with the famous 'bordereau' found in the wastebasket of the Austrian embassy. Rolland later protested against this narrow interpretation. In his mind the essence of the play is the violent conflict between the beliefs of Teulier and Verrat. Shall we have justice at all costs, even though the state may perish? Or shall we save the state, and sacrifice justice? Teulier would see justice done, no matter what the outcome, whereas Verrat would save the nation, no matter what the means. Whatever others may have thought at the time and indeed even much later, Rolland intended the play for a glorification of France, great even when it tears itself asunder (letter to Auguste Bréal, May 18, 1898).

[15] See "Rolland nous dit comment il a écrit 'Les Loups'", *L'Humanité* (Jan. 14, 1937).

Rolland expressed his beliefs in this play, and in a characteristic way, assured Malwida that he was afraid of the hatred neither of the army officers nor of the Jews. The fight had begun; he had broken the first lance; he would break many more, and more dangerously. It is time to fight, he wrote (*Choix de lettres à Malwida,* May 22, 1898, p. 229-233) in a letter that points to his future activities. It is however, difficult to see any broken lances here. Verrat, the man of action, acts dishonorably to attain a worthy end. The theoretical and honorable Teulier is swept away. Quesnel, a possible middle term, accepts dishonor to preserve the nation. For Verrat there is only expediency. He triumphs politically; the moral triumph of Teulier seems bootless and Quesnel's compromise is as unworthy as Verrat's violence. In another letter to Malwida, explaining the beliefs and intentions that inform the play, Rolland defined the subject as that of Destiny which sets in opposition the most imperious duties of humanity and then destroys them all, the one by the other. To give more grandeur to this subject embodied in the struggle between justice and the nation, he had transposed it to one of the most heroic of epochs, that of the French Revolution.

As to the conclusions of the play, Teulier is shown to be correct, but there are cases where the just man is sacrificed in the name of another ideal, less pure but equally powerful, emanating from a collectivity. The one who loses is not the less, but rather the more noble, since he becomes a martyr. Neither Quesnel nor Teulier could act otherwise; both are victims of Destiny, the iron Necessity that constantly sets two opposing duties into conflict. D'Oyron's case differs considerably from Dreyfus'. Rolland wanted to arouse people to reflect about both sides, and to realize that their adversaries may also possess grandeur and that Destiny bears the guilt of humanity's crimes. "Thus I tried", he concludes, "to create a work of funereal appeasement"; the play was not intended as a polemical work (letters to Malwida, May 22, 1898, and Jan. 11, 1899; *Choix de lettres,* pp. 229-233, 253-254).

Les Loups was not played again until after the war of 1914. It had a great impact in post-war Germany because the dramatic conflict of the play was the one Germany herself was then facing:

"Teulier's ideal, or Quesnel's". It was played in Paris, January 1, 1937, at the left-wing Théâtre du peuple (*L'Humanité,* Jan. 14, 1937). More recently it was presented at the Théâtre Lancry, in 1953 (*Mercure de France* [April 1, 1953], 702-704). Its favorable reception was again due in part to the circumstances in which it was played — the German occupation of France and the Resistance Movement were still fresh in the memories of the audience. The play had, the reviewer said, reproduced a conflict from a time that seemed completely in the past; yet here again was the same conflict, revealed in its terrible and universal permanence.

These are not great plays, and their success was small. They did not enable their author to withdraw from a university career. Until his withdrawal, later, music provided the means for a compromise in his life, and musicology became the bridge which spanned, after a fashion, the gulf between the two conflicting parts of his character. It satisfied in some measure his desire to create, as well as his love of music on the one hand and his sense of duty to his family and to his bride on the other.

In a study of Rolland's life, *Les Loups* is more than a historical play. It marks the entry of contemporary events into Rolland's interests, into his creative writings. Contemporary events assume greater importance in his works, until some volumes of *L'Ame enchantée* become historical, sociological documents rather than works of pure literature (although there are some fine pages in them when the critic of society and politics ceases to function). Certain aspects of his character and philosophy make this kind of creative activity inevitable. Contemporary events, he wrote, are part of the artist's ambience, part of the soil from which he draws his sustenance (letter to Malwida, June 20, 1898; *Choix de lettres,* p. 234-235). In spite of his protestations of belief in universal unity and supranationalism, Rolland was always deeply rooted in the present and in his native France. He never denied the importance of one's native land. However, attitudes which limit one to the present or to the narrow limits of country, state, or people, need the correction of a broader vision and wider interests. Rolland endeavored throughout his life to combine these two sources of strength and humanity (letter to Malwida, Jan., 1899; *Choix de lettres,* p. 254-255). In order to be completely oneself, one must not deny family, city, or race, but must strike deep roots into them and absorb all their vital force. Afterwards, the personality thus formed and strengthened can try to embrace the rest of the universe. Rolland not infrequently criticized a certain type of abstract art which claimed to be the reflection of the universal. The only true universal, he said, is composed of particulars, of a multitude of precise thoughts and experiences. Any other form of the universal is a colorless and empty form of the mind. He regretted that he himself had begun too soon to write works that were too general. He was at this time feeling the need for closer contact with daily reality, a feeling which contributed to his interest in a people's theater.

VI

DRAMAS OF THE REVOLUTION (1897-1901)

The epoch and the epic of the French Revolution began to interest Rolland at this time (letters to Malwida von Meysenbug, Oct. 29, Nov. 7, and an undated letter of November, 1898; *Choix de lettres à Malwida von Meysenbug* [Paris, 1948], p. 243-248). He found the most interesting and poetic aspects of Danton, Saint-Just, and Robespierre not in their accomplishments but in the depths of their thinking, in the intensity of their faith, and in the power of their will. He insisted that they must not be judged by their acts; there were too many external obstacles which thwarted their efforts and falsified or distorted their action. As a result of his intensified interest he wrote, during the winter of 1898-1899, another drama of the Revolution, *Le Triomphe de la raison,* presented at the Théâtre de l'Œuvre, June 21, 1899. The play, like *Les Loups,* is essentially a debate concerning Justice and the means to an end — about Reason, Force, and Violence — questions that would concern Rolland during the rest of his life. The action turns on the intoxication of reason which has become a faith. And in certain situations, he wrote, faith is obedience — at least in Latin countries (letter to Malwida, Friday, Jan., 1898; *Choix de lettres,* p. 222).

The subject is the struggle between the outlawed Girondists and the Jacobins. The Girondists, Hugot and Faber, represent two different attitudes towards the revolution and society. Hugot hates the people with conviction and passion; for him liberty is inseparable from reason, and the people fear and hate liberty, reason and intelligence. Faber, on the other hand, more rigorously rational, is less emotional, and more tolerant than Hugot. He is prudent, hesitant about making decisions. He is at first opposed to Hugot's plan to join the other Girondists in an insurrection against Jacobin rule. The Jacobins are his enemies only insofar as they commit acts which he believes to be evil. However, after his decision has been made and a line of action decided upon, he is far more rigid and implacable than Hugot. Faber and Adam Lux, an idealistic and mystic representative from Mayence (the only historical character in the play) and a great admirer of Charlotte Corday, join the Girondists, who have taken refuge in a provincial city. In order to protect themselves from the troops of the Convention and the hostility of the city, they are forced into an uneasy alliance with the Royalists. In the crisis, however, when the only way to save their lives is to aid the English fleet to swing victory to their side, instinct is too strong and Faber turns the cannons against the enemies of France. Hugot realizes that Faber is right, and ceases the struggle against the Jacobins. The Girondists — Hugot, Faber, and Fossette, Hugot's mistress — are condemned to death. Lux, in a mystic rapture, kills himself at the foot of the altar of Reason.

Adam Lux, like Aërt, is the true hero of the free conscience — the only hero Rolland recognized. His is the fight of the free man for an eternal fatherland, beyond and above the 'petite patrie' (Stefan Zweig, *Romain Rolland, the Man and the Work* [New York, 1921]). Like Aërt, Lux is the incarnation of self-sacrifice. "It seems to me that all the suffering I can take on my shoulders is just so much taken off the shoulders of others" (*Tragédies de la foi* [Paris, 1913], p. 212). The other aspects of this desire to sacrifice himself for the benefit of others are his ardent love for people and his own thirst for life — and his fear of living (*Ibid.*, p. 215). This fear, a curious part of his character, is an echo of Rolland's personality. Lux is really afraid of women; he is afraid of life and of nature; he is afraid of Fossette because she is a woman and is closer to the forces of nature. He admires Charlotte Corday, but she is a liberator, a hero, not a woman in his mind. Lux believes that the Revolution had opened the gates of man's prison, and that man had broken the bonds imposed by Nature. But Nature had tricked man, says Rolland; it had pretended to submit in order to dominate more completely. By 'Nature', Rolland meant the force that has resulted in the creation of the universe, of all that exists. In a more limited sense it is the forces inherent in man which by another name are called instincts. In an undated letter to Madeleine Rolland, destined for her alone, Rolland wrote about this aspect of nature.

Nature does not care about you! She perpetually sets traps — our desires... One must be armed against nature, not to combat it, but to defend oneself against it. Only then does one have a feeling of (relative) security, without which no happiness is possible... I do not wish to speak ill of everyday life. I believe that it can be beautiful for a small number of fortunate people. Oh! the good fortune of having common sense, a good mind, someone who can feel and understand all that exists — the good luck to love life and not to be its prisoner — to be free! [1]

He was, he believed, not one of the fortunate ones. The feeling of being imprisoned was deep-seated in Rolland. One chapter of *Le Voyage intérieur* (Paris, 1959, pp. 19 ff.) is entitled "La Ratoire" ('la ratière', the rat-trap) (see J.-H. Barrère, "Romain Rolland et Malwida. Les 'Racines' et le 'Souffle' ", *French Studies,* 1950, pp. 97-112).

The exterior aspect of nature can also be terrifying (as it was for Lux). Readers of *Jean-Christophe* will recall the passage describing the silent struggle in the forest among the various trees and insects. This pessimistic awareness of the suffering and indifference of nature and of life was part of Rolland's heritage from his mother's side of the family.

I too feel everything you tell me about your obsession with universal suffering. I often have it, and in relation to almost anything... As soon

[1] "La nature se soucie bien de vous! Perpétuellement, elle vous tend des pièges, — qui sont nos désirs... Il faut être armé contre la nature, non pour la combattre, mais pour se défendre. Alors seulement on a un sentiment de sécurité, (relative), sans lequel il n'y a pas de bonheur possible... Je ne médis pas de la vie réelle. Je crois qu'elle peut être très belle pour un petit nombre d'heureux... Ah! le bonheur d'avoir de bon sens, une bonne intelligence, un être qui peut sentir et comprendre tout ce qui est — le bonheur d'aimer la vie et de n'être pas prisonnier d'elle, — d'être libre!" (Letter to Madeleine Rolland, written in 1911).

as one is a thinking being, one has a choice only between two attitudes: …to eat or to be eaten. I am both, in turn… Ah! nature is magnificent and atrocious; we cannot judge it; it does not depend upon our intelligence.[2]

He later wrote that there are only two ways to support the tragedy of life : insouciance, or great strength. But Rolland and Mme Cruppi cannot be insouciant nor can they always be forceful ; therefore they must suffer and aid others.[3] This is what Lux tried to do, for he was neither heedless nor very strong.

Nevertheless, Lux is neither the expression of Rolland's entire personality, nor of the essential conclusion of the play. When Marc Elder found the play to be explicitly an extolling of a certain defeatism (p. 242), Rolland wrote to thank him for the study, but pointed out that one cannot attribute to him the words and ideas of his creations.[4] He was, he said, too objective, too Shakespearean to write thesis plays. His true belief was expressed in the words of Hugot, which end the play: "Life will be what I wish it to be. I have outrun victory; but I shall conquer" (p. 254), and which

[2] "Je sens tout ce que vous me dites de votre hantise de la souffrance universelle. Je l'ai souvent aussi, et à propos de n'importe quoi… Dès qu'on est un animal pensant, on n'a le choix qu'entre deux attitudes: celle de la Nature naturante, comme dit Spinoza, ou celle de la Nature naturée, — être celui qui mange ou celui qui est mangé. Je suis les deux, tour à tour… Ah! la nature est magnifique et atroce; nous ne pouvons pas la juger; elle ne relève point de notre intelligence. Mais j'ai l'impression que ce qu'elle a de plus terrible, — la souffrance — est une chose sacrée. Pensez un peu: que la nature mange et soit mangée, rien de plus simple. Mais qu'elle en ait conscience! Cela n'est pas du même ordre." (Letter to Mme Louise Cruppi, Aug. 6, 1910).

[3] "La vie est un spectacle tragique. Pour le supporter, il faut être bien insouciant ou bien fort. Insouciants, nous ne pouvons plus l'être. Forts, nous ne pouvons pas toujours l'être. Alors, il faut souffrir et s'aider à souffrir. Quand je dis que la souffrance est sacrée, je ne dis pas qu'elle est bonne, je dis qu'elle est toute puissante, et qu'elle vient de haut. Nous en sommes les instruments autant que les victimes. La vie ne peut être plus cruelle pour l'homme, que l'homme ne l'est pour tout ce qui vit autour de lui… Il conquiert l'univers en le détruisant. Il est détruit à son tour. C'est la même loi d'airain. On n'y échappe que par la porte de la foi. Mais la porte que je connais — il en est d'autres, — est elle-même tragique." (Letter to Mme Cruppi, Aug. 21, 1910).

[4] Marc Elder: "Romain Rolland", *La Renaissance Contemporaine* (Oct. 1912), pp. 817-829; later in *Deux Essais: Romain Rolland, Octave Mirabeau* (Paris, 1916). Rolland's letter to Marc Elder is dated Oct. 22, 1912.

Rolland quoted to Zweig (letter, July 14, 1918) adding that his own attitude was not that of the 'grand et pur "Défaitiste", Adam Lux', but rather that of Faber and Hugot (*Journal des années de guerre* [Paris, 1952], p. 1534).

The theme of the 'vaincu vainqueur' appears again in this play in Hugot's words. For the moment blind, brute force has triumphed, but the mind, the soul, the eternal spirit will eventually conquer. Both the Jacobins and the Girondists are sincere, brave, and self-sacrificing in the service of a great cause — the good of France, of Europe, of Humanity. No matter which of the two are now conquered, the essence of their efforts will survive and triumph. They are pitted against each other in a death struggle by two equally justified, equally powerful ideals. This conception was an integral part of Rolland's beliefs. It occurs in private letters as well as in his published works. Basically, he said to Mme E. Marchand, we the vanquished are really the victors.[5] After Lux learned that Marat was not a monster of hatred and tyranny and that Charlotte Corday had brought evil, not good, by her act; after he saw his friends remain faithful to the Revolution at the cost of their lives, he understood that evil is not in one man, but in all men; evil is egoism. Goodness exists only on condition of self-sacrifice. Victory, whatever it may be, is evil; defeat is good, providing it is voluntary surrender (p. 241). His suicide follows logically from these beliefs.

Before his death, Lux said to de Maillé and to Hugot that one should never stifle the future, no matter how threatening it may be, under the weight of the past. In reply to de Maillé's objection, Lux said that if one cannot escape from the past, one must die (p. 219). Rolland did not necessarily believe that everything in the future would automatically be better than the past, but he expressed some clear and strong objections to the throttling of the present and the future by the past ("Les Idoles", *Journal de Genève*

---

[5] "Les années qui ont passé sur nous me paraissent vous avoir apporté plus de sérénité; et c'est très beau, après les épreuves que vous avez subies. — Au fond, ma chère amie, les vrais victorieux, c'est nous — les vaincus." (Letter to Mme E. Marchand, March 12, 1912).

[Dec. 10, 1914] ; later in *Au-dessus de la mêlée* [Paris, 1915], pp. 84-96).

The question of justice is also debated — but no solution is offered. Faber asserted that a single injustice makes all humanity unjust, and he is one of the characters whose final words express Rolland's ideas. He is answered by Haubourdin, the violent, super-patriotic Jacobin general, who insists that an evil committed for the good of all men is not an injustice, but is Justice (p. 234). Even Faber sees that Haubourdin speaks with insight.

When the play was performed on June 21, 1899, scenes five and six of the second act were omitted. It is worthy of note that the debate in these scenes prefigures one which Rolland will later have much to say about. They constitute a discussion of the eternal question of the means and the ends. Neither Hugot nor Faber on the one hand nor de Maillé on the other is willing to be limited to legal or parliamentary means. The Procureur-Syndic pleads for less violent action, although his motives are suspect since fear of destruction of life and property animates the citizens of the town more strongly than any desire to aid France, whether by peaceful means or violent.

Among his unfinished works of these years, *Les Vaincus* (1897) was deemed by him worthy of publication some twenty-five years after it was partially written. The conditions in post-war Europe made the play, just as he had written it, timely in 1922 (see *Les Vaincus* [Antwerp, 1922]). The play is the story of a teacher in a 'collège', Georges Berthier, who, being neither wholly with the one nor the other of two forces, is crushed between them. One of the forces is a strike and the social agitation resulting from it. The strike is accompanied by violence that ultimately leads to insurrection. Berthier sympathizes with the workers but is unable to participate wholeheartedly in their movement, not only because of his family and position but also because his intellectualism and his insistence on justice make action impossible. The other force is society; society and its privileged members fight to retain the status quo. Berthier is perhaps less a part of this society than he is of the new proletariat. His wife, Marguerite, however, is the spirit incarnate of the bourgeoisie. Her sister, Françoise, who teaches in a primary school, is the only one of the family who understands his position and sympathizes with him in his helpless struggle. Angiolino, a poor migrant Italian workman, beaten up by the crowd because he was a 'scab', and then befriended by Berthier, assassinates the factory manager to show his love for his new friend. Some rhetorical words of Berthier had led him to regard the manager as the cause of his friend's dismissal from his teaching position. Faced with arrest as an accomplice, hated by his wife, deeply in love with Françoise who in turn is in despair because of the outrageous accusations of Marguerite, unable to share fully in the action of either side, Berthier follows Françoise's wish and they take poison together.

The play is nearly complete; various scenes are lacking or incomplete in Act II and Act III. One is inclined to wonder why Rolland put it away for twenty-five years. The characters are well drawn, better than in some of his other published plays. The dramatic conflict between Berthier and the social order is sufficiently interesting. His hesitations and inner conflicts are well portrayed and carry the spectator along, although Rolland occasionally gives way to a rhetorical style that detracts from the action and intensity of the play. The crisis in his personal life, the incompatibility of his marriage, is directly connected to the larger conflict and contributes to its dénouement. The rhetorical weakness, it is true, is especially noticeable in the various discussions between Jarnac, the leader of the workers' movement, and Berthier. However, since the play deals among other things with the clash of ideas, these discussions can hardly be omitted.

In his introduction, written in 1921, Rolland discloses his reason for not publishing the play in 1897 — a reason typical of this extremely conscientious man. When writing *Les Vaincus* he was disgusted with the ignoble indifference and egotism prevailing in France. At the same time, he perceived clearly the coming era of social convulsions. He knew that this tempest which would destroy the worst in society would also crush the pure, loving souls who, like himself (he said), are frequently bruised by life. He wanted to show the misfortune of those who live in times of social crises, and who are too intelligent and too sensitive not to suffer from the injustices inherent in oppressive society; indeed, they suffer even in any attempt to remedy injustice. They are victims in advance. The professor and his sister-in-law are of this class. Rolland was torn between pity for such future victims and the stoic appeal of the renovating strength of Nature — at once fecundating and destructive. He feared to add to the burden of those who would be sacrificed; his sense of responsibility as a writer would not permit him to publish a work which might have a depressing effect (*Les Vaincus,* Introduction, pp. 14-15).

The introduction affords us glimpses into the origin of the play and the author's intentions. The idea was developed in the spring of 1897, and the play written largely in October and November of the same year. One of the essential themes, the assassination of the factory manager, was inspired by the assassination in 1894 of President Sadi Carnot. Rolland reports a conversation with a close relative of the examining magistrate, who had taken a liking to the 'pauvre petit assassin, bon, simple, franc, naïf, sans haine pour Carnot', who had wanted to avenge Vaillant and his daughter after the press had excited everybody to compassion. Rolland was struck by the tragedy of these two sincere men — the assassin and the victim — both the prey of blind fate: "un innocent tué par un innocent pour expier les crimes de la société", he wrote in his 'Journal' in April, 1897 (*Les Vaincus,* pp. 5-6). Rolland also wished to study in the play the injustice of incompatible marriages — the sacrifice of a good and useful life to a legal pact which has become harmful to both spouses. Why do two people who love each other not have the right to unite freely in spite of social prejudices ? "This question of the inhuman marriage", he noted in 1897, "contrary to the free development of the individual, will be frankly stated in KRAFFT, and solved by facts" (*Ibid.,* p. 9). The reference is to the future novel *Jean-Christophe.* The question was not, however, treated in this novel, but in the second, *L'Ame enchantée,* the first volume of which appeared in the same year as *Les Vaincus,* 1922. His own divorce in 1902 had perhaps relieved him and removed the immediate stimulation for such a study.

In notes dated Nov. 29, 1897, after completion of the play, he wrote that it would be necessary to shift its axis from a specific strike and the problems involved to the question of fanatacism and its awakening, even its necessity in certain conditions. This is the true subject of the play. He had originally intended to give it the ironic title later applied to the play we have already discussed, *Le Triomphe de la raison*. This is not the only example of an ironic title given by him to his works. Although he wanted to write for large numbers of readers, he expected and indeed desired to be completely understood only by a handful of sympathetic and intelligent admirers. His wish to write for all but to be completely understood only by the happy few is an interesting trait, but probably one that is shared by many writers. It is however quite in the nature of his secretive temperament, his timidity, and the opposing tendencies that make up his complex personality.

Other themes and motifs characteristic of his writings are found in the play; some we have already discussed; others appear for the first time. The most important one again is that of the 'vaincu vainqueur' — hence the title. At the end of the play the labor leader Jarnac, facing the troops, says to Boehmer, who sees only death for the workers, that defeat is real only when accepted willingly. Those who, although apparently defeated, refuse to accept their defeat are the true victors (*Ibid.,* pp. 329-330). Boehmer on the other hand affirmed his belief in the corollary that victory in the long run is meaningless: "Le vainqueur est vaincu". To have what is desired is enough to make it scorned (*Ibid.,* p. 332). His affirmation of the uselessness of the struggle against destiny resembles de Maillé's protests in *Le Triomphe de la raison*. Boehmer and de Maillé are not sympathetic characters. This pessimistic attitude was current then, and Rolland set out to combat it. Man, he believed, creates his own destiny. Furthermore, Boehmer is a defeatist, and Rolland was not a defeatist, no matter what he may have been called during the war of 1914. At no time did he wish for the defeat of France; he castigated those who entertained such feelings, and even criticized those Germans who called for the defeat of their homeland. One of the reasons for this accusation may have been the 'German sympathies', attributed to the author of *Jean-Christophe*. In 1908-1909 (*Jean-Christophe* [Paris, 1950], p. 989), Olivier blessed the defeat of France at the hands of Prussia in 1870-1871 because the response of the nation to the defeat had brought the very best of its lifeblood to the surface. To see the good effects of defeat many years later, is not the same as wishing for defeat during the war; it is not defeatism. Such an attitude is of course heavily charged with the belief in the essential value of suffering. Rolland did not condone Prussia; he could not, he wrote, become accustomed to the Germans and their imperturbable self-confidence. It was a great weakness of the German mind and Germany would pay for it. Germans were no longer learning; they know. "We, the French, were the same formerly. We have paid dearly for it. Blessed be the defeat (of 1870-1871). I feel that I was born of it, that it steeled my heart... I believe that it did France more good than Napoleon's victories". What are conquerors? What is the history of the world? What does it teach us? The history of the conquerors, which is the least interesting and vilest part of the world. But who knows the history of the defeated? And yet there lie humanity's only true title to glory.

They alone arouse my taste for life, and do not make me blush for shame at being a man. They alone are men. The others are animals dressed in robes, helmets, and crowns. The history of those who have been defeated, this is the important, rarely written history. To suffer and to aid others are the duties of truly living people,

he told Mme Cruppi (August 21, 1910). Berthier is reluctant to act for fear of inflicting suffering; he preferred to ask Angiolino to help others to be less unhappy (p. 244).

Other themes include the questions of truth, socialism, and certain attitudes of the bourgeoisie. The question of truth is not what is truth, but should the whole truth be told? Professor Berthier, like Rolland at that time, asserts that there are occasions when one lies not only by telling untruths but by not telling the whole truth (p. 156). It was not until the latter had written some of his heroic biographies that he felt that this was an extreme position, and that there are times when to tell everybody the whole truth is unnecessary and even harmful. As for socialism, Jarnac criticized the socialists, most of whose leaders he calls 'arrivistes', accusing them of being socialists only for their own ambitions. This criticism appears later in Rolland's portraits of various socialists in *Jean-Christophe*. The bourgeois attitude portrayed unfavorably is that of the inhumanity of devotion to a certain type of duty — dry, unimaginative, rigid, dominating, and trivial. Marguerite Berthier has many traits in common with Frau Euler in her attitude towards duty (*Jean-Christophe,* pp. 236-241; 341-342; *Les Vaincus,* pp. 204-207). Finally, as we note themes that appear in his works we must recall that the years 1896 and 1897 were critical for Rolland. The crisis was reached with his divorce in 1901. The clash of two temperaments was developing at the time he was writing this play (compare Jacqueline and Olivier after their marriage; *Jean-Christophe,* pp. 1141-1156). The conflict between Berthier and Marguerite clearly shows the state of his feelings.

In 1900, with the play *Danton*, Rolland set out to complete what he now conceived of as the cycle of the French Revolution, which was to end with *Robespierre* in 1939. The plays were not written in chronological order. *Les Loups,* the first to be written, takes its place in the cycle after *Danton* (1900). The play that opens the completed cycle, the prelude, *Pâques fleuries,* appeared in 1926 and the closing one, *Les Léonides,* in 1928. *Danton* was first performed at the Nouveau théâtre, December 29, 1900, for the Cercle des Escholiers. The next day, the Théâtre civique and La Petite République theater presented a benefit performance for the strikers of the Nord province; Jean Jaurès made a brief introductory speech (letter to Malwida, Dec. 31, 1900; *Choix*). Two years later he disclosed his plan for a cycle of dramas about the Revolution (letter to Louis Gillet, May 2, 1902; *Correspondance,* pp. 192-193). He intended it to be a poem of ten or twelve dramas in which would also be seen the transformation of the people from a triumphant force radiant with hope, even though soiled and bloody from the struggle, to a people slowly sinking back in chains because of the oppression of a fate which is composed of all the vices of men. Each of the dramas would be different; there would be a pastoral drama, a military drama, a love drama, a popular drama, and a royal drama. In the preface to *Les Léonides* (1928), Rolland explained the origin of the cycle, the idea for which dated from about 1895. In the summer of 1898, while in the Swiss Jura, he was attracted by the reminiscences of the exiled Baron de Breteuil, which are the origin of *Les Léonides*. This was, he says, the first cell on the cycle; thus the conclusions precedes the beginning and was the starting impulse for the whole group (pp. 8-9).

Danton portrays the crisis in the struggle between the Jacobin Comités de Salut public and de Sûreté générale on the one hand, and Danton and his followers on the other. Essentially it is the contest between Danton and Robespierre. Camille Desmoulins, largely responsible for the condemnations of the Girondists, opposes Robespierre and the Comités and insists on attacking them, hoping thereby to avoid more bloodshed. Danton alone is powerful enough to oppose Robespierre.

When Robespierre visits Camille Desmoulin's home, the real struggle becomes clearer. It is a clash of temperaments. Robespierre is a man of ideas and principles who seeks to impose his ideas and to follow his principles regardless of the effect. Danton and Desmoulins prefer to sacrifice themselves if necessary. Danton withdraws temporarily because he feels that a struggle with Robespierre would ruin the Republic, and his own ambition and successes now seem hollow. He apparently shares Rolland's conception of the 'vainqueur vaincu'. Actually he believes that Robespierre will fail at the last minute.

Robespierre is portrayed as a warm, sincere man, devoted to the people of France and to the Republic of the Revolution. He is outwardly the public official, inflexible and cold. He believes that most of his former associates and friends are traitors. For support he has called St.-Just to Paris. The latter — logical, cold, implacable, and fanatical — is the more determined to root out vice and to preserve the purity of the Republic because he has had to root out the crime and vice of his own nature. The discussion among the members of the Comité de Salut public reveals the prevailing fanaticism. Vadier shrewd, cynical, unscrupulous, and treacherous — excites the others to condemn Danton and his followers. St.-Just is rigorously exacting and legalistic, even though he knows disturbances may result from his action. Eventually he is persuaded to sacrifice his honor for the necessities of the moment (p. 75). Robespierre hypocritically pretends to give up the defense of his friends for the sake of the Republic although, as Vadier sees, in condemning Danton they are following Robespierre's wishes.

Danton and his co-defendants fight for their lives before the Revolutionary tribunal. The people as spectators take part in this scene; their voices and comments are heard, and the fear of a popular uprising is felt. Danton appears in the full force of his magnificent physical vitality, enormous appetites, passions, faith, demagoguery, confidence, and love for the people of France. In spite of his powerful appeal his accusers, who have condemned him beforehand, trick the spectators and the jury, and the death sentence is pronounced. Rolland has compressed the whole terrible idealism of the Revolution and the Robespierrists into the words of St.-Just at the end of the play: "Ideas do not need men. People die so that God may live" (p. 119). This idea, familiar to Rolland, was not congenial. Fourteen years later he attacked such inhuman idealism in "Les Idoles" (*Au-dessus de la mêlée*).

Danton's vitality had a definite appeal for Rolland (letter to Gillet, March 3, 1900; *Correspondance,* p. 67), but he did not write the play to celebrate Danton or Liberty or the Revolution, but to celebrate Life and Death, the Eternal Force of the Universe manifested in the tempest called the French Revolution (letter to Gillet, May 2, 1902; *Correspondance,* pp. 192-193). In his 'journal' (*Le Périple* [Paris, 1946], pp. 56-57), Rolland calls the cycle of plays a symphonic fresco of a cyclone in man's history, and insists on the pronounced epic quality. The two terms, epic and symphonic, are significant when we think of his later works, especially *Jean-Christophe* and *L'Ame enchantée.*

The next play was *Le 14 juillet,* in which Rolland's original purpose was to show the superiority of spiritual over physical force. In answer to unfavorable criticism after its presentation, he insisted that if the capture of the Bastille were measured by the weakness of the resistance, it would be merely a mediocre feat of arms; the marvelous thing is the very weakness of the resistance. The capture of the Bastille was a miracle; the Bastille itself, with only its walls, was impregnable. If it surrendered, it was not from goodness but from weakness and uncertainty in the face of the popular movement, the rebellion of the spirit of justice and liberty which the garrison did not understand. The Bastille was taken with the help of the invisible force that ruins aging states in moments of crisis and decision: a bad conscience. The Fourteenth of July is one of the most memorable examples of the superiority of spiritual force over material power.[6]

The play opens in the Palais Royal, July 12, 1789, in the midst of gambling spots crowded with facile women, shady bookmakers, thieves, and bankers — all the corruption of the Ancien Régime. Underneath the frivolous surface echo the rumblings of a new age of political and social responsibility, of young and joyful revolt against a stultifying past. In the first two acts Rolland paints very vividly the awakening of the Revolution in the hearts and minds of the people. Although still unaware of their strength, they are led by an obscure but overwhelming instinct to overthrow the Bastille. From an amorphous mass, fearing famine and the king's mercenaries, the people becomes a coherent force overflowing with youthful joy.[7] Rolland ends the play with a sort of 'fête du peuple', a "Triomphe de la Liberté", in which the crowd assumes the leading rôle.

In fact, the last scene is almost solely a tableau, for which Rolland insisted on appropriate music. There is no plot in the conventional sense; the play is rather a 'fête populaire', a type of public entertainment in which Rolland was then interested. Furthermore, he wished to present spiritual rather than anecdotal truth; for this reason he takes liberties with historical incidents whenever necessary to present the true spiritual meaning of such an event as the fall of the Bastille. Here the individuals are swallowed up in the 'océan populaire', in which the effect as a whole is more important than the detail of each wave. In *Danton,* on the contrary,

[6]   Rolland: "Le 14 juillet", *L'Art du théâtre* (June, 1902), 107-110. His words are very similar to a statement made by Michelet in his *Histoire de la Révolution française* (Paris, 1868), I, p. 236. See also an article by Rolland, "Quatorze juillet 1789 et 1936", *Europe,* (July 15, 1936), 293-297.
[7]   Ten-year-old Julie, true Parisienne, precocious and sensitive, represents the intuitive, joyful, and youthful aspects of the movement; she is not a symbol of liberty, as some of the critics have believed. Her instinctive love of liberty, her unwitting appeal, her cry "A la Bastille", her complete lack of fear when she enters the Bastille on Hoche's shoulders, make of her a fitting symbol of the new force arising among the humble people of Paris.

the action is concentrated in three or four great men who are portrayed as minutely as possible. *Le 14 juillet* is a grand fresco; *Danton* a powerful but delicate engraving.

Le 14 juillet was to open the epic cycle. *Danton*, the center, is the decisive crisis of the Revolution, in which the leaders sacrifice their faith to their personal resentments and emotions. In *Le Triomphe de la raison,* the Revolution is shown in the provinces, pursuing the outlawed Girondists — and devouring itself. Rolland wrote in the preface for the 1909 edition of the *Théâtre de la Révolution* that he wished to present something like the spectacle of a natural convulsion, from the moment the first waves arise from the depths of the ocean until they again subside and peace descends. There is little romantic intrigue; the interest is in the great social and political problems which have concerned humanity during the last century. The duty of art, if it is to survive, is to raise itself to the level of this new fate, political action (letter to Mme Bertolini, August 17, 1903; *Chère Sofia,* p. 133).

Le 14 juillet was completed in 1901 and produced at the Renaissance Theater on March 21, 1902. The critics, who found little good in it, directed most of their criticism at the very qualities Rolland was striving for. Not until 1936 was it again performed, this time successfully, at the Alhambra Theater, at a time when the vigorous Popular Front movement made the subject one of current interest. The play, presented with music by Koechlin, Honegger, and Lazarus, was witnessed by Léon Blum and other ministers of the Popular Front government.

In this as in other writings, Rolland was inspired less by a desire to create works of art than by an inner compulsion towards action. He assured Louis Gillet later that he had never been without interest in political action, but he was almost never of the same opinion as others. This tendency toward contrary opinions was not confined to politics; it is present in his artistic and literary judgments, in his personal decisions; it seems to be part of the deep hostility in his character. He said that the pen was his only means of action; if he was a musician who did not compose music, he was also a man of action unable to act (letter to Gillet, March 19, 1914; *Correspondance,* p. 273). He strove for more participation by the spectators in his plays, and we find the people taking one of the leading parts in *Le 14 juillet*. In his preparation for its composition he felt his own lack of contact with people (like Olivier, he tended to remain aloof from crowds), and in order to observe the actions of a large group seeking a common goal, he participated in the Socialist Party convention at Paris in 1900. He held a card as delegate from the cabinet-makers' union of Sète, and sat on the left, voting with the Jaurès faction. But the crowd he saw was, he said, the eternal noisy, unthinking mass (see his *Souvenirs de jeunesse* [Lausanne, 1947], p. 241).

His prejudices, however, were merely the reactions of a timid character yet a strong individualist in his first real contact with a crowd, and it is only fair to note that his reactions against groups from the more favored parts of society produced even more energetic condemnations. He had begun to consider the people as a whole — or his abstract idea of the people — before this time. In a letter to Malwida (dated April 30, 1892, *Choix de lettres,* p. 75), however, he had insisted that the people would make the same mistakes and commit the same sins as the bourgeoisie, if only they were able. It was ironical, he felt, that the proletariat was worse than the other classes in this respect. When he wrote about his own *Théâtre du peuple* thirty-six years later, he saw clearly that such a project had been impossible at the turn of the century because there did not yet exist a people conscious of itself and confident in its own destinies towards whom he could turn in his efforts to free himself from the bourgeoisie.[8] Nevertheless, he expressed his own faith in the people, whom he defended at various times (letter to Gillet, April 28, 1902; *Correspondance,* pp. 187-191). In his articles on "Les Salons" (in 1902 and 1903), Rolland called on art to renew its close contacts with the people and the everyday life of its times; in the people alone were to be found strength, energy, joy, calm, and storms. As time passed and the bourgeois society showed clear signs of bankruptcy, he looked more and more to the people (see, for example, a letter to Stefan Zweig, March 28, 1915).

[8]   Rolland, "Pour un théâtre du peuple. Enquête de Paul Gsell. Réponse de Rolland", *Regards* (April 2, 1936).

It is surprising to discover a Rolland who attempted (if un-successfully) to identify himself with the people. His feelings of deep attachment to France, to his native province have been generally hidden from public view. More attention has been paid to his internationalism during the first World War and as expressed in *Jean-Christophe* and *L'Ame enchantée*. Careful readers, how-ever, note the deep attachment of various of Rolland's characters to France (Olivier, Annette Rivière, Annette's sister Sylvie). His love of France is at least one source of the Revolutionary plays. In the period of the Revolution he found the men and events which best embodied the questions he wished to discuss. The themes in his plays were so much a part of his thinking that work on the plays of this cycle would occupy him most of the rest of his life, until 1938-1939.

His sympathy with 'le peuple', the workers and the little people of France and later of the world, became the basis for his future belief in the power and importance of socialism and of Soviet Russia. The conflict within him — to be embodied later in Marc Rivière — is clearly perceptible in his life during the first years of the century.

In the writings of this period we have found various of the themes that will inform many of Rolland's later works. The more important ones are: self-sacrifice in a higher cause; the fear of nature, and a certain fear of women who are so closely identified with nature; the feeling of the suffering which abounds in an indifferent nature; the 'vaincu vainqueur', the questions of the ends and the means, of justice and patriotism, of violence and force. Some of the themes are closely bound to the author's temperament and related to events in his life especially to the crisis which resulted in his divorce in 1901.

VII

PERSONAL CRISIS (1900-1903)

Rolland could never devote himself exclusively to creative writing as he would have liked. Such activity was confined of necessity to his rare moments of leisure. He wrote his plays in the midst of his busy life as a professor. Among his courses he gave one at the Sorbonne (1895-1906) on the history of art, which later became the more specialized history of music after the reorganization of the Ecole normale in 1903.[1] In 1902 he organized the music section at the Ecole des Hautes Etudes Sociales, where he gave his first lecture, May 2: "La Place de la musique dans l'histoire générale". He argued that history should be more than a superficial and exterior review of the political life of a nation; it should show the living unity of the human spirit. Rolland continued to serve as chairman of the section — roughly equivalent to one of our university departments — from 1902 until 1912. In 1900 and for some years he was one of the directors of the *Revue d'art dramatique*. At the same time Rolland and Jules Combarieu organized the first international congress of the history of music, and founded the *Revue d'histoire et de critique musicale,* which became an important means for furthering research in musicology. His was a heavy load, for each course was the equivalent of a new book. Nor was it lightened by his continuing dislike for a university career. In a letter of November 5, 1904, to Mme Bertolini, he criticized French education for the passivity and docility it de-

---

[1] For a list of the courses taught by Rolland at the Sorbonne and the Ecole des Hautes Études, see Jean Bonnerot: *Romain Rolland* (Paris, 1921), pp. 118-119; the *Livret de l'étudiant de l'Université* for the years 1904 to 1912; and the memorial volume, *L'École des Hautes Études sociales 1900-1910* (Paris, 1911).

manded of the students; he particularly detested the 'frightful' competitive examinations. To make unfortunate young men parrot clichés and grow pale over the printed page, when there were so many beautiful and useful things to do, was not to his taste. Education in the modern democratic states has, because of its obligatory nature, the character of the barracks or the monastery, and its virtue is thereby altered. Education, he thought, should be a free luxury, a museum open to the people, not a school with homework and diplomas. His idea of education was of course idealistic and impractical, even to the point of denying the realities of which he was well aware (*Chère Sofia. Choix de Lettres de Romain Rolland à Sofia Bertolini Guerrieri-Gonzaga,* I [Paris, 1959], pp. 202-203). Perhaps for him the most repellent aspect of teaching was the necessity of revealing his thoughts to an audience with which he was not necessarily in close contact. He wondered how he could successfully get through the hour. He was timid, and had such an aversion for speaking that he wanted to leave as soon as he entered the classroom; or in the middle of his lecture, he would like to say: "Silence is so good; let's say nothing; I shall play you some music instead". And he could not understand how anyone could enjoy his lectures.[2]

Personal difficulties added to his already heavy burden. The winter of 1900-1901 was the culmination of a difficult personal crisis. The dissension in his marriage, which had begun some years before, had been growing deeper with the increasing dissatisfaction in his career. By January 18, 1901, he had decided to obtain a divorce. He wrote to Louis Gillet that his love for Clotilde was undiminished — he believed that he must always have love in his heart in order to be truly alive — but he was forced to the step

[2] "Je vous écris, au sortir de mon cours [on Handel and his time]. Je me demande toujours comment j'arriverai au bout de mon heure. J'ai une telle sauvagerie intérieure et une telle aversion pour la parole — pour ma parole — que quand j'entre dans la salle, j'ai envie de m'en aller. Ou bien, au milieu de mon cours, je voudrais pouvoir dire: 'Non, décidément, taisons-nous, voulez-vous? C'est si bon, le silence! Je vais vous faire plutôt un peu de musique.' Vous avez beau m'écrire qu'il y a des gens que mes conférences intéressent: je n'arrive pas à le comprendre; et, au fond, je n'y crois pas" (Letter to Mme E. Marchand, Dec. 12, 1907). See also his description of the same feelings in Olivier (*Jean-Christophe* [Paris, 1950], p. 992); *supra,* p. 35.

by a strong inner compulsion. Whatever the ostensible reasons for the divorce, the root of many of these differences was his absolute and unreasonable demand for personal freedom. His lack of flexibility caused him to exaggerate his need. In a letter to Mme Bertolini (July 7, 1902), he almost admitted this fact: "I am... perhaps more rigorous towards myself, more of a puritan, more of a slave (and perhaps victim) of an ethical ideal. I have paid for it dearly, in numerous enemies and in the ruin of my domestic happiness..."[3] He was determined to maintain at any cost the independence of his life and thinking (letter to Gillet, Feb. 2, 1901; *Correspondance entre Louis Gillet et Romain Rolland* [Paris, 1949], p. 125).

As we have already indicated, one must also seek other reasons for this division in his complex feelings about women. In *L'Ame enchantée* (Paris, 1950, p. 305) he describes Marc Rivière: "... de tous ses sens aveugles d'enfant avide et innocent, [Marc] humait, inquiet, le charme énigmatique de l'être féminin. Il éprouvait pour la femme une attraction dégoûtée. Attraction. Répulsion", and the author adds in his own voice, "Tout vrai homme la connaît". In spite of some early hesitation, we may be sure that by 1922 he considered himself 'un vrai homme'. In his *Mémoires* (Paris, 1956, p. 186) Rolland described Christophe and himself :

Un révolté, fiévreux, gonflé, tourmenté par le travail de la sève, hanté par l'obsession du flux créateur, brûlant de foi, mais intolérant, mauvais coucheur, plein de fureur et de mépris pour la société... s'usant en luttes des moulins à vent... le jeune Don Quichotte... c'est Jean-Christophe. — Et c'est moi-même.

And after Françoise Oudon, the most complete and satisfying love that Christophe ever had, left for a tour of the United States, the young musician felt a sense of calm and freedom. (*Jean-Christophe* [Paris, 1950], p. 1183). Olivier too, who so often reproduces

---

[3]　For more details of his divorce, see his letters to Malwida von Meysenbug, from Feb. 26 to April 18, 1901; *Choix de Lettres à Malwida von Meysenbug* (Paris, 1948). See also *Chère Sofia. Choix de lettres à Sofia Bertolini Guerrieri-Gonzaga*, I (Paris, 1959) p. 78; *Correspondance de Louis Gillet et Romain Rolland* (Paris, 1949), letters of Jan. 18, March 1, 1901; May 2, 1902.

physical and emotional traits of his creator, allows a certain distrust or intolerance of women to pierce the surface: "Les Juifs sont comme les femmes: excellents, quand on les tient en bride; mais leur domination, à celles-ci et à ceux-là, est exécrable; et ceux qui s'y soumettent donnent un spectacle ridicule" (*Jean-Christophe*, p. 1007). Physical desire appears often as a trap in his works. Lux in *Le Triomphe de la raison*, as well as Christophe and Olivier occasionally express this attitude towards love, but it is in *L'Ame enchantée* that Annette, Marc, and the author most consistently refer to carnal love as a trap.

[Annette]... était trop prise par son existence intérieure... Il en serait ainsi, sans doute, tant qu'elle n'aurait pas été happée par le grand piège sexuel... (*L'Ame enchantée* [Paris, 1950], p. 85).

It is of course true that Rolland created other important characters, such as Sylvie, Annette's half-sister, who were free of this fear. Since, however, this feeling was apparently deeply embedded in his temperament, and since he considered himself especially vulnerable, he must have been at times a somewhat difficult husband who probably believed that his wife was unusually difficult. He felt trapped again, many years later, when he wrote to J.-R. Bloch, March 11, 1914: "Je suis harassé. Je viens de trouver encore le moyen de me faire happer par une de ces passions qui rôdent perpétuellement autour des hommes de notre sorte, au cœur et aux sens surchauffés par le feu de leur tête" (*Deux hommes se rencontrent* [Paris, 1964], p. 242). One of the commonplaces of the Romantic epoch is evident here; he feels himself different from (and superior to) others. One might compare the words of Chactas to René in Chateaubriand's *René*, and Jean-Jacques Rousseau's evaluation of himself in his "Avertissement" to the *Confessions*.

Other elements in the author's character and in his life also affected his marriage. His relationship with his mother had generally an adverse influence on his relations with women, and seems to have seriously affected his relations with his wife. He subconsciously held an ideal of womanhood which Clotilde did not fulfill. He revealed this fixation inadvertently to Mme Bertolini (letter of Sept. 20, 1901) after his divorce. "Men are formed by

women", he wrote; "each epoch receives an indelibile imprint
from women". In Contemporary Parisian society there are only
rare and isolated examples of the former virtues of French women
— charming common sense, modesty of sentiments, courageous
and simple loyalty. Generally there are two types of women: the
bourgeois woman with a limited intelligence and "the worldly
woman, the emancipated, modern woman, often intelligent, but
without heart or spiritual life, free of virtues and prejudices. She
no longer believes in any duty or ideal, and is busy only in the
quest for pleasure. Voluptuous and critical, a solvent, she has
shaped the epoch in her image" (*Chère Sofia,* pp. 23-24). That is,
the modern woman, the woman his age, is the opposite in all
ways of his mother, and therefore less desirable, less admirable.

On February 26 Rolland rented an apartment at 162 boulevard
Montparnasse where he planned to move on April 15. In order
to assume the onus of the divorce he left his apartment and his
wife and went to a hotel on February 28, staying only the few
hours necessary to provide the legal basis for the action. He then
went not to his apartment, but to his parents' home. The divorce
was granted between February 28 and March 5, 1901.

He rarely saw his former wife after that. Some months after
the separation he wrote to Maurice Pottecher (Oct. 24, 1901) that
he had seen her for the last time in June or July. The final reference
to this painful event was in a letter to Mme Bertolini dated May
28, 1903. He had just learned of Clothilde's marriage to an or-
chestra director. Although she had been as if dead for him, this
remarriage, he wrote, was like the second death (but without
beauty) of a violated past (*Chère Sofia,* I, p. 117).

He regarded Clotilde's happiness after their separation as painful proof of the correctness of his action.[4] While he had first been
concerned about the effect on Clotilde, he soon felt — probably
erroneously — that true sorrow was principally his; he wrote that

---

[4] "Je ne puis dire que j'use en un seul instant le regret véritable d'avoir fait
ce que j'ai fait, d'avoir provoqué une séparation inévitable. La satisfaction que
Clotilde semble en éprouver maintenant, l'indifférence qu'elle a prise à ma
peine, et la froideur soudaine qui lui est venue pour moi, me montre trop que
j'ai eu raison". (Letter to Maurice Pottecher, April 12, 1901).

he was angry because she referred to him still as a friend. Hate, he said, would at least have been a partial excuse, but indifference appeared to be calculation.[5] He seemed to want her without actually having her; and he evidently did not want another to have her. His reaction appears to be that of a strongly self-centered person. Why should he be angry for her lack of feelings unless he were plagued by guilt concerning his own half- or completely suppressed emotions?

The step had cost him bitter moments, not the least of which was the shock to his principles and to his rigidly uncompromising attitude in regard to right and wrong, especially about marriage. He wrote to Louis Gillet (Feb. 9, 1902, *Correspondance,* p. 171) that divorce was an abominable thing and he condemned it with as much severity as the most uncompromising Christian. Marriage does not exist as long as there is the possibility of divorce and separation, no matter how difficult. It would be more honest to suppress the institution. The idea of free love and of union by mutual consent was less repugnant to him, even as the basis of a new society, than marriage with the possibility of divorce. The present attitude was the hypocrisy of a transitionary epoch and a decaying society.

His attitudes towards friends and the object of his love were equally rigid; he demanded a return of his own absolute attitude. He called his wife's actions the treason of affection; when he gave himself knowingly and wholly to another person, only the spiritual or moral suicide of that person could break the bond. The betrayal caused him unspeakable pain, and hurt him like a personal failure (letter to Mme Bertolini, *Chère Sofia,* I, p. 17). An echo of the break-up of the marriage may be perceived in *Jean-Christophe* in a passage where the word 'race' probably means 'temperament':

[5] "Loin d'elle et de ce charme qui troublait mon esprit, je vois plus clairement le mal qu'elle m'a fait. Là-bas, je ne pensais qu'au sien. Je ne lui en veux pas; mais je ne puis non plus oublier. — Savez-vous ce qui m'a paru le plus cruel de tout, peut-être: c'est cette assurance qu'elle continue de donner aux autres, qu'elle reste ma meilleure amie. — ma meilleure amie! Et que ferait de plus un ennemi? La haine est une demi-excuse du mal que l'on fait; mais quand il n'y a nulle passion, quand tout est réfléchi!" (Letter to Maurice Pottecher, April 19, 1901).

"L'ami est transparent à l'ami; ils échangent leur être. Les traits imitent les traits. L'âme imite l'âme — jusqu'au jour où la force profonde, le démon de la race, se délivre brusquement et déchire l'enveloppe de l'amour qui le lie" (*Jean-Christophe* [Paris, 1950], p. 938).

No matter how strong and inflexible his needs and his beliefs, no matter how ambivalent his feelings may have been, he could not fail to suffer greatly at the breaking of the bonds of some nine years duration. On October 15, 1901, he wrote to Mme Bertolini that he was so saturated with sorrow that the very excess of suffering had produced in him a sort of detachment from the world around him (*Chère Sofia,* I, pp. 34, 51), which lasted for several months. This crisis, he said later, marked the beginning of a new period in his development. Rolland here and in various other writings explains his way of coping with suffering. To seize suffering, to combat it not only by admitting it but by letting it become greater than all his other emotions, transformed it so that the element of pain, whether emotional, physical or mental, disappeared.

Partly as a result of the mental and spiritual anguish Rolland's health suffered. The last months of 1901 found him frequently confined to his rooms. In November, he wrote to Gillet (Nov. 7; *Correspondance,* p. 158) that the doctors (one a heart specialist) had discovered some alarming symptoms; the diagnosis was an incipient pericarditis or pleurisy. Later he wrote that he had again been suffering perturbations of the heart; a spasm of suffocation had seized him (letter to Gillet, Nov. 15, Dec. 12, 1901; *Correspondance,* pp. 155, 160). The suffocation and apparent heart trouble appear remarkably like anxiety attacks in view of the fact that there was no heart trouble in his medical history. Such attacks are not uncommon in times of emotional stress, especially when subconscious conflicts come very close to the surface. Without more modern diagnostic techniques even reputable physicians could be deceived.

Rolland's correspondence at this time reveals an attitude towards nature that is closely akin to romantic melancholy. Undoubtedly a permanent trait of character, it was sharpened by his recent tribulations. It was an attitude of almost morbid love for the more desolate aspects of nature, and a tendency to read his own emotions into the landscape. In a letter to Mme Bertolini (July 18, 1902), he said that mountains and lakes were like living people; everything inspired in him sympathy or antipathy; a mountain was the profile of a face; a lake was an eye; a house, the form of a mind (*Chère Sofia,* I, p. 83). A ruined woods — which appears later in *Jean-Christophe* — was a most beautiful sight (*Ibid.,* p. 88). He also wrote that he liked the rain and the fog, especially when the sun shone softly through at intervals. Nature under this delicate veil assumed a less oppressive apearance; life seemed near to its end, and a melancholy peace reigned — the peace of the cessation of life. Rolland preferred autumn because of its harmony with his feelings; his need for a release from life, from the pangs of creation and the burden of fruition, was strong (*Chère Sofia,* I, pp. 125-126; July 22, 1903). In this attitude we find also a love of moderation that seems contrary to what many critics have expected of him. Something like Baudelaire's 'Regret souriant' ('Recueillement') infuses his feelings.

Of all the forms of nature, the sea and the mountains generally left the strongest impressions on him. Rolland eventually came to prefer the mountains, in which he spent much of his life. At first his reaction was ambivalent; he was not sure that he liked them; the emotions they aroused were too strong to be pleasurable. "I feel", he wrote to Mme Bertolini (July 1, 1908, *Chère Sofia,* I, p. 349), "that above one or two thousand meters, the earth dislikes men; at that height there remain elementary power, impassive beauty, and genial solitude; but there is no longer the breath of tenderness, the arms around one's neck, the loving and fraternal quality which I feel in contact with the dear earth, living and human, of my part of France". In 1907, he wrote from Spain that he was not indifferent to the vast body of the sea, and that he loved the ocean more than he had thought — the Atlantic, not the Mediterranean. He loved it best when it was agitated, like a moving sky and clouds.[6] The stormy quality that attracted him

---

[6] Rolland, "Voyage en Espagne (Journal. Mars-avril, 1907)", *Europe* (Jan.-Feb., 1955), 74.

to the ocean played its rôle in his feelings for other aspects of nature. He liked the wind in pine trees, and attributed the feeling to his northern ancestry. His love for Italy was second to this emotion, perhaps, and touched a different facet of his personality. At times the need for the sharper changes and more rugged nature of the north overcame the softer emotions aroused by the southern climate. He needed the changes of season where nature is young, matures, grows old, dies, and resuscitates; it is more human (letter to Mme Bertolini, May 10, 1911; *Chère Sofia,* II, p. 106). This feeling about the north, where the season changes, seems to correspond to a fundamental character trait which made him receptive to the Heraclitan philosophy of change. We must seek here the probable reason for his decision to reside in Switzerland rather than in Italy after 1919.

His love for nature — a deep and sincere emotion as readers of *Jean-Christophe* well know — was inherited from his family, and especially from his mother.[7] It was almost a religious feeling. He had never found in the trees, meadows, streams, birds, air, and earth, a single moment of melancholy during a gentle summer or fall. This is true, of course, only in a general way; we have seen his mixed reactions to certain aspects of the landscape. He suffered at the thought of returning to the city. But he had to accept the sojourns there, the periodic return of storms and sadness, as the law of life; he must undergo these crises also in order to understand and express the world and to do some small good in it (letter to Mme Bertolini, Sept. 6, 1902; *Chère Sofia,* I, p. 89). The idea here expressed of periodic suffering is another aspect of the familiar pattern of becoming. At the same time he revealed a very curious and unexpected yearning for the unusual, even the cataclysmic, to Mme Bertolini on Easter Sunday, 1903 (*Chère Sofia,* I, p. 106). He had spent part of the preceding night watching the eclipse of the moon, but had received no emotion from the phenomenon. Perhaps the fault lay in the northern sky, he speculated, where the air does not vibrate and the stars do not live. There was no

---

[7] In his 'Journal' (May-April, 1907) of his trip to Spain, he says that his mother arose at five or six o'clock in the morning to enjoy the view of the countryside (*Europe* [Jan-Feb., 1955] 3-77).

mystery. He would like to have something unexpected happen. Would the moon not start rolling out of its orbit through space? Would a star not explode? Would not some frightful monster or column of fire surge up from the bottomless abyss? But the heavenly clockwork continued its monotonous march. Such a wish, with its implication of destruction, appears to arise from feelings of hostility directed towards the world in general.

Certain esthetic and artistic emotions contribued to maintaining his feeling of a semi-detached domination over life, of almost complete freedom, but the balance between sadness and joy, between despair and hope, between subservience to life and domination over it, which he had rather precariously attained late in 1901 and in 1902, was not long continued. It is interesting to note that one of the experiences that contributed to his state of detachment was a performance by Mounet-Sully of *Oedipus Rex* (letter to Mme Bertolini, Feb. 28, 1903; *Chère Sofia,* I, p. 101). At this performance he felt the most powerful theatrical emotion of his life. He felt the serene sky over storms at sea; he seemed to be soaring in light above the grandiose and lugubrious storms of life. Light and fire are both closely connected to sexuality (see Gaston Bachelard, *La Psychanalyse du feu* [Paris, 1938], *passim,* and Bachelard, *L'air et les songes* [Paris, 1943], *passim*). The cause of the sensation of soaring (itself a fantasy connected with sexuality: see A. K. Weinberg, "The Dream in *Jean-Christophe*", *Journal of Abnormal Psychology,* XIII [April, 1918 - Feb., 1919], 12-16), was the play that gave the name to the oedipal complex. Rolland's soul was torn, but he was happy; he was strong and serene, he said. He had the divine inspiration and feeling of being free, of no longer being linked by any bond to life, of being Necessity itself, which governs the universe. After Malwida's death in 1903 he again wrote to Mme Bertolini in the same vein, but the lack of equilibrium is perceptible; he was holding it up as an ideal to be attained, rather than a state he was enjoying. The supreme joy, he wrote, is to live fully, and yet to keep oneself separated from life by dominating the actions in which we are mingled, and by inhaling the very breath of Eternity. Let us try to create for ourselves, he exclaimed, this refuge, this motionless and calm island in the midst of the incessant chaos (letter to Mme Bertolini, April 29, 1903; *Chère Sofia,* I, p. 111). This attitude seems to be much the same psychological process as the conquering of suffering by seizing on it and exaggerating its nature.

This ideal was not solely a retreat from reality into a Nirvana nor a mystic assumption into an ethereal sphere. It was also his perception that life is in man, but that man does not constitute life. We perceive this force within ourselves, and it is our duty to augment and intensify it, be wrote to Mme Bertolini, November 22, 1903 (*Chère Sofia,* I, pp. 150-151). All we can know of this force — and that is sufficient — is whether the strength of the current is growing or diminishing. While the force is intact there is nothing to fear; nothing vile can come from it.

The conflicting traits of his character and temperament were not always in a stable equilibrium. This critical period impaired his health and disturbed whatever balance he had attained. Only at times was he able to attain a certain equilibrium; creative activity (writing, playing music, enjoying some esthetic sensation) was an important stabilizing factor. He was thus able at times to experience a complete but detached view of life and of his part in the universal force. At such moments of harmony he knew the rare joy of a feeling of freedom, attained through an identification of himself with the life force, but not with its physical materializations.

VIII

BIOGRAPHIES AND PLAYS (1903-1906)

It was partly his gratitude for a source of strength in a period of despair and partly his wish to help intensify and clarify the confused and stifled life of his contemporaries that led Rolland to write his *Vie de Beethoven* (Paris, 1903).[1] This biography, which brought his name to the foreground more than any of his works prior to *Jean-Christophe,* has frequently been misunderstood by critics, who have accused him of hero worship and subjectivity. Such criticisms are true, but they reveal a misunderstanding of his purpose. The biography was subjective; it was intended so; it was also the first of the series of the *Vies des hommes illustres,* the purpose of which was to bring hope and light to people oppressed by poverty, by exhausting domestic worries, by stupid and ruinous tasks. Such was his expressed if erroneous aim. He was undertaking to group around those who need help the heroic Friends, the great souls who have suffered and endured for the Good. The *Vies des hommes illustres* are not for the proud and ambitious, he insisted, but for the unfortunate. The *Vie de Beethoven* was not written for science; it was a song of his soul, wounded and stifled, which was attempting to heal its wounds, and which was grateful to its Saviour. It should be noted there that he frequently felt that his own emotions were of universal interest, and that this biography was a cry of pain and liberation addressed to all men (letter to Elise Richter, Nov. 27, 1920). The biography was of capital importance in his life as a writer. The fact is that he had been struggling for some ten years without arousing any

[1]   *Vie de Beethoven* (16e ed., Paris, 1931); pp. i-ii. The preface is dated March, 1927.

echo, and this little work, printed by an obscure publisher, immediately penetrated to the heart of a great spiritual family.

Rolland used the term 'hero' in speaking of his *Beethoven* and gave it very specific sense. He did not call heroes those who have triumphed by force or by mind; he calls heroes only those who were great in heart (*Beethoven,* preface). He was motivated by his feeling of solidarity with all mankind; no man, he said, is separated from others (letter, Jan. 8, 1902; *Chère Sofia. Choix de lettres de Romain Rolland à Sofia Bertolini Guerrieri-Gonzaga,* I [Paris, 1959], p. 49). He can be fully a man only by living with and for all men. Each word or action creates good or evil. The good is life — not the life of one man, but of all men. Anything that increases or intensifies life is good — and this is Love. Goodness, love, and will were more important to him than intelligence. It is true that he was an intellectual, but he wished rather to be an ethical being — he wished to act at all times for the good of others and of himself (letter to Mme Bertolini, Jan. 12, 1902; *Chère Sofia,* I, pp. 50-51). It was not intelligence that he found in the musician, but heroism, poetic imagination, and moral strength. The hero is certainly not the Nietzschean 'Uebermensch', but the man who is aware of, and is redeemed by his weakness (letter to Raymond Pichard, Aug. 27, 1942). Those who have insisted upon the 'germanism' of Rolland's tastes would do well to meditate upon some of his criticisms of Beethoven. In a letter to Malwida von Meysenbug, Sept. 21, 1890, Rolland denied that Beethoven possessed remarkable intelligence; he saw in him great emotion, heroism, a passionate manner, superb and violent disdain.[2] But as a Frenchman he missed what he regarded as the good taste, measure, and critical intelligence characteristic of the French. He was also irritated by Beethoven's attempts at gaiety, the clumsy efforts of a man who did not know happiness. He found the qualities he sought especially in Beethoven's later works. *Beet-*

---

[2]   These letters are not in the *Choix de letters à Malwida von Meysenbug* (Paris, 1948) but in a German translation which was published at Stuttgart in 1932 *(Ein Briefwechsel, 1890-1891. Romain Rolland und Malwida von Meysenbug);* this text was later published in English translation by T.J. Wilson (New York, Holt, 1933).

hoven, which brought the author's name before a broad public for the first time, was a turning point in his life, public and private. It financially and creatively nourished *Jean-Christophe* during its period of gestation. This was not, however, the only biography written then. Rolland wrote to Louis Gillet on August 15, 1904 (*Correspondance entre Louis Gillet et Romain Rolland* [Paris, 1949], pp. 224-225), that he was working on a *Michel-Ange* for the *Revue de Paris* and for Péguy's *Cahiers de la Quinzaine* (Paris, 1906).[3] In the first of the two works he discussed the greatness of the Florentine artist. However, Rolland's insistence on truth forced him in his second biography to show Michelangelo's weaknesses. Many years later he wrote that he had wished to resuscitate the Michelangelo of the *Letters* and the *Rime* — the Orestes, prey of the Furies, the Prometheus gnawed by the vulture (*Beethoven. Les Grandes époques créatrices. De l'Héroïque à l'Appassionata* [Paris, 1928], pp. 190-191, n. 2). His thesis is that the artist was throughout his life a deeply unhappy man who suffered the inner antagonisms of pagan and Christian elements in his character. To this dichotomy Rolland ascribes the oppressive, and passionate restlessness of Michelangelo's artistic creations. In the tragedy of Michelangelo he also saw a Hamlet-like situation: the poignant contradictions between a heroic genius and a very unheroic will (*Vie de Michel-Ange* [Paris, 1926], p. 10).

As well as a vivid, interesting, and authoritative account of the sculptor of *Moses,* this work is of considerable interest to biographers of Rolland. There seems to be a close relationship between the animating spirit of the biography and the volumes of *Jean-Christophe* that he was then writing. Common to both is the comparison of a great soul to a high summit lashed by winds and covered by clouds, where one breathes more deeply and feels nearer the Eternal (*Ibid.,* pp. 187-188). In both he attacks false idealism, saying that the only true heroism is to see the world and to love it as it is (*Ibid.,* pp. 10-11). The 'vainqueur-vaincu' theme also appears here; Rolland remarks about Michelangelo's statue "The Conqueror" in the Museo Nazionale (Florence), that the

[3] For these details see Starr, *A Critical Bibliography of the Published Writings of Romain Rolland* (Evanston, Ill., Northwestern University Press, 1951).

handsome young man, at the very moment of his triumph, hesitates in uncertainty; "Il a vaincu. Il est vaincu" (*Ibid.*, p. 9). This he sees as a symbol of several of his own creations.[4] 'Les grands vaincus' are men of thought and deed, martyrs and exiles, men who reject their epoch, and are rejected by it. The spiritually wounded who celebrate triumphs and who, like Michelangelo and Wagner, have tasted the emptiness of victory are the most bitterly defeated.

He found, however, that the portrait of Michelangelo did not conform to the avowed purpose of the heroic biographies. It was no help to those most in need. Anxiety, so strongly present in Michelangelo, is not a sign of greatness. Any lack of harmony between the individual and the laws of life, even in great men, is not part of their greatness, but of their weakness. Why try to hide the weakness? Is the weaker man less worthy of love? Rolland concluded that the weaker man, on the contrary, is more worthy of love because he has a greater need of it (*Ibid.*, pp. 10-11). Here is the dilemma he faced at the end of the biography. It did not provide a companion for those who suffer. He felt that he was only adding to their woe. Should he have thrown a veil over this aspect of Michelangelo's life? Should he have omitted the more discouraging moments? His answer was a decided 'non'. He had not, he said, promised happiness at the price of lies. He had promised truth, virile and harsh, but pure. If a man can climb to the summit, he will feel nearer the eternal, and he can descend into the plain with renewed vigor for the daily struggle (*Ibid.*, pp. 187-188).

During the same year he published his reflections about a people's theater: *Le Théâtre du Peuple. Essai d'esthétique d'un théâtre nouveau* (Paris, 1903). What relation is there between the theater of his day and the people's theater, as he conceived it? His theater, he wrote, is not an article of fashion or dilettante activity. It is the expression of a new society. It is a question of

---

[4] See his "Hommage à Malwida von Meysenbug", which appeared in *Der Romain Rolland Almanach* (Frankfurt a.M., 1926) (Also quoted by Hans Leo Götzfried in his *Romain Rolland. Das Weltbild im Spiegel seiner Werke* [Stuttgart, 1931], p. 34).

creating a new art for a new world. There are those who would give the people the theater just as it exists, simply by arranging that working people can attend. Others want to create from this new force — the people — a new art. The first group believes in the theater; the second, in the people. The one is the champion of the past; the second, the champion of the future (*Théâtre du peuple,* p. 12).

It is evident that he considered the theater not simply as an art form, but as a medium of expression, the purpose of which lies outside the form. His basic premise was that art does not have for its object the suppression or exemplification of the struggle, but the multiplication and intensification of life (*Ibid.,* p. 131). Rolland, of a rather frail physique, worshipped a strong, vigorous life. Many of the principal characters of his early works, until the end of the First World War, are robust men filled with a taste and gusto for life; Christophe, Danton, Colas Breugnon represented his ideal. When autobiographic elements are uppermost, the characters are generally inclined towards timidity, physical weakness, lack of physical vigor. It is partly this admiration for physical vigor that has made his novels so influential. From his premise there arise certain conclusions. There are three conditions for a people's theater; it must be recreation, it must be a source of energy, and it must be a light for the mind. Joy, strength, and intelligence are the three chief conditions, and they are the ones we would expect of Rolland (*Ibid.,* pp. 103-105). Such a theater must present truths that the people can understand and feel, and in so doing, combat the somnolence of the mind, the indifference, and the fascination of brilliant style which is without any real meaning. People can survive without beauty, but not without truth. The physical energy of man — the basis of our civilization — must be enriched. The superiority of the theater in this respect is that it can boldly take the instincts and present them, molded in the most suitable form.

Rolland surveyed the offerings of serious theaters of the time, and found very little that he considered proper fare. His judgment indicates, it seems to us, a rather competent understanding of the needs of people, if not of the stage. What should be presented to this particular audience, he said, is a form of melodrama. Sophocles and Shakespeare, according to him, wrote true melodramas. Such plays have qualities that people can understand and appreciate; varied emotions, so that the spectators can be relieved of their tears in laughter, and vice versa; true realism; simple morality; commercial probity — that is, substance without extraneous filler.

His ideal was essentially socialism. He insisted in a letter to Alphonse Séché on July 28, 1903 (*Revue d'art dramatique,* Sept. 15, 1903, p. 274; and *Ces jours lointains. Alphonse Séché et Romain Rolland* [Paris, 1962], pp. 23-24), that a popular theater must be socialist in order to live and be fecund. He had been convinced for some time that the theater must not be separated from political action. The theater, as all art and all intellectual and spiritual life, must take part in the struggle even at the risk of losing for a time its highest privileges, especially those of disinterested thought and pure beauty. The first task is to break down everything that opposes the free growth of thought. Later peace can be brought back into art. Thus Rolland called for a 'littérature engagée' long before J.-P. Sartre made the slogan famous.[5] It was too early to expect such a theater, as he soon realized. The change would have to come first in society (letter in reply to a poll on the dramatic repertory, *L'Art dramatique et musical* [Paris, 1907], p. 145). In his efforts to oppose the weak and materialistic individualism of the time, he was carried along by great currents of collective social passions; he had felt them within himself, and he loved their fearful intoxication. This lyricism of the great secret forces, he said later to P.-J. Jouve (1916), is the essence of his theater and of *Jean-Christophe* (Jouve, *Romain Rolland vivant 1914-1919* [Paris, 1920], p. 171). It was only in the face of other currents of collective forces and passions which were completely contrary to his own nature, that he was able in 1914-1915 to realize the extent to which he had been swept along by the earlier ones.

Almost at the same time as the *Beethoven,* Rolland's play *Le Temps viendra* appeared in the *Cahiers de la Quinzaine* (March 10,

---

[5] We are not trying to tie the existentialists in France or elsewhere to Rolland's train. There are, however, certain aspects of his thinking that are somewhat similar to this philosophical movement.

1903). The Boer War had caused him much concern, and his sympathies were with the Boers, especially with President Krüger (letter to Gillet, Dec. 5, 1900; *Correspondance,* pp. 108-110). He had begun work on the play in the summer of 1901 (letter to Malwida, Aug. 31, 1901; *Choix*); it was a protest against war, not a work of hate against England; he wanted to portray men who were capable of wishing to end the war and the resulting injustices, but who were dragged on by a fatality composed of instincts, habits, and customs. The great tragedy of human actions seemed to him (letter to Malwida of August 31) to be that they are generally accomplished in spite of man's will by an irresistible destiny which leads men to ruin.

In the play, Field Marshal Lord Clifford, commander-in-chief of the British Armies, feels the futility, immorality, cruelty, and barbarity of war. Nevertheless, his devotion to his duty is such that he continues to fight in order to conquer a heroic enemy, and to command, in order to preserve some semblance of humane treatment of the women and children in the occupied areas. His sense of humanity, of responsibility for the non-combattants is contrasted sharply and convincingly with the cold and calculated brutality of General Graham. Graham, to protect his troops and to prosecute the war efficiently, is determined to carry out a scorched-earth policy, and to remove from the area all non-combattants. He forces Clifford to take some of the measures he considers necessary, but the results of halfway measures cause additional suffering without achieving the purpose. The result is an intensification of the conflict in Clifford's soul. He becomes so unsure of himself that he asks his friend to watch over him in case he may come to the point of incurring dishonor ("Obéir à ma conscience? Je ne le puis sans trahir. — Obéir à mon pays? Il le faut bien. Mais mon être se cabre", p. 124).[6] Death ends his painful situation when a small boy presses the trigger of a revolver he finds on a table. After Clifford's death, the cruel and repressive measures instituted by Graham fall upon the unhappy population — whose spirit remains unbroken. President Krüger is sympa-

---

[6] *Le Temps viendra,* in *Les Cahiers de la Quinzaine,* Series 4, Cahier 14 (March 10, 1903), p. 124. All references to this play are from this edition.

thetically portrayed as a dauntless man full of faith in the Lord
and in his own cause. But these people are, ironically, caught in
a trap, for they had been equally merciless a century before when
they conquered the land from the natives, whom they reduced to
miserable servitude (pp. 78-79). It is Clifford who points this out
to Debora, inflamed by hatred for the British invader. Of all the
characters, only Owen, a simple foot soldier filled with an ideal
of non-resistance that is truly the spirit of the New Testament and
of Tolstoy — although he himself does not know the author of
War and Peace — is not torn by internal conflict. He is much
simpler than Clifford. When he perceives the folly and injustice
of war — especially after talking to the young Garibaldian who
has come to fight for justice on the side of the Boers — he refuses
to fight. He chooses a certain death for the sake of his faith over
an uncertain life sacrificed to principles contrary to his belief.
The play ends with the Biblical words uttered by Owen as he is led
away with the Boer prisoners, condemned to death: "Le temps
viendra, quand tous les hommes sauront la vérité, quand ils fon-
dront les piques pour des faux, les sabres pour des herses, et quand
le lion s'étendra près de l'agneau. ... Le temps viendra" (p. 148).
Clifford expresses the thoughts of Rolland; when an officer
announces the surrender of the Boer army and includes himself
among the conquerors, Clifford replies that there are no conquerors, only the vanquished. In the play everybody is defeated
spiritually and physically, except Owen, who found security and
joy in his faith.

We recognize familiar themes: the question of violence, of the
means and the ends; the conflict between two equally powerful
opposing forces or situations; the destiny that seems to lead man
to ruin. For the first time there appears a debate that will occur
frequently in Rolland's later works: non-violent resistance in the
sense Tolstoy gave to it. The question of justice is the very essence
of the play. The Boers are struggling against unjust invaders, but
they themselves are unjust invaders. Owen, who welcomes death
in order to maintain his principles and beliefs, is the hero, the
'vaincu vainqueur', although one may be tempted to query the
value of his results except as an example; he is in some ways

similar to Lux of *Le Triomphe de la raison*. Perhaps the most significant aspect of the play is that it again is a subject of contemporary interest, the first since *Les Loups*.

Le Temps viendra has been performed in France less frequently than any other of Rolland's plays, and is in some respects one of his poorer plays. It is marred by preaching and long discourses. On the other hand, the conflicts are capable of arousing interest and sympathy, and the characters are well portrayed. Social criticism enters the scene, but less as an extraneous element than as an integral part of the action. For example, the inextricable threads of finance and conquest are revealed when one of the officers is concerned more with restoring the captured mines for the sake of the London investors than in conquering the Boers for the sake of conquest. The principal flaws are the excessive preoccupation with ethical questions and a certain lack of dramatic sense. No matter how intense the conflicts, how great the sympathy with the protagonist, the author's urge to debate the moral questions that interested him appears only too clearly.

The following year, 1904, Rolland permitted the publication, with only half-hearted approval, of another play, *La Montespan*, written in 1899, in the *Revue d'art dramatique et musical* (letter to Gillet, *Correspondance*, p. 227). It did not satisfy him, although he believed that it had some very good scenes. His principal criticism of it was that it was 'theater', only, and as such not congenial to him. It originated in a transition period, when he was perfecting his technique but losing his 'fire' (unpublished notes on *La Montespan*).

In fact, the play reveals in many ways considerable knowledge of the stage; if Rolland does not count it among his best, it was because it was merely entertainment. The fact that Rolland did not like it emphasizes his deeply-rooted conviction of the seriousness and high purpose of art, and the moral and social responsibility of the artist.

The play is concerned with the struggle of Mme de Montespan to maintain her position at court. Seeking honors for her newborn son, jealous of the King, who had transferred his affections elsewhere, and strongly motivated by her need for power, she has recourse to the Black Mass in an effort to attain her ends. This obscene travesty of the Mass owes its effectiveness to the complete degradation of the personality. Her daughter, Marie-Aube, having seen Mme de Montespan leave her apartments with the sinister La Voisin, follows her to the chapel, where she glimpses the ceremony.

Mme de Montespan desired power in order to rise above men; to flee from them she has climbed the highest summit at the greatest risk. For her, power purifies the soul and mediocrity renders it vile. She believes that mediocrity forces one to the compromises, the circumspection, and the hypocrisy of half-measures, of incomplete actions, and of half-formed thoughts. "There is only one crime in the world", she exclaims (p. 97), "and that is not to be oneself". Again we detect the Rolland who admired the abounding and ardent life of the Renaissance, who insisted on his right and his duty to be himself at all times.

After the Black Mass and its participants are discovered, the Marquise, when brought before the King, still proud and arrogant, points out bitterly and sharply the difficulties she has overcome to gain the power she holds. She insists that all she has done is for the glory of the King. She attacks Louis, the man; it is the King she loves. Louis spares Mme de Montespan, who dies finally from the poisoned wine she had prepared for the King. Her last words reveal the youthfulness of the author; "Oh, my reason, do not swell so with pride! It is not you who have saved me. Reason, so clear, so lucid, imbecile Reason, you who see everything and can do nothing, you are nothing without Destiny" (p. 137).

Rolland himself, in the 'Avertissement', pointed out that he had taken liberties with historical facts. He had kept the characters of Mme de Montespan, the King, and Louvois, but he did not believe that he should be bound by the strict exactitude of historical research unless it was necessary for the internal logic of the characters. Indeed, whenever he saw in the character traits of the model the outline of a passion or of an action which historically had remained incomplete, he took pains to develop it. His purpose here was to paint an ambitious soul watching its power seep away, and the barbarous explosion which occurred in the midst of a very self-possessed and rational society.

His statement contains his whole attitude towards history and the stage. In history, he says, there are two orders of facts; one is of those which portray the essential moments of a nation or of a great soul, those which are engraved in the imagination of a people; the other is of those accidental and ephemeral facts which are like the variations on the principal theme in a musical composition. The latter can be used freely, provided the theme is not touched. It suffices for one to remain faithful to the rhythm of the characters and to the general tonality of the epoch. History is, he concluded, a storehouse of immense forces. It is art's task to loose them. To increase a hundred-fold the forces of life is good, and Truth is life.

Two years later, there appeared his little-known three-act play, "Les Trois amoureuses", in *La Revue d'art dramatique et musical* (1906). The action is laid in the 'grand siècle'. It is well constructed but the subject is slight, differing surprisingly from his previous plays. Mme Henriette, alarmed by advancing age and by the indifference of her unfaithful husband, is easily persuaded by a maid of honor, Antoinette, that the young Prince de Condé loves her and she him. Antoinette hopes to tear the Prince, whom she loves, from the arms of Françoise, who also loves him. Mme Henriette sees through Antoinette's ruse, but in the somewhat morbid days of the declining social order, in the soft and enervating atmosphere of the court, the suggestion is sufficient to arouse the forbidden sentiment in her breast. Antoinette, to convince the Prince that he loves her, plays upon the danger from Françoise, who is half-mad with rage and jealousy. The Prince laughs at her fear of Françoise and her transparent efforts. Françoise approaches the Prince, and when he seems indifferent and desirous of finding pleasure elsewhere, she fires a pistol at him, but Antoinette has earlier removed the ball. The Prince falls, and Françoise, believing him dead, attempts to drown herself. The Prince, seeing her passionate and sincere love, is moved to return her tender emotion.

The difference between this and the other plays — except *La Montespan* — which he considered vastly more important, turns upon his conception of the responsibility of the artist. "Les Trois amoureuses'' does not present or debate a message or any significant ideas, and it presents no particular spiritual values to the reader. It is purely for entertainment, and its principal merit is in its creation of the mellow, languorous, and sophisticated atmosphere of the court, and in the vivid presentation of the characters.

The action is sprightly and the play well constructed. Moments of frivolity alternate with moments of true pathos. Rolland reveals a surprising ability to manipulate a language which is differentiated from his later style by its marivaudage and badinage. The agreeableness of the incidents, the excellence of the plot and of the style are, however, not great enough to conceal the rather thin subject; and the author never considered the play as anything but a pleasant attempt in a mode and genre with which he thought he should have no sympathy. Perhaps it would have been better for him and for his writings had he had more of an appreciation for this sort of writing, with its lightness, and less of the sometimes deadly seriousness of his other works.

The threatening international situation of 1905-1906, which hung over France like a storm-cloud, cast occasional shadows in Rolland's correspondence: "Let us wish good health to ourselves and to our poor country, brutally threatened with destruction", he wrote to Louis Gillet, December 5, 1905 (*Correspondance,* pp. 229-230). Although he was to say later in his *Péguy* (Paris, 1945), I, p. 118, that the threat of war during 1905 touched him very little, we find him writing to Mme Bertolini that he and his friends had been living for several months under the threat of war (March 6, 1906; *Chère Sofia,* I, p. 257). It is true that anxiety over impending conflict did not prevent his trip to Alsace and Germany in the spring and summer of 1905 on the occasion of a Franco-German music festival. His visit was also partly to gain a clearer insight into the two races, French and German, for his novel *Jean-Christophe*. In Alsace the two peoples were to be found, unfused, side by side. At Strasbourg he stayed with Albert Schweitzer, then director of St.-Thomas Church and professor at the Faculté de Théologie of the University of Strasbourg, who played music by J. S. Bach for him (*Péguy,* I, p. 119).

The following year, July, 1906, he again travelled through the

Rhine country. His stay was brief but his impressions vivid.[7] In that exuberant, self-confident Germany, full of scornful fatuity, he seemed to himself to be a poor German of the era before 1870, timid, grave, somewhat ridiculous (*Péguy,* I, p. 102; taken from his 'Journal' of 1906). In August he again went to England, where he stayed in Oxford until the end of September; he then went to London for a week (letters to Mme Bertolini, Sept. 6, 24, 1906). During his stay at Oxford he wrote *Antoinette,* which, if not his very best, has certainly found a favorable reception in France.[8]

Because of the heavy work of the years from 1900 to 1906 Rolland was in a chronically fatigued state. In spite of his vague intentions in 1905 at the time of the Prix Femina, he had not been able or willing to take a leave of absence. Not until 1906 was this feasible, when in the fall he obtained leave for a year. On November 20, 1906, he wrote to Alphonse de Châteaubriant that he hoped the sun of southern Italy and Spain would dispel the northern fogs and dampness that had settled in him. He left Paris in December for Italy (letter to Richard Strauss, Dec. 1, 1906; *Richard Strauss et Romain Rolland. Choix de lettres* [Paris, 1951], pp. 83-85). In March he went to Barcelona (letter to Mme Bertolini, March 12, 1907; *Chère Sofia,* I, pp. 291-294), and travelled through the peninsula until April. His impressions of Spain were very vivid and favorable, and students of Spanish culture may find here some interesting remarks and observations.[9] He was struck by the distinction of the Spanish people, whom he judged superior in many ways to the Italians. In comparison France seemed the least gay, the most tormented of the nations of modern Europe. In this respect his own country was an eternal adolescent.[10]

[7] Letters to Gillet, July 22, Aug. 6, 1906; *Correspondance entre Louis Gillet et Romain Rolland* (Paris, 1949), pp. 231-234; and to Christian Sénéchal he wrote, Sept. 3, 1932: "J'ai peu séjourné en Allemagne. Quelques brefs voyages... Ce que j'ai le mieux exploré, c'est la région rhénane — (j'ai notamment cherché sur place et établi les pérégrinations et la fuite de Jean-Christophe)."

[8] See his "Shakespeare", in *Compagnons de route* (Paris, 1936), p. 32.

[9] See his account in his Journal, "Voyage en Espagne. Journal — (mars-avril 1907)", *Europe* (Jan.-Feb., 1955), 3-77. His judgments of Spanish painting are also interesting — in themselves and for what they reveal about Rolland.

[10] "Dans l'ensemble, je suis frappé de la distinction de cette race. Je la trouve,

He returned from Spain to a busy social life in Paris, where he attended a large number of dinners and receptions — for Richard Strauss, Rimsky-Korsakov, Glazounov, Rachmaninov, and their various kapellmeisters. He saw Richard Strauss most frequently; indeed, the two spent one evening together at the presentation of *Pelléas et Mélisande,* an evening which is reflected in *La Foire sur la place,* when Lévy-Cœur and Christophe attend the same opera.[11] He was fascinated by the gulf between Germans and French in character, temperament, and ideas. The lack of understanding was just as great in music as in any other area. He told Mlle Elsa Wolff that he was trying to throw a bridge over this abyss; although, he said, the truth was that he preferred to remain on the bank peering into its depths.

In these six years we have seen in a state of development and flux the conflicting sides of Rolland's personality, of his thinking and writing. On the one hand there is the admirer of Tolstoy, who feels the artist's responsibility, who takes himself and the world, his art and Art, seriously and rather humorlessly; on the other, the purely creative writer, the admirer of the Renaissance, in whom there arise subjects, themes, and characters, living and well-defined, and who expresses them in subjective biographies and plays that have no self-conscious message. On the one hand, such plays as *Le Temps viendra,* the plays of the Revolution, and *Michel-Ange*; on the other the *Beethoven* of 1903, *La Montespan,* and *Les Trois amoureuses.* His analysis of a people's theater, his very belief in it, are the clear expression of Rolland the artist responsible to society and to his fellowmen. It is partially an attempt to synthesize the two conflicting tendencies. At the same time that these works were being published, he was engaged in writing *Jean-Christophe,* which

en beaucoup de choses, supérieure à la race italienne... Au reste, plus je voyage, plus j'ai le sentiment que de toutes les nations d'Occident, la France moderne est la moins gaie et la plus tourmentée. Elle se brûle et se ronge. C'est une éternelle adolescente." (Letter to Mme E. Marchand, April 2, 1907).
[11]   See a letter to Mlle Elsa Wolff, May 24, 1907, published in *Les Lettres françaises,* Feb. 8, 1951, and a letter to Richard Strauss, Feb. 21, 1909, when Rolland sent him a copy of *La Foire sur la place; Richard Strauss et Romain Rolland. Choix de lettres* (Paris, 1951), p. 93. See *Fräulein Elsa. Lettres de Romain Rolland à Elsa Wolff* (Paris, 1964).

is also partly a synthesis of the two tendencies, and also a result
of the unresolved conflict. As we shall see, the best parts of the
novel are probably those where the social critic yields to the
intuitive artist.

IX

JEAN-CHRISTOPHE (1901-1912)

Jean-Christophe was partially the result of Rolland's attempts to resolve various dichotomies and conflicting beliefs or tendencies. He had wished in the heroic biographies to provide examples of courage and encouragement to those who are weary and sorely tried. But the lives of these great men contained so much suffering, so many pitiful and distressing situations, that he feared the contrary effect. *Michel-Ange* marked the end of the series, except for the life of Tolstoy (1910-1911), which was more a work of gratitude than a heroic biography. Disillusioned with this means of helping his fellow men, Rolland turned now to the imaginary life of Christophe, where suffering could be controlled and a truly inspiring creation offered to the public.

The gradual unfolding of *Jean-Christophe* in his mind is closely linked to his spiritual and esthetic development in these years. The novel was long in maturing; in a letter to Fernando Márquez Miranda, professor at Buenos Aires (June 22, 1927), Rolland wrote that he had taken ten years to construct it completely in his mind before writing the first line of the first volume. In an unpublished part of his 'Journal intime', dated March, 1890, Rolland jotted down some reflections about the novel as a genre, significant in view of the final form of *Jean-Christophe,* and his plans for writing one. Before that time the novel had for its subject matter facts linked together either by rational logic or by the chance of events. On the other hand, what he called the musical novel has for subject matter emotions, preferably generous ones, in their most intense and complete form. The novel must not analyze them, for that would be criticism, but bring them to life in the characters, who are also and simultaneously the prey of the emotions. Every part of such a novel must arise spontaneously from a general and powerful emotion. Just as a symphony is built upon a theme expressing a passion, which is then developed in various ways, so a musical novel must be the flowering of sentiments which constitute its soul. He intended to write such a novel, to express the furious scorn for the world, the tragic disdain of the genius in the isolation of a Moses.[1]

A love story was an integral part of the novel then in his mind (1890), and was partially transformed later into one of the episodes of *Jean-Christophe*. He was writing a musical novel to give vent to his feelings and to purify his love. In order to suppress all personal bitterness, he was writing about a happy and cloudless love.[2] What personal bitterness? Probably he was referring to Sofia Guerrieri-Gonzaga, who had had almost a devastating effect on him. Part of his bitterness was possibly due to his inability to attain and to maintain a relationship with a woman his own age. When he returned to Paris from Rome he was full of sweet memories, but he was unable to resume work on the novel, "Artistes". It was repellent for him to give any of his soul to such a vulgar occupation, so petty, shabby, and unhealthy as the novel then appeared to him. Yet in the principal idea, the genius who dominates and scorns the world, there was ample matter

---

[1] "L'ancien roman a pour matière les faits, reliés soit par la logique raisonneuse, soit par le hasard des événements.

Le roman musical a pour matière le sentiment, — et de préférence les sentiments les plus généreux, sous leur forme la plus intense, la plus complète. Il ne doit pas les analyser (ce serait de la critique), mais les faire revivre sous le vêtement de telle ou telle apparence, de tel ou tel personnage en qui ces sentiments s'incarnent et qui en sont la proie. Toute partie du roman musical doit jaillir d'un sentiment général et puissant, fortement éprouvé. Comme une symphonie est bâtie sur quelques notes exprimant une passion, qui se développe en tous sens, grandit, triomphe, ou succombe, un roman musical doit être la floraison d'un sentiment qui en est l'âme.

C'est ainsi que je ferai un roman (ou une partie de roman), exprimant le sentiment de Moïse, le mépris furieux du génie pour le monde, l'isolement passionné, le dédain tragique. Le travail du romancier consiste à tendre la chaîne sur laquelle se tissera la trame du sentiment."

[2] See the letter to his mother, 1890, from Rome, in *Printemps romain* (Paris, 1954), pp. 343-344.

which he would have had pleasure in treating (*Empédocle* treated this theme).[3] "The Artists" was not suspended, however, and during the following year it began to resemble the life of Beethoven. He wrote to his mother late in June, 1891, that he had been looking for a life of Beethoven or an edition of his letters; he was then engaged on a novel touching on the life of Beethoven. In a letter to Malwida, November 5, 1896, he said that he had a very long novel in progress, which would require several years to write (*Choix de lettres à Malwida von Meysenbug* [Paris, 1948], p. 18). It was the story of a genius; since his return from Germany in the summer of 1895 or 1896 he had almost completed the account of the babyhood. He was then busy with this novel and the drama *Aërt*. They are almost the same, he concluded, but in different areas: one in the domain of action (the novel), and the other in the realm of thought (the play). In what way are they alike? The hero of each is uncompromising, naive, and a thoroughgoing idealist. One is crushed in an attempt to act; his efforts are thwarted because of his naiveté. The second lives almost solely in his music, soon an impregnable fortress for him, by which he eventually conquers all difficulties. Both works were the reactions of a pure, unsophisticated hero.

The first clear design of the novel appeared in May, 1896, and his intent then was greater than the novel as finally completed. He originally envisaged two heroes whose destinies would be complementary: Dream and Action. Furthermore, one book of the novel was never written. He had intended to include, between *Les Amies* and *Le Buisson ardent,* a volume the subject of which was an unsuccessful revolution (Introduction by Rolland to *Jean-Christophe* [Paris, 1950], p. xviii). The only traces remaining are probably the scenes of the riots on May Day, in which Olivier is killed (see also *Souvenirs de jeunesse,* p. 215).

---

[3] "A mon retour à Paris, le cœur tout parfumé de souvenirs d'art et de nature, — mon impossibilité de reprendre le roman: *Artistes,* — même sous la nouvelle forme que je lui ai trouvée à Rome. Il m'est répugnant de donner un peu de mon âme à une aussi vulgaire occupation. Si petit, mesquin, malsain, me paraît à présent un tel roman! — Et pourtant, dans l'idée principale: *le génie dominateur et méprisant du monde,* il y avait ample matière, que j'aurais plaisir (soulagement) à traiter" (Notes to "Empédocle", August, 1890).

On February 24, 1897, he wrote to Malwida (*Choix de lettres*, p. 202) that he had written some hundred pages about the childhood of the main character. It was his intention for the novel and its hero to live with him until the end of his own life, for it was the story of his soul, transposed into a greater man.[4] More than a novel, it was to be the synthesis of scattered events and aspirations of his own life, a symbiosis of the protagonist and his creator. He wanted also to include the whole world, the reflections of contemporary events in his artist-hero's life. Four years later he wrote to Louis Gillet, November 27, 1901 (*Correspondance entre Louis Gillet et Romain Rolland* [Paris, 1949], p. 158), that the principal lines of the novel were drawn. He believed that it would be a beneficial work — if finished. What he would like to do in the novel, which is hardly a novel — as his plays were sometimes hardly plays — was to put into it all his understanding of contemporary life as seen from three or four great peaks. It is not a work of adventure or of psychology or of analysis that he was trying to create, but a sort of mountain chain of souls, each isolated and different, with its own special atmosphere which he hoped would be one of strength, of calm, and of virile, lucid intelligence. The remarks clearly reveal the close bonds between his *Michel-Ange* and *Jean-Christophe*. A year later the plan had taken more definite form, and in a letter to Malwida, September 13, 1902 (*Choix*), the lineaments of the novel as we now know it can be clearly discerned. The novel is, he wrote, the history of a man's life from birth to death. The hero is a German musician, Beethoven in today's world, who is forced by circumstances to live outside Germany, in Paris, Italy, and Switzerland. The atmosphere is that of the Europe of 1902. The hero's temperament is not Rolland's, who said that he lent him only his intelligence. The author's own personality is disseminated in secondary characters. The subject is, in part, the world seen through the eyes of his hero.

[4] "On ne peut parler légèrement, ni donner un résumé de quelque chose qui doit être bien plus qu'une œuvre pour moi, — une vie. En vérité, il me semble que ce roman ne peut être terminé qu'avec ma vie. Je crois que si j'avais dix ans de vie encore, je pourrais faire là une œuvre sans précédent." (Letter to Mme Bertolini, Aug. 2, 1902; *Chère Sofia, Choix de lettres de Romain Rolland à Sofia Bertolini Guerrieri-Gonzaga*, I [Paris, 1959], p. 86).

The novel was to consist of six or seven parts, each concerning a period of his life and development, and each set in a different world. Every part, although closely attached to the whole, would be able to stand alone. Each volume would have for its center an important episode, or one of the characters who play a capital rôle in the protagonist's life. Everything in the novel was to be closely related to the development of the hero.

Earlier in the year (Jan. 15, 1902; *Correspondance*, p. 166), he wrote to Gillet that the whole was sketched, up to the death of the hero. It would probably consist of four distinct parts — like the parts of a symphony. He intended to write the second and fourth parts first.

By the end of the summer of 1902, in Switzerland, Rolland had almost completed one of the important episodes (he does not specify which one). He felt great joy at what he had accomplished — good or bad. He had the deep satisfaction that comes from the awareness — or the illusion — of understanding some part of the world (letter to Gillet, Aug. 29, 1902; *Correspondance,* pp. 210-211). You know, he wrote, that I insist, although an idealist, on realism; and on living truth, although a romantic. He wanted to give his work a subtitle equivalent to *Life*. Two weeks later he wrote to Mme Bertolini, September 6, 1902 (*Chère Sofia. Choix de lettres de Romain Rolland à Sofia Bertolini Guerrieri-Gonzaga* [Paris, 1959], I, p. 89), that he had written one of the five or six proposed parts of the novel. He hoped to finish it by the same date of the following year. On August 6, 1903, he wrote to her that he was watching Christophe grow; his words reveal an almost maternal tenderness that seems to result from a lack in his own emotional life, an innate dissatisfaction which may have been one of the causes of his divorce. It seemed to him that Christophe was his own little son. Alas! he said, how he is going to suffer; I cannot, as a mother does, live in an illusion about his future. Just think, it depends upon me to make his life happy, if I wish, and I cannot. My heart is heavy; but I know that he will be a valiant little man, and that he will not let himself be overcome, whatever happens (letters to Mme Bertolini, June 26, August 6, 1903; *Chère Sofia,* I, pp. 120, 129). He was sure that Mme Bertolini would be a good mother, and asked her advice about a name for his little hero; he wanted something solid and robust, like Jean-Christophe.

The first volumes, "L'Aube", "Le Matin", and "L'Adolescent" appeared in Péguy's *Cahiers de la Quinzaine,* February, 1904, and January 10, 1905. At this time all the notes were prepared and the outline ready for the complete work, but the only other volume actually written was the one that is now *Le Buisson ardent* (volume nine; Christophe's flight to Switzerland and his passionate love affair with Anna Braun) (letter to Mme Bertolini, Feb. 3, 1905; *Chère Sofia,* I, p. 213). The next volume, *La Révolte,* appeared in 1906 and 1907, after his extended travels in Germany. In 1906, at Oxford, he completed *Antoinette,* which takes its place between *La Foire sur la place* and *Dans la maison. La Révolte* first, and then *La Foire sur la place* provided Rolland with the opportunity of proclaiming unpleasant truths to all sorts of people, first about Germany, and then about France, especially Paris. Despite some slight uneasiness about the effect of such criticism, he secretly enjoyed the possibility of airing, untrammeled, his views of Parisian art and society.[5]

By the summer of 1907 he had completed *La Foire sur la place* and part of *Dans la maison* (letter to Gillet, Sept. 19, 1907; *Correspondance,* p. 241). The three volumes were to correct and complete each other mutually. The third would render justice to the preceding volume, in which Paris is so sharply criticized. He was unable to finish *Dans la maison* in time for it to appear simultaneously with the two other volumes (letter to Mme E. Marchand, Oct. 17, 1907); it finally appeared in February, 1909.

The next volume, *Le Buisson ardent,* caused Rolland real suffering. He had felt keenly the trials and tribulations of Christophe in some of the other volumes, and he rejoiced in advance over the last one, which was to resolve all the discords. It was to repay him for the suffering the other volumes had caused; each one, he

[5] "Je suis bien content que le premier cahier de la *Révolte* vous ait plu. Christophe ne fait que commencer à dire la vérité aux gens: et déjà, il y a pas mal de protestations. Ce sera bien autre chose, l'an prochain, quand il arrivera à Paris. Il y a tant d'années que j'attends le moment de dire enfin tout ce que je pense de l'art parisien! — J'ai conscience de la force morale, qui couve dans la France. Tâchons de la réveiller" (Letter to Mme E. Marchand, Jan. 5, 1907).

told Gillet, had brought him gray hairs. Christophe's crises had been as upsetting for Rolland as for Christophe — indeed, more, for his body was weaker than his hero's. *Le Buisson ardent* was one of the most distressing of the volumes; yet he was unable not to write it.[6]

The principal reason for the long delay in completion is to be found principally in the subject, Christophe's overwhelming and illicit passion for Anna Braun; this sudden intrusion of a deep physical love which sweeps all before it touched too closely part of the author's inner and secret nature. The need for love penetrated every fiber of his being and every part of his multifarious activities. But he also suffered from this need; indeed he feared women, and we occasionally hear the cries of suffering that escape from him at times when his guard is down. In a letter of May, 1895, to André Suarès, for example, he had spoken of his feelings for the two Guerrieri-Gonzaga sisters, one of whom "so peacefully tore my soul to shreds". (Compare the letter to J.-R. Bloch, Mar. 11, 1914; *supra,* p. 41).

Was this torment one of love? or was it the suffering of inner tensions? In a later text, July-August, 1924, in which he tells of a friendship with a beautiful actress in order to illustrate what he believed to be his fundamental need for freedom, he incidentally revealed something of his own ambiguous attitude towards women and marriage. His friend was frank, and without any subtle or hidden intentions. She was a tall, robust, bold, laughing, affectionate and devilishly noisy woman, he said, (the exact opposite in all respects of his own mother). They got along well together, and yet they were really very far apart. One day, he recalled, he felt himself crushed under an indefinable weight, until late in the afternoon when he discovered the reason. The previous night he had dreamed that he was married to this charming friend. Married! he exclaimed. It was crushing (not because of happiness or excite-

[6] Letter to J.-R. Bloch, Oct. 21, 1911. See his letter to Gillet, July 9, 1911; *Correspondance entre Louis Gillet et Romain Rolland* (Paris, 1949), p. 248; and *Péguy* (Paris, 1945), I, p. 251.

ment); he regained his breath only when he was sure that this 'happiness' would be spared him.[7]

He was putting so much of himself into the novel, into both Olivier and Christophe, and releasing by this means so many of the tensions, inhibitions, and repressions of his own nature and life, that he lived all the joys, struggles, and sorrows of his two heroes. In spite of the generally beneficial effects of the exteriorization of his own emotional problems, the nervous energy necessary for the process drained his physical strength. He hoped also to write a work in which there would appear a serene, Raphael-like, Mediterranean genius, a figure which would do more good than the original conception of *Jean-Christophe,* but he was apparently unable ever to write this other *Jean-Christophe.*[8] He was unable, possibly because of his own lack of sincerity or because of his refusal or inability to see or understand his own tensions and fears. The two principal characters of *L'Ame enchantée,* Marc and Annette, do not answer this description. Marc is a far more tormented soul than Christophe. The only remains of his intention is perhaps the partially transformed character of Christophe in the last volume, *La Nouvelle journée.*

La Nouvelle journée, which was to resolve all the discords and dissensions of the novel, was already formed in his mind in 1911 (letter to J.-R. Bloch, Nov. 18, 1911). As Rolland points out later in his introduction to the novel (Paris, 1950), p. xviii, the puritanism of the first books is relaxed in the third group (*La Fin du voyage*); with the calming effect of maturity, the music of the

[7] *Le Périple* (Paris, 1946), pp. 87-88. This incident seems to be the basis of Christophe's love affair with Françoise Oudon, actress; Christophe's life with her, without benefit of marriage, seems to have been somewhat more complete than Rolland's.

[8] "Ah! quand serai-je sorti de ce cercle de luttes qu'il me faut nécessairement franchir dans Christophe? Ce que je demande le plus à la vie, c'est d'avoir dix ans avant ma mort pour vivre loin de Paris, dans le Midi, et de pouvoir écrire l'*autre* Jean-Christophe que j'ai toujours rêvé; le Jean-Christophe méditerranéen, heureux, serein, le *Raphael* (je l'appelle ainsi, en attendant, comme j'appelais l'autre Beethoven, avant qu'il fût né: quoiqu'ils soient l'un et l'autre bien distincts de leurs grands-frères d'autrefois.) — Cet *autre* Jean-Christophe ferait tant de bien, — tellement plus que le premier" (Letter to Mme E. Marchand, March 8, 1908).

whole work becomes more complete and more subtle. In a letter to Stefan Zweig, March 9, 1922, Rolland speaks of the sensualism of Colas Breugnon (in the novel of the same name, 1913), and of the sexuality of Christophe, 'these forces essential to complete harmony'. He had himself undergone such a passion and crisis as Christophe's, although less tragic, he wrote to Paul Seippel on February 10, 1913, not long after the appearance of the last volume of the novel. 'Less tragic' — the words reveal his own lack of understanding of this aspect of his character; in view of his unsuccessful marriage, of another broken love affair, and of a second marriage only when he was sixty-eight years of age, one may well wonder if 'less' should not be 'more'. In *Le Buisson ardent,* Christophe had undergone all the suffering and consolations of the believing Christian: sin, penitence, forgiveness, and a new life.[9] Rolland insists that the visitation of the Divine Spirit to Christophe in the bitterest hour of his life (conclusion of *Le Buisson ardent*), was conceived in the deepest sense of the Christian religion. But Christophe's new life is more than the life of a sinner, repentant and saved. It is the attainment of a Goethean serenity which is beneficent in its effects on others. The stresses and strains of his earlier life, the tensions and discords within his personality and in his social relations are almost all resolved in the sun of a new day; its warmth can benefit not only those who have suffered, but also those who have yet to reach that stage.

Rolland experienced vicariously his hero's fall, repentance, and redemption, and looked at life with new eyes. Immediately after the completion of the novel, he wrote to Seippel (November 9, 1912) that he had been freed by Christophe from the enormous burden of the past. He seemed to be on the threshold of a new moral and esthetic world into which he hoped, God willing, to enter. You cannot imagine, he assured Seippel, what an exalted joy I feel within me at the sight of eternally new life on all sides.[10]

---

[9] Paul Seippel: *Romain Rolland* (Paris, 1913), pp. 160-164. Eugen Lerch, *Romain Rolland und die Erneuerung der Gesinnung* (Munich, 1926), p. 47. See also Rolland, *Péguy,* I, p. 284, n. 95.

[10] Quoted by Paul Seippel, in "Jean-Christophe", *Bibliothèque universelle et Revue suisse* (Oct.-Dec., 1912), 449-470.

The musical nature of his novel, so frequently and so vaguely mentioned consists not in the hero's interest in music or in Rolland's references to that art, but rather in the structure of the novel. Themes are introduced, analyzed, and developed. Dissonances between conflicting themes in one volume are resolved in the harmonies of a following volume. For example, *La Foire sur la place,* which is an acrid critique of the superficial writers, artists, and politicians of the 1880's and 1890's, is also France seen through the eyes of the candid and somewhat unlearned and prejudiced Christophe. The following volume, *Antoinette,* is France seen from within as a Frenchman sees it, but it is perhaps not yet the true picture, in depth and focus, of France. *Dans la maison* resolves these conflicting images in the rounded and subtly-drawn view of France as seen both by the outsider Christophe, and the insider, the idealistic Olivier, in whom, as Rolland says, there is so much of the author.[11] The views of the two friends, their opinions and perspectives are modified by their mutual influence to a new vision. The conflicting themes, the two visions of France, are thus resolved in a harmonious unity.

Rolland was conscious of the nature of the process of his artistic creations. How can one judge my work and my mind, he asked, if one is not a musician? Music is not merely the subject of some chapters of my novel, or of my criticism; it is the very form of my mind; it penetrates the essence of my thinking and of my art; it is the key to my literary composition.[12] In a letter to Louis

11 "Vous trouverez dans le premier cahier de *Dans la Maison* certaines confessions d'Olivier, qui sont aussi des confessions personnelles, et vous expliqueront, mieux que je ne puis le faire, mes pensées d'enfance et d'adolescence" (Letter to Jean Bonnerot, Feb. 3, 1909). "J'ai retourné à Humblot 2 vol. de *Jean-Christophe* revus et corrigés, pour un nouveau tirage (*Antoinette,* et *Dans la Maison*). Cela m'a fait relire, avec intérêt, ce dernier livre. J'ai trouvé qu'Olivier me ressemblait beaucoup plus que je ne me souvenais" (Letter to Mlle Madeleine Rolland, Feb. 14, 1917). To Zweig, who was preparing his biography of Rolland, he wrote (June 10, 1920): "A l'arrivée à Paris, dans les années 1881-1884 ou 5, se place la crise d'adolescence, qui fut très dure et même dangereuse. J'en ai exprimé quelque chose dans l'ébranlement moral et religieux de Christophe, ainsi que dans certaines confessions d'Olivier. Je sais des minutes d'alors où j'ai été bien près du suicide."

12 "Comment juger de mon œuvre et de mon esprit, si l'on n'est musicien? La musique n'est pas seulement le sujet de quelques chapitres de mon roman,

Gillet, July 30, 1913 (*Correspondance,* p. 236), he expressed the hope that someone would reveal clearly not only the moral but also the artistic personality of Christophe, and the originality of the novel, especially its symphonic construction: preludes and postludes, guiding themes, symphonic and rhythmic developments. This was the constant form of his thinking while writing.[13] When critics speak of his musicality, he said, they are generally referring to the superficial analogies with the lives of various musicians. His 'music' is marked by his intuitive feelings in the souls he describes, the subject that he embraces, and the symphonic, harmonic, and rhythmic language used in treating them.[14]

Not only does the handling of the ideas and themes resemble musical composition; even the physical make-up of the novel follows devices used in music. "In my work", he wrote to Stefan Zweig, "and especially in *Jean-Christophe,* the divisions (paragraphs and chapters), the lines which run on into the following page, the spaces provided in the text, all are extremely important. They are the articulations... Can you imagine a musical edition, where, in order to save space, half and quarter rests would be omitted? Yet that is what the German translator... and the publishers did...". He suffered, he said, when he saw the German edition; the islands of consciousness still surrounded by night had been shoved together by the printer and made into a single continent. In the first pages of the volumes *Dans la maison* and *La Nouvelle journée,* the odes to friendship and to music were inserted into the mass of the novel instead of forming imposing approaches to it. Certain 'postludes' were treated in the same way; their harmonies were supposed to be leisurely unfolded in the quiet

---

ou de quelques volumes de critique: elle est la forme même de mon esprit, elle pénètre l'essence de ma pensée et de mon art, elle est la clef de ma composition littéraire... Ce à quoi je tiens beaucoup, c'est à ce qu'on montre le caractère musical de la composition de *Jean-Christophe* et de son style" (Letter to Mlle Madeleine Rolland, Dec. 13, 1918).

[13]   For his statement of this fact before 1909, see his remarks to Jean Bonnerot, published by Bonnerot in "Romain Rolland. Extraits de son œuvre", *Les Cahiers nivernais et du centre.* 13th and 14th cahiers (Oct.-Nov., 1909), 16.

[14]   Letter to Fernando Márquez Miranda (June 22, 1927).

reflections of the day's end.[15] The rhythms, the musical phrases, are constituted by divisions, indicated by spaces — since there are no typographical signs for rests in literary works. To disregard them is to disregard an essential part of the composition.

His form of composition is not musical only; it is also cyclical. He discussed this characteristic in the letter to Fernando Márquez Miranda. His art was, he said, essentially epic, architectural, and musical. He had created a new architecture of the novel, or rather, an epic poem written in prose. He was reasonably sure that in a hundred years people would become aware that the construction of *Jean-Christophe* corresponds to laws of balance and proportion that are as sure and as strict as those for Gothic cathedrals. The same error has been committed concerning the style. Because it is frequently very different from the hackneyed expressions of academic, classic, and Neo-Latin style, no one has taken the trouble to study it for itself, for its essential originality and musicality.[16]

---

[15] "... les divisions (de paragraphes et de chapitres), les rejets à la page suivante, les blancs ménagés dans le texte, ont chez moi (et particulièrement en *Jean-Christophe*) une extrême importance. Ce sont les articulations des membres. — Conçoit-on une édition musicale, où, pour gagner de la place, on aurait supprimé les pauses et les soupirs! C'est pourtant ce qu'ont fait, tranquillement, sans m'avertir, Grautoff et Rütten und Loenig! ... Je vous avoue que je souffre, quand je vois, dans l'édition allemande, ce que deviennent ainsi les premières pages de l'enfance, — ces îles de conscience qu'entoure encore la nuit — agglutinées par l'éditeur allemand en un seul continent; ou, au début des volumes (*Dans la Maison, La Nouvelle Journée*, etc.) ces odes (à l'amitié, ou à la musique) enclavées dans la masse du roman, au lieu d'en former les propylées. De même, pour certains "Postludes", dont les accords doivent sans hâte s'étaler dans le recueillement de la journée finie" (Letter to Stefan Zweig, February 4, 1918).

[16] "Mon art est essentiellement *épique, architectural,* et *musical...* J'ai créé une architecture nouvelle du roman, ou, plus exactement, un poème épique en prose... J'ose dire que, dans un siècle, on se rendra compte que la construction de *Jean-Christophe* répond à des lois d'équilibre, à des proportions aussi fermes et aussi strictes que ces monuments gothiques. Même erreur pour le style. Parce qu'il s'écarte volontairement des 'poncifs' du style académique, classique, néo-latin, on n'en a point senti (on ne s'est pas donné la peine de l'étudier en soi) l'essence originale et les lois musicales. Quand on parle de ma 'musicalité' on en reste aux dehors, aux analogies superficielles avec des 'vies de musiciens' ... Ma 'musicalité' — (ce n'est pas assez dire) — ma 'musique' est marquée à la fois dans mon intuition propre des âmes que je dépeins, des sujets que j'embrasse, et dans la langue symphonique, harmonique et rythmique que

He distinguished as the principal cause of the cyclic nature of his creations the fact that he knows of no life form, individual or social, save in the process of flux; one cannot define any being by his situation in a point of time, but only by his trajectory; and the trajectory must be followed from its point of departure to its point of arrival. The very social atmosphere which envelops the characters is in movement.[17]

His style is not to be judged by the same standards and criteria as more conventional works. As in music perhaps, and as in the epic certainly, details are subordinated to the general movement. He is far from the hard perfection of the Parnassians, and equally far from the extreme importance attached to the individual word by the symbolists. However, a careful analysis of the style would, we feel, reveal an equal importance of detail. But, just as in good music, the detail exists not for itself but for its contribution to the tonality, the structure, and the expressive quality of the whole work, so Rolland's style contributes to the emotion and the movement of the whole, without many details standing out in relief.[18] The general movement, he wrote to Alphonse Séché on February 4, 1912, is more important for him than the detail of the sentence, and each volume has its own rhythm. He attached more importance to the main lines of the composition than to delicate shadings. If transition passages are sometimes treated

---

j'emploie pour les traiter..." (Letter to Fernando Márquez Miranda, June 22, 1927).

[17] "La raison de ma forme de composition *cyclique* est que je ne connais aucune vie, individuelle ou sociale, qu'en '*devenir*' constant ('Werden'): tout est toujours en mouvement; on ne peut donc définir aucun être par sa situation en un point de temps, mais par sa trajectoire; et pour embrasser celle-ci, il faut la suivre, du point de départ au point d'arrivée. L'atmosphère sociale même, qui enveloppe les personnages, est, comme eux, en mouvement" (Letter to Fernando Márquez Miranda, June 22, 1927).

[18] "*Jean-Christophe* ne doit pas être regardé à la loupe... Certaines œuvres sont faites pour être vues de loin, parce qu'il y a en elles un rythme passionné qui mène tout l'ensemble et subordonne les détails à l'effet général. Ainsi, Tolstoy. Ainsi, Beethoven... Je ne me compare pas à ces grands vieux. Mais on peut être de la famille de ces grands vieux, et n'être qu'un pauvre petit diable. Je suis de la famille, — je sens très bien mes défauts de style. Mais jusqu'à présent aucun de mes critiques français — (si, un seul, mais il n'est pas connu) — ne s'est aperçu que j'avais un style" (Letter to Mme Cruppi, June 15, 1911).

with a certain carelessness (because of his haste to finish the novel before his death), the summits of the action are never neglected. For each volume there are some twenty different revisions; he continued to rewrite until he felt that nothing, not even a comma, could be changed in the text. I believe, he wrote, that it would be more accurate to say that I do not consider art as an end but as a means.[19]

In judging his works we must also examine the goal of his writing and his means of attaining it. Rolland wished to write an imaginary heroic biography. However, the imaginary hero is not the only important figure. Rolland had begun to find true heroism in more humble people, and Tolstoy's influence is visible in their importance. Rolland's intention was to show that true heroism exists everywhere, in all sorts of obscure people.[20] Gottfried comes immediately to our mind, and the elderly Schulz, who idolized Christophe and his music, who gave much and demanded little, accepting the tribulations of life without complaining. Louisa, the devoted mother, is another important secondary figure. Such people embody a rather important idea that is essential in the novel, namely: Do what you can, to the best of your ability, every day, without yielding to discouragement or succumbing to monotony. These people are especially frequent among the French in *Jean-Christophe*: Mme Arnaud, Cécile Fleury, Marthe Langeais — and it must be noted that the majority of these figures are

---

[19] Letter to Alphonse Séché (Feb. 4, 1912); *Ces jours lointains. Alphonse Séché et Romain Rolland* (Paris, 1962), p. 61.

[20] "Dans votre analyse de *Jean-Christophe*, vous laissez de côté le peuple des 'humbles' qui entoure les deux figures centrales. Or, il tient une place remarquablement grande dans l'œuvre et dans ma pensée... On a trop uniquement les yeux fixés sur celui qu'on nomme le Héros. Mais mon intention a été justement de montrer que l'héroïsme n'est pas le privilège d'un petit nombre d'*'Hommes Illustres'*: bien loin de là! (Et c'est une des raisons pour lesquelles j'ai abandonné ma série de Biographies des 'Illustres'). L'héroïsme est répandu partout, chez les plus simples, chez les plus humbles; et nulle part il n'est plus pur et plus divin peut-être que chez eux — chez un vieux Schulz, chez Gottfried, chez une Madame Arnaud, ou chez la chère maman mourante de Christophe. Christophe l'a bien senti... Et la grandeur propre de Christophe lui-même n'est pas tant dans son art (qu'aucun de ses lecteurs ne peut connaître) que dans son humanité simple et profonde, naturellement fraternelle aux milliers d'humbles héros inconnus..." (Letter to Stefan Zweig, June 1, 1920).

women. Rolland's mother could perhaps have taken her place here, and her influence over her son was such that various characteristics of the novel are undoubtedly traceable to this relationship. Antoinette is the principal example of self-sacrifice, devotion, heroic acceptance of life and its hardships. Yet Antoinette's sacrifice is also, in part, the result of Olivier's demanding and rather clinging nature; she is almost literally swallowed alive by him. And in the author's own life it was only his never-ending, at times only partially successful, battle that prevented his own mother from almost literally swallowing him. In the novels, the heroism that these persons display, each in his own way and within the limits of his ability, is salutary and beneficial. But they are not to be taken as examples. Each has his own capacities, and Gottfried's are not Christophe's. The word 'hero' is ironic in the mouth of a Gottfried; it is sufficient to say 'a man'; the number, Rolland said, is not large.[21]

From the esthetic point of view, these characters are not marked by the flaw that at times mars the presentation of Christophe and Olivier. Christophe is often simply a vehicle for the author's ideas. He is also a kind of symbol for the generation that Rolland wished to describe.[22] With the possible exception of Gottfried, who has a Tolstoyan message, the secondary characters exist both for themselves and as functions of Christophe. Grazia at times becomes a symbol, but never overwhelms Christophe or the reader with long discourses — as Christophe does in his letters to her. Ada, Sabine, Minna, Jacqueline, Mme Arnaud, Anna Braun, Louisa, Melchior, the grandfather, Otto, are their own excuse for being. The characters themselves were intended to be more important than the ideas (but Rolland also said, and not infrequently practiced, the contrary). In a letter to J.-R. Bloch, December 6, 1913, he wrote that no French critic had paid any attention to the

21   Letter to Roger Bodard (Oct. 12, 1933), published in *Combat* (Sept. 1, 1936).
22   Rolland admitted as much in a letter to Paul Seippel (Feb. 7, 1913): "Je souris, quand je me vois traité parfois... d'anti-intellectuel. Anti-intellectuel, Christophe l'est peut-être, parce qu'il a une tâche précise à remplir, parce qu'il est le type un peu symbolique d'une génération, parce qu'il est, dans une certaine mesure, une machine de combat."

persons in the novel, but only to the ideas. But the ideas exist only as a function of the characters. Even when the ideas are not expressed by the characters, when they take on an objective form, they are the ideological atmosphere in which the characters of the novel live. "The thoughts are not mine. I do not express my thoughts in formulae, but in the beings, whose repulsions and attractions form a symphony. The rhythms and harmonies, in the universe of souls, form the plane where my thought moves."[23]

With *Jean Christophe* the series of heroic biographies, true and fictional, is almost at an end. Only *Colas-Breugnon,* written in 1913, can be further included. The novel that will later form a counterpart to *Jean-Christophe, L'Ame enchantée,* is no longer a heroic biography. The life of Mazzini, for which he collected material for several years, was never written. The volumes of Beethoven exegesis will no longer be conceived in the same spirit as the *Beethoven* of 1903. Social problems become increasingly important in his thinking, and shape his literary creation more and more as time and a World War bring the multitude of problems into sharper focus.

But the other Olivier-Christophe, Rolland, was living his own personal life during the years of the writing of the novel. At least two young ladies were interested in him. One, Hélène B[arrère], believed that she could make him happy in marriage; but this was not then in his emotional power to consider. In a letter to Mme Bertolini, Mar. 3, 1908 (*Chère Sofia,* I, p. 331), he insisted that she could never be happy with an artist of his sort, a man per-

---

23 "Les idées, qui n'existent, dans *Jean-Christophe,* qu'en fonction des personnages! Les uns les louent, les autres partent en guerre contre elles, comme ce Souday, sans se douter un instant qu'elles ne sont pas plus miennes que je ne suis Christophe, Olivier, Schulz, Lévy-Cœur, et toutes les femelles, — mais juste autant. Je les perçois en eux. Même lorsqu'elles ne s'expriment pas par leurs bouches, lorsqu'elles empruntent une forme objective, et tranchante, d'un ton absolu... — elles sont, en quelque sorte, l'atmosphère idéologique où vivent et respirent les personnages du livre — de chaque livre. — D'où ces contradictions, qu'on m'a reprochées, — et dont je jouis. Ma pensée à moi, je ne l'exprime pas dans des formules. Je l'exprime dans des êtres, dont les attractions et les heurts forment une symphonie. Les rythmes et les accords, dans l'univers des âmes, voilà le plan sur lequel se meut ma pensée" (Letter to J.-R. Bloch, December 6, 1913).

petually haunted by his ideas and whose critical nature never disarms. Moreover, she should find someone younger and simpler; he considered himself an old man whose life lay behind him (he was only 42 at the time). Other letters (*Chère Sofia,* I, II, *passim*) reveal his slightly anxious determination to avoid any closer relationship with the young woman, and a gradual shutting off of all relationships, even by letter. At about the same time, he was deeply interested in a young English woman, a writer and friend of his sister's, Ethel Sidgwick. In a letter to Mlle Madeleine (July 15/16, 1909), Rolland referred to the idea of marriage, expressed his uncertainty, and finally decided not to go to England for fear of seeming to urge his cause too vigorously — an odd reason if one is truly serious! Nothing came of the project, although Rolland continued to correspond with Miss Sidgwick until 1939. It is likely, given his temperament and his mother's domination, that nothing could have come of the association. On December 22, 1909, he wrote to Mme Bertolini that, although he had been thinking of remarrying — he loved the English woman's beauty and spiritual nature — he had almost given up the idea (*Chère Sofia,* II, p. 52). He alleged the many and sometimes sharp differences between the French and the English temperaments as the principal reasons for his decision. Rolland's half-hidden feelings about women — fear and distrust of them — had not been mitigated by his marriage and divorce. In almost none of his works does there appear a reasonably normal, pleasant or happy love affair. We have seen the ambivalent emotions of Lia and Aërt, and the similar nature of the love of the two young people in "Le Siège de Mantoue", Olivier and Ariane. In *Jean-Christophe* and *L'Ame enchantée* very few succeed in marriage. In *La Nouvelle Journée* (the last volume of *Jean-Christophe*) Emmanuel even finds his love a burden. Olivier's marriage, like Rolland's, ends in divorce. Grazia's marriage is only fairly successful, and she is left a widow; her love for Christophe never comes to fruition.

In the occasional satisfying relationships, it is frequently the woman who takes the initiative — even with the violent, impulsive, powerful Christophe. It is Françoise Oudon who first comes to visit him after their chance meeting. During the adulterous affair with Anna Braun, it is Anna who comes to Christophe's bedroom until the very end of their affair.

Rolland was never able during these years to give himself unreservedly to his writing. The ever-present question of his academic career and a livelihood plagued him. At this time negotiations were proceeding to appoint him director of the music history department being created at the Institut français de Florence. The negotiations were successful; in fact, the director, Julien Luchaire, also asked Rolland to give a series of lectures during the winter of 1909, an invitation which he refused for the rather odd reason that he believed Luchaire wished mainly to exhibit him to the public.[24]

At the same time there was suggested to him the possibility of a professorship at the Conservatoire de Musique. When this position failed to materialize, Rolland wrote that he was not disappointed, since he was not sure that he wanted the extra post. He felt that he could not abandon the Sorbonne into which he had been warmly welcomed, and two chairs would not leave him sufficient time for writing (letters to Mme Cruppi, June 22, 23, and July 4, 1909).

During the winter and spring he had finished preparations for his course on Handel (to be given in the next two years) and was planning to publish the material. He was also busy preparing the history of the following period in Germany, studying the precursors of the great classic composers of the end of the eighteenth century (letter to Ethel Sidgwick, July 18, 1909). As a result of his work in musicology and his professorship at the Sorbonne, Rolland was proposed for the Cross of a Commander of the Legion of Honor, an honor which interested him only slightly (letter to Mme Bertolini, July 17, 1909; *Chère Sofia,* II, pp. 41-42).

In June, 1910, he requested another year's leave from the Sorbonne, and it was granted (letters to Mme Bertolini, June 11, Aug. 18, 1910; *Chère Sofia,* II, p. 70, 78). He spent the summer in Switzerland, very tired from his work in two areas; he intended to complete the last two volumes of *Jean-Christophe* the following

[24] Letters to Mme Bertolini (June 13, and Nov. 14, 1909); *Chère Sofia,* I, pp. 34, 48.

year (letter to J.-R. Bloch, Oct. 1, 1910). But chance ruled other-wise. On October 25, 1910, he was caught between two automobiles on the Champs-Elysées and severely injured (see a letter of Made-leine Rolland to Mme E. Marchand, Oct. 26, 1910). A fractured left arm, a dislocated leg, minor bruises and contusions, and shock kept him in bed at his parents' apartment for almost three months. It was here during December, scarcely two months after the acci-dent, that Granié completed the portrait of Rolland which has done him such frequent disservice (letters to Mme Cruppi, Dec. 15, 20, 1910). It is not surprising that Rolland seems a very neurotic, introspective, and ethereal being in this portrait.[25]

His complete recovery was slow, and he undertook various cures in Switzerland and Italy. Not until August, 1911, does he seem to have completely recovered. He wrote to J.-R. Bloch on August 10, 1911, from Schoenbrunn that the sun had been beneficial, that his left arm was better, and that he was again playing the piano about as well as before. Among his Italian acquaintances, he visited Grazia Deledda, the author, and Eleonora Duse, the actress. In Florence — where he lectured — he renewed his acquaintance with the young Florentine writers of *La Voce,* especially Giuseppe Prezzolini and Gaetano Salvemini, then professor at the University of Pisa.[26] He wrote a detailed account to Mme Cruppi, April 11, 1911, in which we find his enthusiasm for Professor Salvemini especially interesting. He said that he admired Salvemini, an un-fortunate and courageous man who had escaped from the earth-quake at Messina, but who had lost his wife and children in the catastrophe. He was working without discouragement and with a

---

[25] Various of his literary enemies carefully called the public's attention to the neurotic appearance of the author of *Jean-Christophe* in the portrait by Granié. Rolland later sued the offending driver; the court awarded him the verdict, but his opponent appealed. Rolland won the appeal early in 1912, but was not sure that the case would not go to a superior court. (See letters to Alphonse de Châteaubriant (March 3, 1912), and from J.-R. Bloch to Rolland, published in *Europe* (May, 1948), 25-29.

[26] *Jean-Christophe. Dans la Maison,* I, *Cahiers de la Quinzaine* (Feb. 16, 23, 1909), Series 10, Cahiers 9 and 10, pp. iii-v, at the end of the second volume. Most of this was omitted from later editions. See my *Critical Bibliography of the Published Writings of Romain Rolland* (Evanston, Ill., 1950), p. 123.

great deal of energy for the good of his beloved South Italy.[27]

By this time Rolland's leave from the Sorbonne had expired and he was considering his plans for the next winter. His writing had advanced sufficiently — and had been sufficiently well received by the public — to enable him to think about resigning. He could be useful in a professorship, but could not continue to write and lecture at the same time (letter to Mme Cruppi, June 2, 1911). Four days later he expressed sincere regrets concerning his possible resignation. Although he suffered from the limitations his professorship imposed upon his freedom, he was aware of the service that these very limitations rendered him by preventing him from isolating himself completely. Moreover, he respected professorships in higher education, and it was very difficult for him to break with the university.[28] His youthful jibes at the Sorbonne and the professorial career no longer echo in his remarks. By the end of June he had succeeded only in convincing himself and the Sorbonne that he should take another year's leave for his health and his work (letter to Mme Bertolini, June 28, 1911; *Chère Sofia,* II, p. 112). He felt somewhat guilty at the thought of breaking with the University when it was the object of extremely violent attacks. Reactionary coalitions developing during the past two years had been attacking the university because they saw in it the temple of free thought, the keystone of democratic teaching (*Chère Sofia,* II, p. 112).

Not until July 1912, did Rolland come to a definite decision,

[27] "J'aime surtout le jeune directeur: Prezzolini, et Salvemini, professeur à l'Université de Pise, un malheureux et courageux homme qui a réchappé au tremblement de terre de Messine, en y perdant sa femme et tous ses enfants, et qui, sans se laisser abattre, travaille et lutte avec une énergie extraordinaire, pour son cher Midi italien..." (Letter to Mme Louise Cruppi, April 11, 1911). Salvemini seems to be the origin of Bruno Chiarenza of *L'Ame enchantée,* whose life history is largely summed up in the words about Professor Salvemini in this letter.

[28] "Tout en souffrant des entraves que mon métier de professeur mettait à ma liberté, j'ai toujours eu conscience du service qu'elles me rendaient, malgré moi, en m'empêchant de m'enfermer dans mon isolement. J'ai d'ailleurs le respect du grand professorat, et je ne rejette pas de gaieté de cœur, son honneur et ses charges. Il m'est plus pénible que vous ne pouvez croire de rompre avec l'Université" (Letter to Mme Louise Cruppi, June 6, 1911).

prompted largely by one of his periodic urges for more complete freedom. On July 19, he wrote to Louis Gillet (*Correspondance,* p. 253) that he had just sent his resignation to the Sorbonne, and that it had been accepted. He evidently found relief and joy in his new state. If it was the fulfillment of an old wish, it was also the result of other circumstances. He had found in the musical world at the Sorbonne more enemies and carping critics than he would have expected. No defenders had come forward in his behalf, and he had neither the time nor the inclination to answer the attacks.[29]

During February, March, and April, 1911, Rolland's "Tolstoï" appeared, first in the *Revue de Paris* and then in book form. It had a certain success, and was particularly prized in Russia and by the family of the Russian writer. As a result Rolland began to come into closer contact with various Russians. He noted in his Journal, January 15, 1912, that he had lunched with Charles Salomon, Daniel Halévy, and Michael Stakhovitch; the latter was one of Tolstoy's intimate friends. Stakhovitch said that neither he nor any of the family's friends had ever read a book which portrayed the intimate soul of Tolstoy so truly. They wished Rolland to visit them in Russia. He considered the possibility of the trip — although he disliked many things about the Russians, especially the chaos of their thoughts (see *Europe,* April, 1949, pp. 1-7) — but he was not sure enough of his health to accept the invitation (letter to J.-R. Bloch, June 26, 1912, published in *Europe* [May, 1948], 29-30).

The decade from 1903 to 1913 was principally the period of the composition of the fictional heroic biography, *Jean-Christophe,* and the life of Tolstoy. Part of the original conception, a musical novel, was of a work in which is expressed and developed a dominating sentiment; the figure and sentiment was to be like that of a Moses — the powerful, lonely figure of a genius — although more passionate and angry than the Vigny's *Moïse.* Christophe fits the conception and Rolland's original idea; the model for part

[29] Letter to Louis Laloy, copied by Rolland in his "Journal intime" (April-Sept., 1912); p. 58 of the typescript. Laloy, hoping to follow Rolland in his position at the Sorbonne, had written to him to express his friendship. Rolland noted ironically that he had never found much support in Laloy.

of his life and personality, Beethoven, reinforces the romantic quality present in Rolland and in his first long novel. Among the most important aspects of *Jean-Christophe* is the musical nature of the structure, composition, and style of the work.

As a professor of musicology and of art, Rolland was successful at the Sorbonne and the Ecole des Hautes Etudes. His courses were well attended, and a number of people were to express their admiration for them and for the professor. The university and its demands were the great but not insurmountable obstacles to his purely creative work. Indeed, in comparison with the time at his disposal after the First World War, the pre-war years must have seemed relatively calm and undemanding. Nevertheless, after having long planned to withdraw from the university in order to live by his pen alone, he resigned in 1912. The separation troubled him; he discovered that he had taken deeper roots in that institution than he had believed possible.

X

MÈRE ET FILS

As we have previously suggested, one of the strongest influences on Rolland's life was his mother. To her he attributed the best that was in him.[1] He wrote to Paul Seippel that he would never be consoled for her death; to her he said he owed his music and his faith, and a special debt of gratitude for her courageous and faithful companionship throughout his whole life.[2] But besides the obvious influences — his early interest in music, his mother's determination that he should finish his education in Paris, the fact that she pinned all her hopes for the family on him — there are other aspects of this relationship that have been insufficiently investigated and explained. *Jean-Christophe* may furnish us with the clue to this relationship.

When we consider Christophe and his various loves we find that in only three instances is the physical love actually consummated in sexual union, and these three are irregular liaisons. Ada and Christophe enjoy the first sensual love of youth, beyond all conventions; although Christophe's love is deep and sincere, there is never any question of regularizing the union. His affair in Paris with the actress Françoise Oudon is a more serious repetition of the liaison with Ada; again there is no question of a regular union.

[1] "Hommage à Malwida", *Europe* (March 15, 1934), 305-335; also in *Letters of Romain Rolland and Malwida von Meysenbug* (New York, 1933); "A l'Antigone éternelle", in *Les Précurseurs* (Paris, 1919); and a letter to Paul Seippel (June 28, 1919).

[2] "Vous savez tout ce qu'elle était pour nous; elle remplissait toutes nos pensées. Je lui dois le meilleur de ce que je suis; la musique et la foi. Et je lui dois surtout d'avoir été ma compagne courageuse et fidèle d'épreuves, pendant toute ma vie" (Letter to Paul Seippel, June 28, 1919).

Both affairs end in separation, although not entirely through Christophe's fault. His passion for Anna Braun was adulterous, and their love was akin to hatred; they were swept along without finding any deep joy in love or sex. Christophe's love for Sabine did not come to fruition; he was unable to open the door between their bedrooms at the propitious moment. In Paris he did not understand the very plain invitation of the 'grisette', whom he had met at a concert, to go up to her room (p. 800-801). Later he sacrificed his love for Jacqueline in favor of Olivier. His great love for Grazia remained unconsumated, not because of Christophe, but because Grazia refused any union. Not always is the failure Christophe's — but the fact remains that the only sexual consumation of love is in the irregular liaisons, which, with the exception of the affair with Françoise, do not contribute greatly to his happiness. We remember that Rolland's marriage ended in divorce after some nine years, and that he did not contract another durable relationship, except by letter, until his marriage in 1934.

Nevertheless, he believed firmly that his deepest and most essential need was of love, that he made a religion of love, that he needed to love more than to be loved. "Pour moi, j'ai plus besoin encore d'aimer que d'être aimé. Ce que vous appelez, un peu cruellement, ma 'solitude de cœur froide et cruelle', vient de cette religion de l'amour, que j'ai toujours eue, et que je ne profanerai jamais" (letter to Mme Bertolini, Jan. 11, 1908; *Chère Sofia. Choix de lettres de Romain Rolland à Sofia Bertolini Guerrieri-Gonzaga,* I [Paris, 1959], p. 329). This need undoubtedly existed, but when the object of it was a young unmarried woman, multitudinous objections arose in him and his love was almost always saved for an ideal woman, one never destined to appear, for her existence in his mind was a creation of his unconscious to enable him to refuse the very real women whom he knew.

Pas amoureux du tout! D'abord, je suis comme Christophe, je n'ai pas le temps. Et puis, je connais trop... ces petites dames: je les vois, non pas seulement comme elles sont, au moment où elles m'écrivent ou me parlent, mais comme elles seront demain; et cela ne me ravit pas. Celles dont je serais amoureux, ce sont celles que je ne connaîtrai jamais, ou que je ne connaîtrai que par le plus grand des hasards: les silencieuses, les calmes, les âmes musicales (letter to Mme Bertolini, July 1, 1908; *Chère Sofia*, I, p. 350).

Or, in the real woman, he ignored the realities of sex; "La présence de ce qu'on aime arrache à l'imagination son dard envenimé; la fièvre du désir tombe; l'âme s'absorbe dans la chaste possession de la personne aimée", he wrote about Christophe and Cécile Fleury (*Jean-Christophe* [Paris, 1950], p. 1460), and the two slept at least one night in adjoining rooms, "sans que l'ombre d'une pensée trouble les effleurât" (*Ibid.*, p. 1137).

Neither Christophe nor Rolland had children — despite Rolland's apparent longing for them. Christophe was a substitute for a flesh-and-blood son, as Rolland admitted in a letter to Mme Bertolini, August 21, 1904 (*Chère Sofia*, I, p. 189). He felt a real love for children, and when the son of his close friend Alphonse de Châteaubriant was ill, Rolland showed great affection and concern, even making a special trip to Zurich to buy toys for the child. He also had an extraordinary affection for small animals and birds, possibly a substitute for more enduring emotions and relations. Alphonse de Châteaubriant narrates an incident when he and Rolland went to considerable effort to get a moth out of the room without hurting it (Châteaubriant, *Des Saisons et des jours* [Paris, 1953], pp. 47-48).

Why was this man, apparently of such a loving, warm temperament, neither a husband nor a father? Why did his marriage last less than nine years? Why do his characters rarely succeed in heterosexual love, and almost never in marriage? The answer seems to be that his mother's overwhelming influence had resulted in and from an oedipal complex, a mother fixation of which the phenomena here discussed are more or less typical symptoms, that made these normal relationships very difficult, at times impossible. We find situations of this type in his works. In *L'Ame enchantée*, Annette Rivière refuses to marry the father of her child. She then becomes the dominating element in Marc's life, and the father is relegated to a peripheral rôle. Later, after Marc's death, his child Vannia becomes one of a trinity: "Le petit univers à trois était complet, comme un accord. Anne, la vierge et l'enfant" (*L'Ame enchantée,* p. 1371). Anne (mother of the virgin Mary) is Annette; the virgin is the daughter of an old friend of Annette's; the child is her grandson. And this scene occurs after Marc's death. Marc's father is rejected a second time, by his son, when Marc is old enough to make his own decisions. The completeness of Annette's rejection of Marc's father is again revealed, long after the events that led to his birth:

Annette pensait, de bonne foi, qu'elle ne pensait pas à Roger Brissot : elle ne lui voulait pas de mal, puisque pour elle il était mort. Mais c'est le plus terrible : subconsciemment, elle l'avait tué; elle lui refusait l'air des vivants'' (*L'Ame enchantée* [Paris, 1950], p. 1150).

Marc's later struggles to free himself from his mother are frequently confused in his mind with the political struggle to free Europe from the domination of an effete bourgeois class. His struggles in politics and against Annette are all in vain; even after death at the hands of fascists, he continues to be dominated by Annette. Marc's work and soul are continued by his mother. It is true that he had married and had had a child by his wife, Assia, but his interest in his son was slight, and his feelings bordered at times on repugnance. It will further be recalled that the relationship between Aërt and Lia was of a strongly maternal sort; Aërt himself was afraid of sexual union; he was frightened and angered when the stadhouder had an amenable young lady, quite naked, introduced secretly into his bed. (To be sure, other reasons for his reactions were alleged).

When we consider this attitude towards the question of sexual relations, we are again led to the conclusion that no matter what Rolland may have said elsewhere about sexuality as essential to the whole man, his psyche tended to be repelled by physical love. We have pointed out the failure of his creations to achieve any very satisfactory sexual life, and we wish here only to add this further piece of evidence and to note that such an attitude towards sexual contact is part of the oedipal complex, in which women tend to be identified with the mother and the subsequent apparently incestuous desires are repressed as repugnant.

Rolland himself wrote in *Souvenirs de jeunesse* (Lausanne, 1947), pp. 11-12, that his mother surrounded him with walls of defense against death, which were also prison walls. During his residence at the Ecole normale, Rolland wrote regularly to his mother. No matter that she visited him during visitor's hours, and that he spent the vacations and other free days at home, Mme Rolland was not satisfied without letters from her son. Nowhere perhaps are the quality of their relationship and her dominance shown more clearly than in the letters to his mother from Rome (1889-1891). In his *Souvenirs de jeunesse* (p. 60), he says that not a day passed without a letter in which he gave a complete account of his thoughts and doings. The correspondence became a burden, and a note of irritation at her worry and her demands becomes audible. "What do you want me to do?" he asked indignantly. "If I tell you I am bored, you are upset. If I tell you that I am not bored, you continue to worry. You are always worrying, about yourself and about me. Either I am unhappy and lonely, or I forget you and no longer love you. What can I do? And what can I say that will please you?" (*Printemps romain* [Paris, 1954], p. 72; Dec. 9, 1889). At another time he reproached his mother for criticizing his pleasures and for expressing her doubts about his conduct (*Ibid.*, p. 217; Feb. 27-28, 1890). "Permit me to be a man, as much as I can". He was aware that her love was jealous. "That will not prevent me from keeping my childhood love for you", he reassured her. At other times her worry and admonitions merely aroused amusement, or amused irritation, as in his letter of June 4, 1890 (*Ibid.*, pp. 302-303), in which he answered her fears that Malwida would convert him to Protestantism. Her jealous desire to be the sole occupant of her son's heart and mind frequently rendered her unjust. The relationship between Christophe and his mother Louisa is an echo of these feelings and attitudes. In the volume *La Révolte,* when Christophe came home one evening, happy and exuberant after a rather sterile, unhappy period, "Mon Dieu! fit-elle, inquiète. Je parie qu'il est de nouveau amoureux" (*Jean-Christophe,* p. 376). She is uneasy because she fears his happiness is the result of his love for a woman! Some of Rolland's letters to his mother were sent general delivery, according to their agreement; they were read and destroyed in secret by his mother — although he kept partial copies. He complained about her doubts of his conduct, character, and development. At times he revealed his love and veneration for her, and his ambivalent feelings. He considered her not only as his mother, but as a superior woman, capable of understanding and discussing sympathetically his problems. He wanted to consider her his best and most intimate friend, but it was difficult for him because she introduced into their relationship a feeling of authority which hurt his pride (*Printemps romain,* pp. 342-344). Thus, in spite of occasional attempts to break away physically and psychologically, he remained emotionally bound to her. He paints this relationship and himself in *L'Ame enchantée* in the character Julien Davy, who was so dominated by his mother that the love between Annette and himself never resulted in their union.

[Annette] se disait que, jusqu'ici nul ne connaissait cet homme, pas même cette mère, dont il parlait toujours, et qu'elle commençait à jalouser. Lui-même... ne se connaissait pas. Qui se fût douté que, sous cette écorce rêche, il y eût une âme tendre, délicate" (*L'Ame enchantée,* p. 241-242).

In fact, Rolland, at the age of forty-one, felt himself old (he had probably never felt young), and he was beginning to feel more need of closer relations with his mother; "Pour moi, je vieillis sans doute; mais je n'aurais pas plaisir à m'en aller seul, en ce moment, — à me séparer de ma mère. A mesure qu'approche le moment inévitable de la séparation éternelle, on sent de plus en plus le besoin de se serrer l'un près de l'autre!" (letter to Mme Bertolini, July 27, 1907; *Chère Sofia,* I, p. 309).

Rolland's correspondence with his father is far less voluminous and never has the intimate tone of his letters to Mme Rolland. It is not until the First World War that we find many mentions of the elder Rolland among his son's notes, 'journal intime', and letters. It was not until after the war and his mother's death that the father began to assume a more important place in the son's affections. Rolland himself pointed out the minor rôle of his father in his *Souvenirs de jeunesse* and *Le voyage intérieur* (Paris, 1942). This secondary rôle of the father is frequently found in relationships in which the oedipal situation is dominant.

Mme Rolland's communion of sentiment with her son filled all the moments of her life after those doubtless devoted to the memory of her dead daughter. When Rolland left for Rome, she said she was like an empty house. Yet her husband at that time was a hearty man, of good spirits, and apparently devoted to his family. After the son's departure, and during the summers in Switzerland, Mme Rolland seemed to have drawn farther away from her husband, or her husband from her, and to have concentrated all her thoughts and affections on her son and her dead daughter. The effect was unwholesome both for the mother and for the son. The young man, although torn by pain, insisted on going to Rome, but he said that he was always full of remorse and felt himself more closely linked to her than before.[3] Rolland had by then encountered his mother's opposition to his marriage. He was finally able to achieve a successful marriage only long after his mother's death, and with a woman much younger than he, in 1934.

A certain tendency towards homosexuality is also a frequent component of the oedipal complex. Since the patient is unable to make the proper transfer to love of a heterosexual nature at a normal time, having been to some extent trapped in the oedipal stage of development by the circumstances of the family constellation, a considerable degree of attraction for the same sex remains in the character. It is interesting to note rather obvious cases in the two most important fictional works of our author. In *Jean-Christophe,* the friendship of Olivier and Christophe; in *L'Ame enchantée,* the friendship of Franz and Germain. Christophe "...a les attentions féminines pour Olivier" (p. 1012), and Rolland repeatedly uses the word 'ménage' (household) to describe their apartment. Germain's words about Franz lead Annette to think he is speaking of a woman. Franz's first letter, a love letter, to

---

[3] From his *Mémoires* (Paris, 1956), pp. 74-75. In *Le Voyage intérieur* (Paris, 1942), p. 134, he spoke of the true separation which began when he left for Rome. The desire for something new and different (and we suspect, the desire for independence) was greater than the sadness he felt. He was pained at causing suffering, as was Christophe, when his mother begged him to stay; and he says that the description in the novel is the all-too-faithful narration of the days preceding his own departure.

Germain, left Annette breathless. Moreover, Franz "...avait à l'égard des femmes une sauvagerie qui s'alliait à l'attrait" (p. 578). Marc, Annette's son, also appears to have strongly marked homosexual tendencies (*L'Ame enchantée*, v. p. 426).

These hints of Rolland's temperament and character, complex and informative as they are, do not yet reveal the whole man. His personality seemed to consist in a series of sharply opposing tendencies, some of which are apparently — but only apparently — mutually exclusive. He was aware of the difficulty of anyone's understanding him when he wrote to Mme Bertolini (Feb. 12, 1913, *Chère Sofia,* II [Paris, 1960], pp. 169-170) that he was so complex he did not willingly reveal his true self. How could one be at the same time rebellious and pacified, passionately fond of life and detached from life, a believer and ironic, a Tolstoyan and an admirer of Renan? But these tendencies were harmonized in him; there was no conflict but a harmony or hierarchy. Among the apparently contradictory elements in his character was a duality of which he became aware during certain moments of ecstasy or fright, when he felt himself separated and above his ordinary self, flooded with joy. It is a state that Christophe experienced at times as a young man (pp. 69, 264, 382, 508, among others). In what might have been an accident in a railroad tunnel, Rolland suddenly felt a strange joy, and a separation of the spiritual from the physical body; "Ce fut comme si un voile se déchirait dans mon cerveau. Je pensai: 'Ecrase-moi, si tu veux. Je ne suis point d'ici. Mes yeux et mon corps sont dans la nuit de ce tunnel. Mais mon Moi, ma Vie, est en dehors; il plane dans l'air libre, dans le soleil; rien ne l'enferme; il est dans tout'" (letter to Mme Bertolini, Sept. 20, 1901; *Chère Sofia,* I, p. 26). There are frequent references in Rolland's letters and fiction to the physical body as something shameful or disgusting. Christophe, for example, "...avait honte de son corps malade. Il pensait: — Comme je serai content, lorsqu'il mourra" (*Jean-Christophe,* p. 816). It should be noted that such an attitude is frequently part of the oedipal complex.

His reticence and outward inflexibility sometimes stood in the way of an immediate understanding of his personality. His somewhat feminine temperament and sensitive nature — probably augmented by his mother's influence — combined with a man's body had made life very difficult for him as a young man. He spoke of himself as of being poorly armed for life, impressionable, feminine, naive, blushing easily; he had had to impose a strict discipline on himself in order not to be devoured by life. In the preface (1939) to his *Mémoires* (Paris, 1956), p. 15, he becomes in a metaphor a spider contemplating its web. The word 'spider' occurs twice, once in an unusual form 'arachne', which leads us back to the mythological tale of the woman who was transformed into a spider. The spider is both a symbol of woman and a symbol of devouring woman; the web is one of the traps of the devouring spider, and Rolland here makes of his life a torn spiderweb. Also in his *Mémoires* he describes his emotions in terms of the female orgasm: "Mes notes sont pleines (surtout en 1888-1889, où j'étais devenu maître de lire jusqu'au fond de ma nuit) de ces spasmes d'amoureuse broyée dans les bras du géant" (*Mémoires,* p. 23). Doubtless he imposed the discipline on himself also to conceal from others and from himself these characteristics. By this discipline he kept a certain stiffness, an armor which he rarely removed. That is why, he said, it was so beneficial for him to breathe freely in Christophe's body (Letter to Mme Bertolini, July 7, 1908; *Chère Sofia,* I [Paris, 1959], p. 352).

No wonder that he prized calm and harmony above all. The mere attempt to harmonize these contradictions in one person is sufficient to make anyone tense and nervous. Furthermore, his senses were excessively acute. His sense of hearing, and presumably of pitch, was particularly sensitive; noises were painful (letter to Mme Cruppi, Nov. 6, 1913). Like Christophe, the peace and tranquility of a person or a place were very attractive. The desire for the calm beauty of the Roman Campagna (frequently expressed in his letters and also by Christophe) was great. The harmony of a personality was the most important aspect for him in his relations with others.[4] In 1919, he momentarily attained this ideal state of harmony and equilibrium (letter to Mme Cruppi, Sept. 26, 1919).

[4]   See a letter to Mme Bertolini (Aug. 17, 1902); *Chère Sofia. Choix de Lettres de Romain Rolland à Sofia Bertolini Guerrieri-Gonzaga,* I (Paris, 1959), pp. 87-88.

Timidity and innate aggressiveness were largely responsible for his somewhat retiring appearance, but did not prevent him from taking part in action by letter and occasionally directly, whenever his faith or his convictions were challenged. Inwardly, even during the heat of discussion and especially in the face of the action to be performed, he was extremely tense. As a younger man his emotions were revealed by the trembling of his hands and even by tears in his eyes, although generally those around him were unaware, he believed, of the inner storm. His thinking at such times became, he said, very lucid, but occasionally was manifested in violent expressions which pained him, but which he did not really regret. His true thoughts were expressed at such moments. He held himself in a state of readiness to meet the painful necessities of action and struggle. He had constantly to check the force of his emotions by his will and his rational intellect. Undoubtedly one of the character traits that impelled him to such defensive actions was his pride.

He freely admitted his timidity and his innate abhorrence of action to Mme Bertolini on November 13, 1915, when he wrote that he would have liked, as a child, to hide from the rest of mankind in order to dream — a not infrequent reaction of a child who feels rejected by one or the other parent, and in whom many fears have (unwittingly) been aroused. The violation of his own nature caused him to feel a peculiar pleasure in overcoming suffering (*Chère Sofia*, II, p. 236). The Rolland who wrote thus of pleasure in suffering overcome will long remain in French thought and letters. His best works, the two long novels, and such plays as *Le Temps viendra*, *Le Triomphe de la raison*, *Danton*, *Le 14 juillet*, and *Le Jeu de l'amour et de la mort*, are infused with this spirit of the mind and soul, triumphant over pain and sorrow. Cogent reasons for his going to Rome over his mother's protests now become clear; one is his conviction of the necessity of entering upon a more active life in order to develop the less robust part of his character. His mother's pain and the mental anguish he suffered because of it are another. It is sometimes necessary to provoke suffering in order to overcome it. The complex of guilt, sadness, and secret pleasure at his mother's grief, the pleasure of overcoming his own suffering because of her, and a secret triumph over the demanding woman are further reasons for this important step.

His nature was essentially contemplative and speculative, but his sincerity, his independent spirit, and his instinct of justice forced him to enter the field of action — although his emotions would have persuaded him to remain aloof. The results were crises when he was caught between opposing forces as in the Dreyfus case, during the First World War, and in the period of his support of Soviet Russia.[5] He never understood why he seized such occasions to throw himself into the midst of turmoil and thus to attract the animosity of both camps (see *Souvenirs de jeunesse,* p. 232). In part it was because of his stubborn attachment to his own ideas and to his own faith; in part it was because in the attempt to defend his ideas and beliefs, carried away by his essentially violent nature, he violated his natural reticence and timidity. Like Christophe, he was swept along to say more than he had intended. He apologized to Mme Cruppi in a letter, November 26, 1913, for the violent expressions in a previous letter. He had been upset, and had allowed himself to be carried away by the discussion, as in the good old days (he said) of his youth, when he had sometimes come to the point of breaking lances against his own cause.[6]

His character in this respect was of the stuff martyrs are made of. As he matured, in the years following his sojourn in Italy, he became more and more uncompromising in spite of certain other softening effects of the previous period. His brief contacts with the world, he wrote to André Suarès, January 6, 1896, had dissipated every breath of dilettantism. As he saw reality more clearly, he felt that he did not live the same life as others.[7] His natural

---

[5] See his *Journal des années de guerre* (Paris, 1954), pp. 114-115.

[6] "...je me laissais emporter dans la discussion, comme aux beaux temps de ma jeunesse, où j'en arrivais parfois, dans la violence de ma sincérité (et de mon esprit de contradiction) à rompre des lances contre ma propre cause."

[7] "J'ai changé; il y a en moi une susceptibilité morale qui s'est développée jusqu'à la maladie; quelque chose qui est à nu dans mon cœur, et que la moindre chose exaspère. — Je n'aurais jamais hésité à l'École, à aller voir Barrès, et tous ceux de son espèce... par simple curiosité, et même avec une

tendency was to wish to understand and to dominate the world by thought, not by action. Hence his desire to judge the men of the French Revolution by their thoughts, not by their deeds. To understand everything that exists — he wrote to Mme Bertolini, July 7, 1902 — even one's enemies, those whose ways of feeling, living, and thinking are the most antipathetic to you, to understand those who misunderstand you, who mock and detest you, and whom your anger would cause you to attack, head down and club swinging, if your intelligence did not help you to understand, excuse and love them — that is the greatest voluptuousness that can exist in the soul (*Chère Sofia,* I, pp. 77-78). There is apparent in these words a surprising amount of violence, and even greater restraint and rigid self-control. At the same time, May 2, 1902, he wrote to Louis Gillet (*Correspondance entre Louis Gillet et Romain Rolland* [Paris, 1949], p. 193) that his joy and his duty on earth was to understand the world as far as possible, and to try to defend and preserve reason, attacked and outraged by all. Each time he could understand and feel a new truth, a religion, a new God, he was happier, calmer, and stronger — for no truth could trouble his faith, which embraced all faiths.

Such an attitude, and the calm and detachment it implies, were to remain an ideal for him rather than a reality. The world and the times he lived in — as in any other epoch — would not permit such an Olympian attitude on the part of a man endowed with quick sensitivity, the power of empathy, and a keen sense of justice.[8] In all that he wrote he oscillated between violent anger

---

sorte de sympathie désireuse de chercher le bien sous le vice apparent. Aujourd'hui, cela m'est impossible; les rencontrer est une torture; les aller chercher me serait une honte... mes froissements avec le monde ont dissipé en moi tout souffle de dilettantisme... je n'ai pas une âme de laïque. A mesure que je vois plus clairement la réalité, je sens que je ne vis point de la même vie qu'elle" (Letter to André Suarès, Jan. 6, 1896). In a letter to Louis Gillet on March 3, 1900; *Correspondance entre Louis Gillet et Romain Rolland. Choix de Lettres* (Paris, 1949), pp. 67-68, he wrote: "Je sais que je manque de souplesse et de bonne grâce, que je suis dur et étroit; ...Mais il s'agit de savoir si l'on doit *être* pour les autres, ou pour soi. Qu'ai-je besoin de m'accomoder aux autres? J'ai besoin de m'accomoder au Bien."

[8] See a letter to Mme Bertolini (Aug. 17, 1902); *Chère Sofia,* I, p. 87. See also the letter to Malwida (Jan. 8, 1894); *Choix de lettres à Malwida von Meysenbug* (Paris, 1948).

and love. He was greatly attracted to and admired those who possessed this calm (letter to Mme Bertolini, July 27, 1907; *Chère Sofia,* I, p. 309). Grazia, in *Jean-Christophe,* is the embodiment of this state; Annette Rivière reaches a stage very close to his ideal. During the last twenty years of his life, Rolland himself achieved a large measure of the calm and harmony of spirit that was his ideal, although he was never egotistically detached from the trials and sufferings of his fellowmen.

Such a state is the result of a balance among many opposing emotions. It was not, in his mind, a servile ataraxy, not a simple abandonment of oneself to the calm of nature. On the contrary it was an active state, in which all the opposites are mastered and the peace and tranquility of nature shine forth from the individual for the benefit of others (letter to Mme Bertolini, April 9, 1902; *Chère Sofia,* I, p. 64).

We are again brought face to face with a temperament that is the result of inner conflicts, of opposing tendencies, desires, and emotions that were only occasionally brought into an unstable balance or uncertain harmony. Having been rendered essentially inadequate for the rough and tumble of the world largely by his mother's pervading and dominant personality — it is symbolically revealed in his rather frequent use of the words 'swallowed up', 'devoured' (*englouti, dévoré*), which express the fear of being devoured or absorbed by the powerful female — Rolland, as a child and even as a young man, feared the world. He feared it also because of the overprotection, combined with the burden of too much responsibility imposed too early; he would therefore have liked to hide. But his innate aggressiveness, sharpened by the hostility felt at being forced out of the protective ambience and by the timidity instilled (unwittingly) in him by his family, forced him to face the world and to act. Most of the actions he was involved in were violent ones, whether discussion, analysis, criticism, or political action; for who is more aggressive and hostile, than a timid man, finally goaded to action that he both fears and desires? Frequently the result is violence out of proportion to the cause.

The oedipal complex that appears from the study of the author, his family, his letters, his works of imagination, is responsible in no small measure for the retiring, stiff, and tense man who was to arouse the anger and hostility of Germans, French, and neutrals during the First World War, and who would again anger all sides after the Bolshevik Revolution. A victim and a victor, of himself and over himself, of others and over others, he created, supported, and fought for much that was good, and struggled against much that was unjust, but at considerable personal sacrifices.

XI

THE FIRST WORLD WAR (1913-1921)

In April, 1913, Rolland left Paris for the more restful surroundings of Switzerland. The rest he hoped for was not granted; he was not in good health and was plagued by insomnia, because of cerebral hypertension, he thought. By the end of June he had resumed his work — he was writing *Colas Breugnon*.[1] He visited at this time, partly in preparation for the novel, his native Clamecy, and the Morvan region: Autun, Château-Chinon, Avallon, and Vézelay, in September.[2] The visit to these regions of Burgundy and the work of writing *Colas* seemed to mark the end of a period in his own development. He wrote to Mme Bertolini (September 23, 1913), that he had gone to this region first because of piety, and to test his thinking, and then because he was writing a sort of heroic libertine poem in which he was trying to revive a type of the French race, from which he himself was descended. He wished

[1] Letters to Mme E. Marchand (June 8, 1913); to Mme J.-R. Bloch (June 25, 1913); to Alphonse de Châteaubriant (June 8, 25, and July 26, 1913); and to Louis Gillet (Sept. 24, 1913); *Correspondance entre Louis Gillet et Romain Rolland* (Paris, 1949), p. 264. For this period see the valuable work by P.-J. Jouve, *Romain Rolland vivant 1914-1919* (Paris, 1920). However, his health at this time was normal and his mind unusually lucid: "Le curieux, c'est que le reste est bon, et le cerveau parfait, — lucide comme un lynx, et tranquille comme Baptiste... Je suis en train sans doute de fabriquer un nouveau Romain Rolland. Je suis en mal d'enfant... Mes insomnies tiennent un peu à une hyperesthésie de l'ouïe. Je guette les moindres bruits, de la cave au grenier" (Letter to Mme Cruppi, Nov. 6, 1913). 'Mal d'enfant' (childbirth pains) referred to himself may well reveal some uncertainty as to his own virility.
[2] Letters to Châteaubriant (Sept. 17, 1913); to L. Gillet (Sept. 24, 1913); *Correspondance*, p. 264; to Mme Bertolini (Sept. 23, 1913); *Chère Sofia. Choix de lettres de Romain Rolland à Sofia Bertolini Guerrieri-Gonzaga*, II (Paris, 1960), pp. 185-186.

to pour into this work the very depths of his Burgundian heritage before resuming his forward march (*Chère Sofia. Choix de Lettres de Romain Rolland à Sofia Bertolini Guerrieri-Gonzaga,* II [Paris, 1960], p. 184).

The period that was closing was the period of the heroic biographies; *Jean-Christophe* and the gay and hearty *Colas Breugnon* are essentially imaginary heroic biographies. It was for him a period of inner struggle and tension dominated by firm and uncompromising individualism. His points of view were informed by a belief in the high purpose of true art. The heroes of the period were largely romantic; they were individuals, usually isolated, who developed in spite of society, who were in constant conflict with society, but whose action was chiefly limited to the realm of artistic creations.

He wrote in his 'Journal intime' under the date of June 29, 1913, that he had reached a point of absolute detachment from life, which he said he yet loved and venerated. But he was tired, fatigued with the miserable envelope of his body, and his soul was no longer sufficient for him; he would like to change or to exchange his whole being.[3] Like Christophe, he called on God who had used him for His ends to take him and break him, and use another stronger and better instrument (*De Jean-Christophe à Colas Breugnon* [Paris, 1946], p. 142; and see *Jean-Christophe* [Paris, 1950], p. 221). Now, as at other times, the need to dream and allow nascent ideas to formulate themselves was strong, although his other tasks left him only two hours a morning, twice a week, for this work.[4] In spite of fatigue, poor health, and insufficient time, he finished *Colas Breugnon,* which was not to appear until 1919, before June 29, 1914, when he wrote to Mme Cruppi that

---

[3] *De Jean-Christophe à Colas Breugnon* (Paris, 1946), p. 142.
[4] "J'ai le besoin maladif de rêver, de m'absorber dans mes rêves. *Or, je ne le puis pas, je ne le puis jamais sans luttes* [Rolland's italics]. Sachez-le, mon amie, depuis le 1er octobre, je n'ai pas pu donner plus de deux matins par semaine, plus de deux heures par matin, à l'œuvre qui me tient à cœur. Et (cela semble incroyable) cela a été presque toujours ainsi" (Letter to Mme Cruppi, November 19, 1913).

he was doing nothing for the moment except to enjoy the June sun and air, close to the strength-renewing earth.[5]

The change in Rolland's writings was accompanied by a change in his style. He was perhaps not aware of it then, but as he looked back thirteen years later the change became clear to him. He wrote to Fernando Márquez Miranda (June 22, 1927): "I note that there are two clearly different periods in my style — one runs from the *Vie de Beethoven* to the end of *Jean-Christophe*; the other begins with *Colas Breugnon* and runs to *L'Ame enchantée* (excepting *Clerambault,* the product of a troubled period of transition, and the fruit of meditation rather than a work of art). The best books of the first style are *L'Adolescent, Les Amies,* and the second part of *Le Buisson ardent* [all parts of *Jean-Christophe*]. The best of the second are the episode "Belette" in *Colas Breugnon, Le Jeu de l'amour et de la mort,* and especially *Mère et fils* [*L'Ame enchantée*], and *Liluli.*"[6] The change in his style does not correspond exactly to the change in attitude and content. As we have pointed out, *Colas Breugnon* in the latter respects belongs to the first period, but in its style to the later period.

During this transition period other changes were taking place in his personal life. In January, 1914, he met and fell in love with an American actress, Helena Van Brugh de Kay, whom he

---

[5] "Et votre ami, étendu au pied d'un grand vieil arbre, au tronc couleur de miel, aspire à la lumière, rêve et se prépare, une fois de plus, à faire peau neuve. Car *Colas Brugnon* étant fini, je laisse sa défroque et cherche une autre dans laquelle me couler. En attendant, je suis libre de toute forme, et je goûte le plaisir délicieux de me baigner dans les éléments tout purs: boire l'air, baiser la terre" (Letter to Mme Cruppi, June 19, 1914). For a more complete account of the publication of *Colas Breugnon,* see my *Romain Rolland and a World at War* (Evanston, Ill., 1956) pp. 1-2, 174.

[6] "Je note d'ailleurs qu'il y a dans mon style, deux époques nettement différentes, qu'aucun critique n'a songé à différencier: — l'une, celle qui va de la *Vie de Beethoven* à la fin de *Jean-Christophe*; — l'autre qui commence à *Colas Breugnon* et va jusqu'à l'*Ame enchantée* (en exceptant le seul *Clerambault,* fruit d'une époque troublée et de passage entre les deux styles, qui est œuvre de méditation beaucoup plus qu'œuvre d'art). — Les meilleurs livres du premier style sont l'*Adolescent, les Amies,* et la seconde partie du *Buisson ardent.* — Les meilleurs livres du second style sont: l'épisode '*Belette*' de *Colas Breugnon, Le Jeu de l'Amour et de la Mort,* et surtout *Mère et fils* et *Liluli*" (Letter to Fernando Márquez Miranda, June 22, 1927).

refers to in his diary and letters as "Thalie" and "Psyché". It was a love affair which never came to fruition but ended tragically some six years later. On January 8, 1914, he wrote to Châteaubriant that he had finally met the little American actress, who was one of his most intelligent correspondents. She was charming, with a dash of what he called Anglo-Saxon madness. On January 30 he wrote again to Châteaubriant, even more enthusiastically, about her. In what she writes, he said, there are true pearls of emotion and poetic vision together with comic naiveté and glaring errors. By April 5, his feeling of delighted attraction had become a sweeping passion, enveloping him; he was carried along in the warm flood of love like a pebble on the beach (in his words). His love was returned, he said; but he could scarcely believe it. When he went to Switzerland in May, he was waiting for Thalie to join him at Vevey for one or two weeks (letter to Châteaubriant, June 6, 1914).[7] In 1916 he seriously considered a permanent union with her; but the *graine de folie* he had perceived, and which became more evident as he knew her better, caused him to hesitate. In this hesitation we are also aware of his mother's influence; he discussed with her his feelings and doubts about the advisability of the marriage. Fearing perhaps that his own judgment might be biased, he wanted her opinion. She vigorously opposed the marriage; however, Rolland began to prepare for a meeting with Thalie, the first since early in the war years. His anxiety was sharpened by his dislike of inflicting pain; he was worried about the effects of an adverse decision on the young lady should the marriage be deemed inadvisable. His mother saw nothing but misfortune in the union, and Rolland himself, by mid-August, was very dubious about it. He had already postponed the meeting for a year, and in spite of his love for her he seemed, without being aware of it, determined to break the match. He wrote to his sister (August 11, 1916) that he did not need his mother's arguments against the marriage; he had been

---

[7]   See: Alphonse de Châteaubriant: *Lettres des années de guerre, 1914-1918* (Paris, 1952); Châteaubriant: *Des saisons et des jours... Journal, ...1911-1914* (Paris, 1953); Châteaubriant: *Cahiers verts, 1906-1951* (Paris, 1955); Rolland, *Journal des années de guerre* (Paris, 1952).

weighing all the arguments on both sides for several months, and the negative arguments seemed the stronger.[8] For two weeks he had been seeking desirable quarters for the four of them. He wanted the meeting to be in a quiet spot, where neither of the two had previously been together. He thought especially about Lungern, which his mother and he had visited several years before.[9] He wished his sister and mother to be close at hand for reasons that reflect his uncertainty: he hoped to avoid gossip; he wanted his mother's opinion; he wished for Madeleine's help in softening the shock in the event of a contrary decision; and he desired the affectionate intimacy between the three women (wife, mother, and sister) if he should decide upon the marriage. One notes that in his letter to Mlle Madeleine, August 1, Rolland wished to avoid meeting Thalie in a place where the two had been together before, but he had no such reluctance where his mother was concerned. Apparently he wished to soften in every way possible the blow which he secretly, perhaps unconsciously knew would be dealt to the young woman. The meeting, if it materialized, did not seem to be conclusive, for Rolland continued to see her until the summer of 1920.

At the outbreak of the war, Rolland had been in Geneva for several months. From that city he wrote to his father on July 26 that he was urging his mother to come to Switzerland now because he was worried about the international situation. He was at Vevey when hostilities broke out; except for two days, he stayed in Switzerland for the duration of the war, after some initial in-

---

[8] "...elle ne cesse pas de se tourmenter et de me faire les plus sinistres prédictions. Je n'en ai pas besoin, car il n'est guère d'argument pour et contre que je n'aie ressassé dans ma tête depuis des mois; et en vérité, c'est le contre qui l'emporte plutôt" (Letter to Mlle Madeleine Rolland, August 11, 1916).
[9] "Il est préférable que la rencontre ait lieu dans un pays tranquille, où nous n'avons pas été ensemble. Dans cette région, j'ai cherché, et j'ai pensé notamment à Lungern, ...sur la route de Brünig au lac de Lucerne. Maman et moi nous y sommes promenés, il y a quelques années... Et de quelque façon que l'épreuve se termine, je voudrais que vous ne restiez pas en dehors. En cas d'affirmative, ce serait la source d'une affectueuse intimité entre vous et elle. Et si je reconnais au contraire qu'il est déraisonnable de songer au mariage, tu pourrais m'aider à panser délicatement sa blessure. — Je souffre de faire du mal" (Letter to Mlle Madeleine Rolland, August 1, 1916).

decision and in spite of a certain desire to return to France to share in the common burden of his compatriots. However, there was never any real hesitation; he knew that he must stay in Switzerland in order to be free to make his ideas heard. He returned only briefly to Paris, July 28-29, leaving Paris late on the afternoon of the twenty-ninth, to arrange some personal matters and to collect his more important papers (Sven Stelling-Michaud. "Le Choix de Romain Rolland en 1914", *La Pensée,* No. 132 [April, 1967], 26-27). His service to the state in his university teaching had taken the place of military service; in 1914 he was forty-eight years old, and his age and poor health would also have kept him from active duty. In Switzerland he attempted, generally in vain, to preserve the voice of freedom and moderation in a world gone mad.[10]

In August, 1914, Rolland was not immediately overwhelmed by the catastrophe whose extent was not then apparent. He hoped that the insolence and rapacity of Germany would be punished. The new prussianized Germany seemed to him criminally oppressive (letter to Louis Gillet, July 30, 1914; *Correspondance entre Louis Gillet et Romain Rolland* [Paris, 1949], p. 286). The assassination of the socialist leader Jean Jaurès, July 31, was a great misfortune (*Journal des annés de guerre* [Paris, 1954], p. 31), and the next year Rolland penned a tribute to him (*Journal de Genève,* August 2, 1915; collected later in *Au-dessus de la mêlée* [Paris, 1915]).

He was loath to remain inactive in exile, detached from all roots and all action. He cast about for a means to be of service to his country and to his fellowmen — not only to his compatriots. He learned that the Red Cross at Geneva had organized a section to aid both civilian and military prisoners of war of all nationalities. Here was a means of service which seemed compatible with his ideas. By October 3, 1914, he and his sister were installed in Champel-Genève, and he had begun to work in the agency (*Journal... de guerre,* pp. 73-76). Here he worked until July 3, 1915, reading, sorting, and answering thousands of letters that poured in from all parts of Europe.

[10] We have studied in detail Rolland and this time in *Romain Rolland and a World at War* (Evanston, 1956).

After his resignation from the Red Cross a year later he returned to Vevey; and here and in Villeneuve he spent the remaining years of the war. His task from the first was, he considered, to maintain the rights of reason and justice. This he did in numerous articles, which seem anodyne to readers of forty years and a Second World War later. The *Journal de Genève,* partly through the good offices of Rolland's friend Paul Seippel, opened its columns to him during the first two years — until the boldness of his ideas and external pressures caused their good relationship to deteriorate. In these essays, Rolland protested that man's patrimony was created by man and then destroyed by man himself. He laid the blame on imperialism (Prussian, Russian, or any other), and paid tribute to the heroic stand taken by Belgium. He was at this time convinced of the justice of the French cause, but he differentiated sharply between the individual German citizen and the German government — which he disliked and feared. As he himself said much later, he was not 'above the struggle', but above the passions that produced and intensified the struggle. It was a stand that cannot be understood or welcomed by the rank and file of people in the nations involved, nor indeed even in neutral nations. He attempted also to bring before the combatant nations any men or movements representing a sane and rational supranational ideal, or ideals of understanding or organized charity and aid to enemy prisoners. The most immediately obvious results of his articles were disapproval, condemnation, and attacks against him in the press. Typical of the passions of the time were his controversies with Bernard Shaw,[11] Hauptmann, Henri Massis, and Loyson, who accused him of pro-Germanism in regard to the German 'Bund Neues Vaterland' — an organization soon outlawed in Germany as subversive.[12] Criticisms of his ideas and his attitudes came from both sides of the trenches, from militarist and pacifist, from leftist and rightist, socialist and capitalist. The reasons in each varied, but

[11]   Starr: "Romain Rolland and George Bernard Shaw", *The Shaw Bulletin,* II, no. 3 (September, 1957), 1-6.
[12]   See Pierre Grappin: *Le "Bund Neues Vaterland" (1914-1916). Ses rapports avec Romain Rolland* (Lyon and Paris, 1952), pp. ii-149; and Marcelle Kempf: *Romain Rolland et l'Allemagne* (Paris, 1964).

their object was the same: whoever is not with me (all the way) is against me (completely). The award of the Nobel Prize for literature for the year 1915, which was actually made November 9, 1916, also aroused hostility.

Events in Russia during the spring and summer of 1917 aroused Rolland's interest; he corresponded with some of the exiled revolutionaries in Switzerland, and in fact was partially involved in the departure of Lenin for Russia. He hailed the Revolution there as an attempt to create a more just and sane social order. It must be understood that he in no way called for violent social revolutions in other European countries except in Germany. He flatly stated that it was his belief that revolution in France would aid the Germans. More than anything else he condemned violence, especially unnecessary violence.

The most important problem at this time, he thought, was to bring the war to a close before France was ruined; a lengthy war might even bring about a moral renovation of Germany, and again redound to the harm of France. A German victory would consolidate Prussian imperialism and block any further social progress in France and in Europe for decades. Revolution in Germany was therefore to be encouraged. With his usual ability to arouse antagonism by telling what he considered to be the truth to partisans on both sides of the question, he created considerable animosity among the Bolsheviks and their supporters. Ardent non-Russian Communists such as Henri Barbusse accused him of lukewarmness, whereas the conservative bourgeoisie looked upon him as little less than a fire-eating revolutionary. It is true that in these years he felt strongly the necessity of a complete change in the existing social order as the only possible way of remedying current abuses and evils.

As dissatisfaction grew in 1917 in all countries, official and unofficial pressure mounted against those who sought to explore the possibilites of ending the war or of promoting peace. The 'Peace Offensive' was viewed as a dangerous movement, and ardent patriots attacked the subversive utterances of those who would work for the end of hostilities. Since Rolland was more and more active in bringing to public attention such men, books, and movements as had peace for their aim, he was frequently attacked. The label of defeatism was gratuitously awarded by various opponents. Others fought against the 'Peace Offensive' by attempting to tie such men as Rolland to the Bolsheviks and their efforts in Russia.

The term 'defeatist', which was applied to him with some frequency, was very odious to him. He felt, despite his innate tendencies to the contrary, that it is always better to be active than passive, especially in the midst of almost boundless evil. His duty was not to work for the defeat of Germany and the victory of France and the Allies, but to work for the mitigation of the evils of the present and to aid in preparing a future in which such calamities would not be repeated. He considered it important to bring to public attention any German efforts in this direction — an idea very unpopular in France.

Only three creative works were completed during the war. They were *Clerambault, Pierre et Luce* — both published in 1920, but the first begun in 1917 and the second in the spring of 1918 — and *Liluli,* begun in 1917 and published in 1919. *Liluli* is a social satire, directed largely against warmongers and those factors in society which arouse and maintain hysterical hatreds and unreasoning emotions. In fact, Rolland satirizes many of the elements of contemporary society in a style which reminds one of *Colas Breugnon,* and which uses the iterative and repetitive devices made familiar by the poet Charles Péguy. One crowd chants: "Ora pro nobis, Sankt Luther-Blücher, Koerner, Schopenhauer — Bebel, Hebbel, Hegel, Haeckel — Sankta Gewalt, Sankt Oswald — St. Kant, St. Krupp, Krieg und Kultur..." The other mob sings: "Saint Julien, saint Gratien — Hygin, Crépin, Longin, Lucain — Balbin, Quentin, Quirin, saint Lin..." etc. (pp. 73-74). The language is a very important element. The sole value of *Liluli* (if any), Rolland wrote to Stefan Zweig, is less its thought than the special form — the dancing rhythm, the salty language and spirit of intoxicated truth which animates it.[13]

[13] "Le seul prix de *Liluli* (si elle en a un) est moins dans la pensée que dans la forme toute spéciale, dans le rythme dansant, le *vert* langage et l'esprit de vérité ivre qui l'anime... Sans le rythme rieur, l'argot du cru et la folie, le

Maître-Dieu appears as an oriental pedlar selling images of God. Truth, disguised as Harlequin, is under the domination of Maître-Dieu and his supporters: the journalists, diplomats, and lay-powers. Even Polichinelle, free and independent laughter, fears Truth. Reason, blindfolded, disregards everything but her own calculations. Love is portrayed as an idiot, and Life (perhaps Bergsonism) is a huge, running, headless man. Diplomacy, high finance, academic and political orators and intellectuals are satirized; the latter, at the beck and call of the great Dervish, sing in chorus: "How very brave, to go down to the grave, before one must shave. Let us die, Sirs, 'tis the sweetest of fates" (p. 134). Liluli is Illusion, who leads the dance with the aid of her minions, and especially the goddess Llop'ih, public opinion — horrible harpy — and the enchained brains (fanatics and bigots of all sorts). The Hurluberloches (the Germans were called 'Boches' in 1914-1918) on one side of a chasm, and the Gallipoulets (the Gallic chicken, if not the Gallic cock) on the other exchange confidences and food and build a bridge. Before they can cross it, the Fat Ones and the Diplomats work so well that the two peoples exchange insults and blows. *Les Gras* are saved; there will be no fraternizing with *Les Maigres* (the Thin Ones). Maître-Dieu changes garments in mid-bridge and blesses both sides. Even Jeannot the peasant, who stubbornly tills the soil, is led to fight, and Polichinelle, who avoided the recruiting sergeants and Llop'ih, is overwhelmed when all collapses, and only Liluli remains.

In spite of the bitterness which such a rapid survey of the play may seem to indicate, and which many of its readers felt in the years following the First World War, Rolland insisted that there is no bitterness under the irony — at least, there was no bitterness in him. It is difficult, he said, to make others understand the special state of mind of a French Voltairian who finds in the comic aspects of the world and in its irony a joy, pure and unmixed. He assured Zweig that there was not a drop of bitterness or

---

discours de Polonius ou les dialogues des peuples tombent à plat" (Letter to S. Zweig, July 5, 1920). For a good analysis of *Liluli* see E. Richter, "Romain Rolland", *Germanische-romanische Monatsheft* (1920), 299-312.

melancholy in his joy; he was filled with laughter while writing *Liluli*.[14]

Clerambault is the tale of one man's struggle with his conscience during the war. Clerambault, a successful writer, self-satisfied but not smug, an idealist unprepared to maintain his idealism in the face of public pressure, but sensitive, sincere, gentle, and an inactive humanitarian caught up in the hysteria of the war, becomes a very vocal patriot. After his son's death at the front he questions the absolute justice of the French cause (for was not the cause of France the cause of humanity?) and the nature of war. His struggles both with his conscience and with the prevailing ideas and attitudes of war-time France form the subject of the second part of the novel. When he decides that all the participants, including the French, are wrong and that war is immoral and unjust, he acts on his new convictions and gains the reputation of being a pacifist, a defeatist, and a traitor. In the inflamed atmosphere the inevitable happens (as it happened to Jaurès in July, 1914), and he is assassinated on Good Friday. His sacrifice of self — for he was not unaware of the danger — was freely made for the good of all, and is a religious gesture. It is significant that he was killed on Good Friday; it is his crucifixion for his convictions and thus the beginning of the resurrection to a new life, a sacrifice made for the good of all. *Clerambault* seems to have been the author's expression of man's efforts, at personal sacrifice, to raise himself above the past.[15]

The book is a consideration of war and its effects, an analysis of patriotism, and a novel about one man's efforts to avoid being swallowed up entirely by the collective soul. His conversion, despite great opposition and inner tensions, is to ideas essentially

[14] "...Voltairien français — Français de vieille race — qui puise dans le comique du monde et dans sa libre ironie une joie pure, sans mélange. Mais je vous assure qu'en vérité il n'y avait pas dans la mienne (dans ma joie), quand j'écrivais *Liluli,* une once d'amertume ou de mélancolie. Je riais, voilà tout... j'étais heureux" (Letter to S. Zweig, June 10, 1920).

[15] "Une grande âme religieuse comme la vôtre devait saisir aussitôt le sens religieux de ce livre. Oui, la scène du Vendredi Saint est bien la cime mystique de l'œuvre; et les dernières lignes du volume (les paroles finales d'Edme Froment) en rappellent les harmonies" (Letter to E. R. Curtius, July 25, 1921).

like those Rolland had been upholding and would continue to uphold. Clerambault is the free conscience which refuses to submit to the tyranny of forces, just or unjust. And ultimately such spirits are the sources of change in society and of revolution in states and governments. The novel is an appeal for the struggle of the free individual conscience against the mass. It is the struggle against the tendency towards such manifestations of mob psychology as shocked the world some years later in Hitler's Germany. Rolland, animated by a humanist's ideal, with an artist's intuition and sensitive perception of events to come and of currents in their yet embryonic stages, took up the fight against one of the most disturbing problems of the twentieth century.

Pierre et Luce, whose origin we have discussed elsewhere, is, like "Le Siège de Mantoue", the story of a young love, happily unconcerned with the war that rages on all sides. Pierre, eighteen years of age, loves Luce, somewhat younger, but more mature; Pierre's older brother, Philippe, is the man in the trenches. Pierre is ana dolescent of the type which Rolland has so frequently portrayed; just at the threshold of young manhood, but close enough to early adolescence to retain something of the slightly feminine quality of that age. Sensitive, easily caused to blush, tender, and yet uncompromising in his ideals, horrified by the cruel aspects of life, Pierre is closely related to Aërt and to Marc Rivière. He is still at an age when death is preferable to submission to what he feels are the degradations of life (p. 147). Luce, on the other hand, is more robust, more realistic, and more optimistic; she is more determined, positive, and practical, much like Lia in *Aërt* or Annette Rivière and her sister Sylvie. In part this is the result of the different milieus in which the two were reared, and in part it is a difference that seems to be an expression of Rolland's conviction that the truly significant force in social relationships is woman, 'das ewig Weibliche'. It may be the result of some innate and obscure tendency of his character, or it may be one of the manifestations of an oedipal feeling; certainly "es zieht ihn hinan", to paraphrase the words from the second *Faust*.

One factor which makes such creations truly feminine in spite of a certain masculine outlook is the accompanying maternal instinct which now and then amounts to a passion, and which is colored by the author's outlook. This normal emotion occasionally rings false when it is felt not for a child or even a small, helpless animal, but for a lover, a sweetheart, or a husband. Luce feels this equivocal emotion very strongly for Pierre (pp. 88, 171), and the tragic idyll ends on such a note: "D'un mouvement maternel, elle serra de toutes ses forces la chère tête contre son sein..." But the two should have been lovers, and the maternal emotion is out of place. Let us note again, without undue emphasis, that here too physical love remains unconsummated and unsatisfied because of the lover's hesitancy, because of events, and perhaps because of the author's own problems.

In the spring of 1921 Rolland released for public sale a work he had finished shortly before the outbreak of the war, *Colas Breugnon*. This novel is the Gallic, Burgundian pendant, in miniature, to *Jean-Christophe*. Colas, the main character, is just as fond of life as was Christophe, but perhaps in a lustier, more sensual, certainly more insouciant fashion. He is not tormented by inner struggles and compulsions. There is none of the occasional puritan stiffness of Christophe. Colas is really the man Rolland would have liked to be, and somewhat of the man his father was, at least as far as the non-intellectual side of his personality is concerned. Colas is a spontaneous, untrammeled expression of the gaiety of a people close to the earth — hearty lusty lovers of life and the vine. All the old Burgundians who slept in his veins, Rolland said in a letter to Châteaubriant, May 12, 1912, had awakened; and he himself shook with laughter while writing it — although he appeared as stiff and solemn as a Protestant preacher when he left his writing desk.[16]

Colas Breugnon is the story of a year in the life of a fifty-year-old Burgundian wood-worker (about the age of Rolland when he

[16] This self-restraint is a very deep character trait. We find him writing, in his 'journal' at the École normale supérieure:
On ne me connaît guère, à l'École Normale... on ne voit de moi que la correction de conduite, la régularité du travail, la probité laborieuse, l'honnêteté froide de la vie intellectuelle, — sans se douter de la contrainte dure que j'impose à tout ce qui bondit en moi, hurle même quelquefois contre les autres et contre moi *(Le Cloître de la rue d'Ulm. Journal de Romain Rolland à l'École normale (1886-1889)* [Paris, 1952], p. 301).

finished it in 1914). It was inspired in part by his trip to the Nivernais region and in part by his own father and grandfather. Colas preserves his fundamental good humor in the face of life's adversities: an unhappy marriage, war, pestilence, illness, death, and the destruction of his creations. Unlike Christophe, he would never say: "Qu'est-ce que la vie? Une tragédie! Hurrah!" but that life is a wonderful thing, to be lived to the full. We can say of Colas what Rolland said of the book: a book without claims of changing the world, a book, frank and gay which laughs at life because life is good (*Colas Breugnon* [Paris, 1919], p. ii-iii). In spite of his much-vaunted love for the vine, and in spite of his generosity, Colas is shrewd and calculating, stubborn but able to adapt to new situations when necessary. He is distinguished not only by his innate joy, his ability to laugh and to see the ludicrous and the humorous sides of tragedy, but also by his robust good sense. He is an artist; he is not lost in a dream, but his own creations are sometimes more vital to him than other aspects of everyday life. There are many similarities between Rolland, Christophe, and Colas. Rolland wrote to Stefan Zweig that Colas is a French Christophe; the soul had changed covers, but was the same soul. At the age of twenty or thirty he had dreamed of expressing throughout his works, from one character to another, the same Divine Force, the Eternal Soul; the Old Adam, Proteus-Unity, would have been recognizable in different guises.[17]

This miniature Christophe also reveals something of his creator. Colas is unhappily married, although the reasons are somewhat different from those which caused Rolland's divorce. Colas' wife was sharp and bitter because she loved Colas, who did not fully return her love. His heart had remained entangled with another. Until the time of her death, Colas spent most of his time away from his 'vieille', consciously or unconsciously avoiding her.

[17] "Une petite remarque seulement sur *Colas Breugnon* (L' 'Intermezzo'). Peut-être n'est-il Intermezzo qu'en apparence. En fait, c'est un Jean-Christophe français. L'âme a changé de peau; mais elle est la même âme. Quand j'avais 20 ou 30 ans, je rêvais de promener dans mes œuvres de corps en corps la même Force divine, l'Ame éternelle; j'aurais changé ses yeux, ses sens, ses fenêtres ouvertes sur la vie, mais les initiés eussent toujours reconnu le vieil Adam, l'Unité-Protée" (Letter to Stefan Zweig, April 15, 1920).

Rolland's own father seemed to have spent relatively little time with his wife, especially after Rolland left for Italy in 1889. Colas, unlike Christophe, manages to found a family; he has four sons and a daughter. But like Christophe, who was unable to open the door to Sabine's bedroom at the propitious moment, Colas was unable to pluck the one he loved as a young man, when she was waiting for him in the warm summer orchard. The would-be lover fled — and regretted the action the rest of his life.

A vivid appreciation of the natural beauty of the Burgundian countryside is sensitively expressed in the work. The seasons are gracefully yet forcefully delineated. The action unfolds in the lush hills and valleys of the Nivernais, near Clamecy and Vézelay, between Auxerre and Nevers. The material comes from this region; the language, the proverbs, the character of the men and women who fill its pages. The spoken language comes directly from its popular sources, Rolland assured Stefan Zweig (November 21, 1919), just as it was spoken forty years previous to the writing of the book. The style has frequently been criticized, and it is true that it is a poetic style (Rolland referred to it as a poem); the rhythm is frequently more that of poetry than of prose. There are inversions, uncommon word order, alliterations, repetitions, metaphors and similes. The rhythm is occasionally somewhat breathless, almost jerky, yet seems to fit the subject or the incident. As a critic wrote concerning a 1955 edition, the tale is a long poem, and it sometimes surprises the reader. But after one becomes accustomed to it and finds his way in it, *Colas Breugnon* is effective.[18]

The years of the First World War formed a period of transition for Rolland; they were very difficult years for him, and brought great changes in his views of man and society. His deep-seated belief in the responsibility of the artist became the most compelling force in his life, and remained the guiding principle of his post-war activities. Only his musical works such as the volumes of Beethoven exegesis escape this preoccupation. Four major works mark this period. *Colas Breugnon,* which he described as the first work in

[18] Claude Juppet: "Colas Breugnon...", *Europe* (January-February, 1955), 251-252.

his new style, belongs to the second period in this respect, but is truly of the first (pre-war) period in its subject, being essentially a heroic biography, although fiction, and gay and light. *Pierre et Luce* continues a theme which had appeared as early as "Le Siège de Mantoue", and thus further connects this period of transition with the past. *Liluli* on the other hand is completely of the new period in style and subject, and looks to the future, especially to the last volumes of *L'Ame enchantée*. Indeed, it anticipates even more directly a work that is less well known, a satire that might almost take its place in the ranks of science fiction à la H. G. Wells: *La Révolte des machines* (Paris, 1921).

XII

THE REVOLUTIONARY CYCLE
AND THE ENCHANTED SOUL (1921-1938)

His mother's death on May 19, 1919, caused Rolland a long period of pain and indecision. He returned to Paris then for the first time since the summer of 1914. His sister and he soon began to look for a more permanent dwelling than the Swiss hotels where they had spent the past five years. Paris was odious to him, and he wished to establish himself in some more congenial physical and spiritual climate. His choice was Villeneuve, Switzerland; but not until August, 1921 did he sign a lease for the Villa Olga in Byron Park, where the two took up residence the following May, 1922.[1] He remained there until his return to Vézelay in 1937.

He was again in poor health, suffering from a respiratory ailment and incipient tuberculosis. In fact, he had been ill since early in the fall of 1921.[2] The illness, which had flared up late in 1919, had its causes, he said, in the difficult period of crisis after his divorce; it had been partially overcome by the creative urge which had resulted in his writing *Jean-Christophe*. The therapeutic agent was frequently intense spiritual or intellectual activity.[3] This rhythm of

---

[1] Letters to Mme Cruppi (May 12, 28, June 7, 1921); letter to Stefan Zweig (May 8, 1921); letters to J.-R. Bloch (July 7, August 10, 24, November 4, 1921).

[2] "Moi-même, j'ai été sérieusement malade, depuis la fin de septembre; et je suis encore incomplètement rétabli. Toujours la suite, ou plutôt une reprise du vieux mal qui s'était envenimé, il y a deux ans: (l'origine remonte aux premiers temps de mon séjour, au bould. Montparnasse, et à la grave crise morale et physique, dont je ne me suis guéri que par la volonté créatrice d'où est sorti *Jean-Christophe;* mais l'organisme en a toujours gardé la blessure, prête à se rouvrir, aux heures de crises nouvelles)" (Letter to Mme E. Marchand, December 24, 1921). See also a letter to J.-R. Bloch (Nov. 4, 1921).

[3] "Que la vie et la force me soient seulement données, pour un peu de temps encore! Elles sont en train de revenir à grande vitesse, — selon mon rythme

an illness followed by an upsurge of creative activity is of frequent occurrence in his life. The period from 1921 to 1922 seemed to him in these respects to be a repetition of the period from 1901 to 1902. In both, he was surrounded by the ruins of his (and Europe's) past, and found the energy to clear them away and to begin a new life.

Among his writings of this period, he completed a scenario — written in much the same spirit as *Liluli* — sharply critical of certain trends in modern society and civilization: *La Pensée dé-chaînée ou La Révolte des machines* (Paris, 1921). From November, 1921 to August, 1922 he carried on negotiations concerning the scenario with the American Play Company of New York, but they came to naught. The scenario depicts how, in a sort of Wellsian fantasy, the gigantic and efficient machines created and built by men revolt and drive out their masters and creators, threatening to gain complete control of a world no longer man's. The satire apparently directed against machines turns out to be a satire of man's inability to control his creations. Rolland was not opposed to machines in modern society, but to their abuse; machines themselves are neither good nor bad, they simply exist. Rolland found more beauty and poetry in machines than in certain aspects of the art of his time — the 'tinware' of Bayreuth, for example. He found the dynamic quality of machines, especially of airplanes, almost intoxicating.[4]

Now, after an interruption of twenty years, Rolland resumed work on the cycle of plays from the Revolutionary period. In 1925 there appeared *Le Jeu de l'amour et de la mort,* which, like many of his works, had been going through a slow process of maturation in his mind. The original idea goes back at least to 1903. In a letter

---

intérieur, qui fait que chaque assaut de la maladie, repoussé, augmente mon énergie. Il me semble que je suis en 1902, — que je m'en débarasse des ruines d'une période de ma vie — et que je m'en vais m'en tailler une autre. — Mais sans hâte. Je ne travaille pas pour le succès d'un temps. Je travaille pour ma loi et ma joie" (Letter to S. Zweig, December 11, 1921).

[4] "J'admire les machines. Je trouve certaines d'entre elles les plus belles œuvres d'art de notre temps. (Quoi de plus beau qu'un bel avion?) Je jouis de leur enivrant dynamisme. — Je les trouve beaucoup plus riches en possibilités poétiques que le glaive de Siegfried et toute la ferblanterie de Bayreuth" (Letter to Lucien Price, October 3, 1934).

to Mme Bertolini he wrote of the story of the proscribed Girondist, Louvet, who in spite of the danger to his life returned secretly to Paris and to his love. "J'ai toujours", he wrote, "désiré consacrer un de mes drames de la Révolution à la passion. Elle y a pris parfois un caractère de folie sublime" (letter of September 21, 1903; Chère Sofia, I, p. 139). The play, a tragedy in twelve scenes, takes place in Paris in 1794, after the proscription of the Girondists. In its construction Rolland remained close to the inner construction of classic tragedy. The action occurs entirely in Jérôme Courvoisier's apartment during the afternoon and evening of one day. The action is unified, the outer conflict being between the three principals: Jérôme, his wife Sophie, and the proscribed Girondist Claude Vallée. Both men love Sophie; and Sophie loves both, in different ways. The inner conflicts are, in Sophie between her love and her duty; in Vallée, between his love and the imperious call of Life; and in Jérôme, between his ideals and reality.

One of the important themes of the play — typical of Rolland's humanistic meditations — is the conflict between the State and the individual. It is foreshadowed in the first scene between Horace, a Republican soldier, and Lodoïska, a young widow whom he loves. He prepares to depart for duty despite Lodoïska's pleas; his love for the Republic is greater than his love for the woman.

Sophie is disillusioned about her husband (Rolland drew on Lavoisier and Condorcet in creating Jérôme de Courvoisier); she had brought her youth, her rich hopes, her devotion, to a man worthy of admiration, respect, and love. But Courvoisier had sacrificed her to his faith in science and in the Revolution (and it must be remembered that he is sixty and she thirty-five years of age). A similar conflict had been the one between Rolland and his wife. However, Vallée, too, has sacrificed Sophie to his faith, to his belief in the Revolution. She had refused his love, and now, believing him a victim of the brutal forces of the time, accuses herself bitterly of wronging Vallée and herself — she had sacrificed herself to her duty, to conjugal fidelity.

Vallée's return precipitates the crisis in her soul. Vallée, when his love is returned, finds life beautiful; his hatred and disgust for mankind disappear, and only the will and the need to live and to love remain. Courvoisier, on the other hand, lost the will to live when the Assembly voted Danton's death.

When Lazare Carnot asks Courvoisier to support the condemnation of Danton, the latter refuses and assures Carnot that he will stigmatize the dictatorship of blood and tyranny, even at the cost of ruining their work and the Revolution. The two men are fundamentally divided. For Carnot the individual's rights are non-existent without the force of the state, but for Courvoisier they cease to exist if they are sacrificed to the force of the state. Carnot defends man's progress and the doctrine that the ends justify the means; Courvoisier defends justice; the means are more important than the ends — a position Rolland reaffirmed in 1922, and which he had debated in such works as *Les Loups*.

Courvoisier, wishing to save his wife but not himself, insists that Sophie and Vallée escape — for he is aware of their love. Sophie rises above her love and chooses her husband; the two, reunited, calmly await their fate. Their past life and love rise again from the ashes of their defeat. Jérôme consoles Sophie, and gives us the keynote of the play and one of the keys to Rolland's thinking. Life, he said, is given to us to overcome. They themselves have conquered life. This is again the theme of the 'vainqueur vaincu', or its corollary the 'vaincu vainqueur'. The triumph over life manifest in this play is a forceful contradiction to those who have argued that Rolland always sings of a mystic surrender to the forces of life, good or evil. It is perhaps a passive triumph, but still a triumph, though mystic and spiritual.

Later in the same year (August 12, 1925), Rolland wrote to J.-R. Bloch that he had finished a one-act play, *Pâques fleuries,* which was to be the prologue to the cycle of Revolutionary plays. He was also ready to write the epilogue, *Les Léonides,* the pendant to *Pâques fleuries.* It was, in fact, partially written at this time. The two plays were thus closely associated in his mind, being intended originally to form one spectacle. Two of the characters, the Count of Avallon (later Prince de Courtenay), and Mathieu Regnault, who are opponents and quasi-conspirators at the end of the first play, will again face each other defiantly, on the common ground of exile, in the second.

The action of *Pâques fleuries* is laid in 1774, twenty-three years before the events of the closing play of the cycle. Rolland placed the action under the aegis of Jean-Jacques Rousseau, 'le précurseur halluciné', and his choice reveals certain traits of character. First, the mention of Rousseau the precursor strikes the reader. The title of one volume of war-time essays is *Les Précurseurs*. In fact, much of what Rolland considered to be his significant and important work during those years was to call attention to writers and thinkers who were giving evidence of foreseeing and interpreting the future. Much of his academic writing was concerned with forerunners; for example the article "Les Précurseurs du théâtre du peuple" (*La Revue d'art dramatique,* June 15, 1903, pp. 177-188). We must not, however, belabor the point, since any artist may be the forerunner of a movement, a style, or another artist. Perhaps of more significance is the fact that the whole cycle stands *sub invocatione* Jean-Jacques Rousseau. In studying Rolland's life and writings, one is at times forced to the conclusion that there is within him a deep sympathy with the early currents of Romanticism, and particularly with Rousseau (*supra,* pp. 21 and 101).

The classic nature of *Pâques fleuries* is striking. Despite its division into twenty-three scenes and one act, it is essentially a five-act tragedy. It moves through less than twelve hours of time, from afternoon to midnight of the same day. All the visible action takes place in the horse-shoe shaped esplanade of a Louis XV garden, with a colonnade forming the peristyle of a pavillon. The main conflict is between the Comte d'Avallon and his father, the Prince de Courtenay. As a *basso continuo* there murmurs the distant thunder of the rising revolution, distinctly perceived only by the elderly Jean-Jacques and the young Mathieu Regnault. The Comte d'Avallon is in conflict with his father the Prince on political and ideological grounds. The Prince cannot support the King and the policies of the Monarchy formed so largely by the King's mistresses. Exiled from Paris, he cannot employ his energies extensively. The son, on the other hand, has identified the Nation with the Monarchy, the Monarchy with the King, and is resolutely working for ends diametrically opposed to his father's. The Count, in the prime of his life, is powerless to work to his full capacity and to satisfy his innate tendencies to act and to command. He can only wait for his father's death in order to become the responsible master of the estates. But his personal situation is complicated by the existence of a bastard half-brother, the Chevalier de Trie. The clash between the two men is sharp, and the prize is the estate, itself being gnawed away by the rising bourgeoisie. The frivolous society, whose true ideals have been lost, is unable to oppose the new class. Popelin the notary is enriching himself and educating his nephew, Mathieu, in the law, at the expense of the brilliant, carefree, and basically indifferent Prince. Popelin hears only the clink of coins in his dealings with the Prince and the Count; but Regnault hears the rising clamor of resentment against old abuses. The stylized vices and qualities of the old order, and the cruder but more vigorous and self-conscious men of the future society are well portrayed in the two men. The Chevalier in his indifference resembles his father the Prince more than does the older son, the Count. The latter is a more capable man and a more serious adversary of Regnault and the new society, for he is more aware of the importance of the economic aspect.

The Count's situation is changed by the tragic death of his half-brother. The Prince's game-keeper, Guérin, inflamed by jealousy and hatred, kills the Chevalier who had seduced his sweetheart, Rose. The Count, however, is morally responsible for the Chevalier's death.

The style of the play and its language are very similar to those of *Le Jeu de l'amour et de la mort* and *Les Léonides*. The attempts to make La Maréchale speak poetic language in irregular sentences that are at times blank verse, are not always successful. As a stylized version of the elegant language and badinage of the older generation it is at times effective, but it is frequently tiresome. This lyric style is justified, for example, when La Maréchale participates in the fête; but when this style is continued in a discussion between herself and the Countess, designed to portray the great indifference felt or attained by those of her generation and position, the reader may be pardoned for his irritation at the rather pale imitation of the insipid verse of the epoch.

The title of the last play of the Cycle de la Révolution, *Les Léonides,* comes from the name of the shower of shooting stars which emanates from the constellation of Leo, visible from November 11 to 13, a phenomenon thought to be the disintegration of a comet. The play itself is an expression of the final disintegration of a society, the Ancien Régime, while the citizens feel that their benefits radiate over all Europe and all humanity; the title is symbolic of the essential attitude of the author. The play is more conventionally constructed than *Le Jeu de l'amour et de la mort,* but lacks some of the latter's rigorous classic tightness. The time of the action is the fall of 1797; the place, the Bernese Jura mountains not far from Soleure, first in the courtyard of a farm, and then in a terrace-like clearing on the mountainside.

The violent forces that have swept through the people of France for several years have left two men of opposing sides in the Swiss mountains: the Prince of Courtenay (the Comte d'Avallon of *Pâques fleuries*), and the Conventionnel, Mathieu Regnault. But the gigantic winds, after attaining their ends, have blown themselves out. It remains only for those who were separated by opposing currents to become reconciled and to go ahead in a common direction that will benefit France and humanity. This reconciliation, the main theme of the play, is accomplished through the children of the two principals, the Count, son of the Prince of Courtenay, and the two children of Mathieu Regnault, Manon and her half-brother Jean-Jacques Regnault. The Prince too is strongly attracted to Jean-Jacques, and this is the second factor in their rapprochement, which will be consummated later partly as a result of the boy's death.

Relationships between Mathieu and the Prince are prevented from becoming worse by Manon and the Count, who love each other dearly. Jean-Jacques, a victim of vitiated city air, loves the open air and country life; like Rolland, he is especially fond of autumn. His life is fulfilled when he effects the reconciliation of the two enemies, the two opposing worlds; then, like others of Rolland's creations, he can and must depart.

It is the Jacobin who expresses the author's conclusion: the invincible Force, which grips all of us, uses for its own ends and for progress the lowliest instruments (p. 219). This does not mean that man is totally and merely the plaything of destiny and blind force. Rolland's characters — especially Courtenay — like Rolland himself, believe that man is not powerless in the grasp of a blind fate. Man's will is part of destiny; he helps make the forces that move the world and man (p. 48). Closely related to this theme of man and his destiny is that of the 'vaincu vainqueur'. The two ideas are combined in the Prince's words, that one fights on even though defeated. What is approaching (in this case, Napoleon Bonaparte), whether called God or Devil, Progress or Force, Life or Death — is the vital force, Life and Creation, which Rolland felt at the core of all being, and which ultimately renders victorious even those whom external circumstances and life itself seem to have crushed.

One of the 'vaincus' is the fifteen-year old Jean-Jacques Regnault. As one of the bonds between the opposing worlds of Courtenay and Regnault, his is the triumph which endures after death. He is a brother of Aërt, Olivier, and Marc. He is young, tender, sensitive, and he dislikes violence and hatred. He is frail, but has a lucid and somewhat precocious view of life. The rôle of such persons is similar; they die that the work or the ideals they stand for may continue. Like Marc and Rolland, Jean-Jacques cannot endure the idea that he may cause others to suffer. All are sensitive to their natural surroundings (Marc less than the others, for he was completely Parisian). Rolland himself explains their similarities in the preface. They are the sons of the same man, of the man that he was at that moment, 'shortly before the dawn', when Christophe had not yet begun his voyage.

The last play to be written for the Revolutionary cycle was *Robespierre,* which was not completed until late in 1938 — the preface is dated October 26. It takes its place between *Danton* and *Les Léonides.* At the age of seventy-two, Rolland completed the cycle with the drama which, in his mind, was to constitute the summit. He had been living with the subject for many years, and the critical year of 1938, with the tragic meeting and pact at Munich in September, added perhaps the necessary stimulus for its completion.

The play opens with the execution of Danton, 16 Germinal, an II (April 5, 1794), and closes with the execution of Robespierre, three months later, 10 Thermidor (July 26). It is a drama in three acts and twenty-four tableaux, the last one written with the requirements of a People's Theater in mind. The technique reveals his desire to write for the cinema or radio. The twenty-third tableau, after Robespierre's imprisonment, consists of a series of visionary flash-backs of his life to bring to the audience certain capital events or situations and explain his present personality and actions. Even his myopia is expressed by the blurred vision of audiences and crowds.

Rolland also wished to rehabilitate Robespierre in the light of more recent research. Throughout the play he appears as a sincere, kind, idealistic man, with a normal share of human weaknesses. Part of his inner distress, carefully hidden behind his reserved, cold, slightly pedantic manner, was the awareness of the evil inevitably caused by his actions which were nevertheless always for noble ends (happiness, liberty, justice, and a humane social order). He thus resembles our author, and we wonder if Rolland did not find in him a kindred soul. His fanaticism is his boundless desire to help his people, to aid humanity, and to live solely by his principles. There seems to be a strong relationship between the choice of the subject and the author's spiritual life. By his own admission, Rolland was outwardly stiff and reserved — although the intensity of his gaze, his penetrating blue eyes have been noted by all those who met him. The sincerity and idealism, the unyielding, uncompromising intransigence, his ardent desire to aid in creating a freer and better social order, his belief in justice, all these traits resemble remarkably the subject of his play. Robespierre wishes to act within the framework and the spirit of the law. Couthon, on the other hand, does not hesitate to use extra-legal measures. Robespierre also faces the dilemma that Rolland had encountered: whether to tell the whole truth or not, when the effect upon the public would be depressing (p. 138). Like Rolland, Robespierre also feels that 'le feu de l'âme' is the essence and principle of all great actions (p. 139). Rolland paints in this play another human relationship that he prized perhaps above most others, and which he succeeds in portraying vividly and sensitively, that is friendship, the friendship between Saint-Just and Le Bas.

The early twenties also saw the beginnings of Rolland's second cyclic novel. *L'Ame enchantée*; the first volume of which, *Annette et Sylvie,* appeared in 1922. Rolland wrote to Mme Louise Cruppi, August 18, 1921, that he had finished the first part of the novel, which was to have four parts; he already knew quite intimately the companion he had created for himself — that is, Annette Rivière. Concerning the novel, he said that true creation is a spontaneous germination of the raw material of the mind, and an embodiment on paper of the figures that fill the mind, consciously and sub-consciously. Working over the first draft of the manuscript later is the work of an artisan, not of a creative artist.[5] Creation was a physical and psychical process for him; in fact, in his *Péguy* (Paris, 1945, I, p. 220) he indicates that it is closely allied to sexual creation, and he uses a sexual figure to describe it. Péguy, he wrote, had just expelled a new creation.[6] Following this spurt of inspiration, the second volume *L'Été* was nearing completion in August, 1923 (letter to Maxim Gorki, Aug. 15, 1923). During this time, which was a period of isolation in his personal life, he had also finished *Mahatma Gandhi,* the biography of the Hindu leader. At the same time he was vigorously trying to avoid being drawn into the vortex of action. Work on the novel provided the necessary substitute for action. He emigrated (in his words) into the life of the heroine, of whose existence he could not doubt, the 'Enchanted Soul' (*Le Périple* [Paris, 1946], p. 147, and a letter to Herman Hesse, March 5, 1924); the novel continued to grow until the last volume, in 1933.

[5] "Je continue mon roman... Il avance trop lentement, à mon gré. et il y a toujours tant à dire! Et je ne suis pas arrivé aux moments les plus importants. Il faudrait s'enfermer hermétiquement, six mois un an s'il le faut, avec son rêve, et ne permettre à rien de vous en distraire. On a besoin de faire le vide, autour, de fixer sur lui seul toutes les forces de son attention. Gare si elles se détendent! On aurait beau avoir, écrites par avance, toute la chaîne de l'histoire et ses péripéties. Si l'on n'a plus le contact, on n'enregistre plus rien des ondes électriques. Tout est perdu. 'Votre fille est muette'" (Letter to Mme Cruppi, September 6, 1921).

[6] See also *L'Ame enchantée* [Paris, 1950], Introduction, p. ix.

In *L'Ame enchantée* he embodied his dreams and ideals; in fictional characters he traced in part his own development. Through the novel we penetrate further into Rolland's creative activity, into his personality, and into his relationship with his mother. The novel is indeed perhaps more important in a study of his personality than in a study of literature, although it has amidst its less living parts some very fine moments.

It must be noted that he called the first volume a prelude (*L'Ame enchantée* [Paris, 1950], p. 5). There is a subtle difference in the tone of the first two volumes. In *Annette et Sylvie* the half-sisters, daughters of the society architect Raoul Rivière, are presented from the author's point of view. In the second volume, *L'Été,* we explore more deeply the protagonist's soul. The author's intuition enabled him to place himself at the core of a woman's personality and to perceive her and the world about her through her eyes. The essence of the volume is love; it is Annette's summer and harvest of love.

The third volume, *Mère et fils* (1927), was completed before May 25, 1926 (letter to J.-R. Bloch, May 25, 1926). The subject is Annette and the world around her; both Annette and the world are the protagonists, in opposition to each other in attitudes of distrust and hatred, each seeing clearly the faults and virtues of the other. The difference between this and the first two volumes is sharp and clear. Here and in the following parts, society, the European society of the period between the two World Wars, assumes a position of preponderant importance; the protagonists and antagonists are merely parts of the society of the time.

The Enchanted Soul is the history of the progressive disillusion-ment of a human soul, in this case a woman's. It is the gradual freeing of the body and soul of all the bonds and clinging vines of the past. It is a process like maternity, to which Rolland compares it, and often it is a life-long process:

C'était aussi une maternité : celle de l'âme cachée. L'être est enfoui comme un grain au fond de la substance, dans l'amalgame d'humus et de glaise humains, où les générations ont laissé leurs débris. Le travail d'une grande vie est de l'en dégager. Il faut la vie entière pour cet enfantement. Et souvent, l'accoucheuse est la mort (*L'Ame enchan-tée*, pp. 217-218).

Before the process can begin, the soul must become enchanted, immersed to the full in the illusions of this world. This process is symbolized in the opening pages of *Annette et Sylvie* (pp. 3-4). Seated drowsily by the open fire after her father's death, Annette, in a moment of relaxation so complete that her subconscious takes over the reins, fantasizes herself naked in a woods by a deep pool of dark water. She plunges in, dives to the bottom, and then must fight her way to the top through clinging, impeding water grasses. The water weeds that impede her ascent are the bonds, habits, atavisms of the past; they are rooted in the life-giving ooze of the bottom. This is also a dream of birth, a fantasy of the emergence of the foetus from its protective but hampering amniotic fluid. It may also symbolize the plunge into the subconscious, stripped of all protective illusions — a process that occupied her whole life. A similar dream or fantasy occurs again at the end of her life, when shortly before death, she again floats in the deep pool. But this time the water is red — the blood of life — and she is not stifled. The fantasy then also symbolizes life, into the hidden sources of which she had sprung, and to which she is about to return. Our supposition is strengthened by the symbolic use Rolland makes of water. The water in the pool flows off towards the sea and Annette flows with it. Previously Rolland had called the ocean Maya, l'Un, Om (rivers are the life of living beings — the Ocean contains all that exists). "In this meandering dance of the Mind-Ganges, which flows tumultuously towards the Ocean, it is not the Ocean which attracts Annette, it is the river. She marries it; she hears in her arteries the tread of the Great Army" (see *L'Ame enchantée*, p. 1359). This is the answer to Annette's question at the time of Sylvie's death. "Yes, there is the child — the child of my child... the fruit of the sea... But where is the sea? Where am I...?"[7] Annette was standing near the shore of the Sea of Being, the Ocean of Illusion. Its breath swept over her and pulled her towards

---

[7] *L'Am enchantée*, p. 1405. The child born from the sea is the literary development of the childish concept of birth as the confusion of water (hence fish, which come from the water) and babies, both of which issue from the body. For the feminine and maternal rôle of water, see Gaston Bachelard: *L'Eau et les rêves* (Paris, 1947), pp. 154-80.

the repose of mystical illumination and escape. Only later does she realize that her true nature lies in the River of Physical life and action.

Rolland's composition is again that of a musician, as in *Jean-Christophe*. The structure of the novel, like a symphony, is an orderly structure of what at first seems to be disorder. The subject, the stripping of the illusions and enchantments of a world of illusion from the soul and mind of the central character, is stated, developed, repeated in various secondary characters, as for example when Sylvie begins late in life to find pleasure in illusions and, in music. The movements vary from the *allegro* of the first volume (in spite of the slightly sombre beginning, the movement and the theme are sprightly); the *andante con moto,* and *grave* of the second, through the recapitulation in the final part of the last volume, with its *adagio* full of tragic hope. Again, as in *Jean-Christophe,* the cyclical and epic nature of the novel is important. It is epic in that we follow the hero or heroine from youth to the moment of death, epic in its breadth and scope, and epic in the dual nature of the protagonist. Just as there is a dual hero in the epic, so in *Jean-Christophe* we have Christophe and Olivier; there is essentially a dual hero in *L'Ame enchantée*, for the half-sisters Annette and Sylvie are complementary; they are also completed by Marc. Both Marc and Olivier disappear before giving their full measure, but leave an ineffaceable impression on the other persons, and especially on the dominant soul — Annette or Christophe — and through them, on their contemporaries.

The fact that Rolland was torn by various dichotomies is clearly visible in the novel, where almost every situation has its opposite. It is bi-polar throughout; each theme or incident has its inverted counterpart. First there are the two half-sisters (did not Rolland make them half-sisters so that they could be two opposite sides of the same phenomenon?). In Annette the emotions and intuition dominate the intelligence although it is lucid and strong, whereas in Sylvie the rational intellect never really loses control over the feelings. Marc, her son, perhaps represents a partial synthesis of the two, but unfortunately he is the least attractive character. A similar pair of opposites are Germain (the wounded French soldier) and Franz (the German prisoner of war, artist, and friend of Germain). Germain is a rational, intellectual Frenchman; Franz, an intuitive, emotional, poetic German. Is it fortuitous that Germain dies and Franz lives? that Annette falls in love with Franz? Marc himself attains his full development partly as a result of his love for Assia, the Russian émigrée, who is in many respects his opposite; Marc remains what Rolland calls a 'sterile intellectual', until, under the combined influences of Assia and of his mother, he achieves a partial synthesis of thought and action. Assia, after being won over to the Bolsheviks, puts all her energy into action. The differences between the two are finally reduced to the lowest common denominator as they gradually come to occupy somewhat similar positions. In these two are embodied the fundamental contradictions of their creator's character: individualism versus collectivism, thought versus action, intuition versus rationalism (he calls it 'l'intelligence'). They are embodied also in various secondary characters: Philippe Villard and Julien Davy. Villard is a coldly calculating intellectual though not without intuition, and a man of action, indomitable will, and great energy; Julien, equally intelligent, is too intuitive and too much a critical spirit to force himself to action, although he too, when he sees what he believes to be right, hews to the line and, like his creator, lets the chips fall where they may. These differences also exist between the generations. Julien's daughter Georgette, in many respects the spiritual if not the physical daughter of Annette, resembles her rather strongly, but with all the differences of two generations. Georgette, like Annette, has a true passion for maternity, but unlike Annette, not for love, not for the love of a man — she is content to mother Assia's son Vannia. She is interested in athletics; her mind is clear and lucid, but her emotional and intuitive life weaker than Annette's. Vannia, the third generation, has gone farther along the road toward the acceptance of a new form of society. Reared actually as a bourgeois individualist by Georgette, Vannia allows his mother's and his half-brother's strong influence to draw his youthful and pliant personality along the path towards a collective society. He reaches in his youth the stage of development that

Marc reached only at the height of his maturity. Vannia in turn attracts Georgette along the path towards revolutionary Russia. Thus Annette's spiritual heirs, aided by their very differences carry on the work for an improved society, the work which had become her own and for which she had reared and sacrificed her son — conceived by a fleshly father who was rejected and forgotten.

Julien and Bruno Chiarenza form another pair of opposites who complete and correct each other. Julien is pessimistic, Bruno optimistic and the more effective for that reason, said Rolland. Both are lucidly intelligent, and they represent a certain great generation of French and European intellectuals. In Julien mind dominates the emotions and instincts; in Bruno the heart and the intuitions are more active. Both are hesitant to act, but Bruno goes beyond action in his travels along the paths of mysticism and Julien is too clear-sighted to ignore the futility of action. Thus neither is able to act effectively, and it will be Marc, strongly influenced by both men, who will carry out a vigorous program of political action. After his death Annette continues to act in the same direction as the two men of her generation.

Rolland's dual nature appears in another recurring figure and situation, namely: the metaphor of the house.[8] In contrast to his demand for freedom and to his insistence that man is a free agent, we find that he conceives of some of his characters, or all of them at certain times, as being the dwellers of a shell, a house, a limiting frame. Society itself is compared to a house.[9] The relationship between parent and child, especially between mother and son, with its limiting, cramping effects on the child, appears in this metaphor (p. 1341). When the author steps into the novel, he says to Annette about Marc: "He dwells in you. The house, it is true, has nothing perhaps which resembles him. But he is there. He looks at me, through the window." Again, in the same volume (p. 1365),

[8]   See J.-B. Barrère, "Romain Rolland et Malwida. Les 'Racines' et le 'Souffle' ", *French Studies* (April, 1950), pp. 97-112; and Barrère, "Les 'Racines' et le 'Souffle' ", *Mercure de France* (August 1, 1954), 668-689.
[9]   See for example, *L'Ame enchantée,* pp. 92, 724, 809, 1165, 1246, among others.

Marc's son has the same eyes and features as his father: "He looks at you. Even before he has spoken, one feels, one knows that a new guest, a new era have entered the house."

Certainly the dominant figure is Annette the mother. She so dominates Marc (unavoidably) as a boy and as an adolescent that his struggles to free himself are particularly difficult. Fundamentally he does not wish to be free. In this respect, he seems to be an expression or an extension of the author's own fixation; Rolland appears to have been partly conscious of this function of his hero. Marc's whole evolution is to identify himself with his mother, who — quite unconsciously — leads him to his death, and in spite of her pain and sorrow possesses him thus alone and entirely.

Marc exhibits various traits associated with the oedipal complex. Most notable is his horror of the sexual act. The author insists on his need for purity and integrity, but the act itself is pure or impure only in the mind of the participant. Marc's horror of it seems unnaturally great, as for example when he and and his friend Sainte-Luce find shelter with two pretty modistes, friends of the latter. Overcome by his natural appetite and the physical attractions of one of the girls, Marc follows his companion's unabashed example — and then, despite all protests, flees disgusted, not by the girl but by the act (pp. 803-805). He cannot even think about it without repugnance. Such a feeling arises because his mother was, first of all, a woman for him, and secondly, an authority — the same kind of authority that Rolland had had to rebel against in his youth: "...this foolish little cock who refused to receive money from a woman. Is a mother a woman? Well, for him, yes". (p. 946). It is his mother that Marc unconsciously seeks in Assia. After his marriage, Annette explains to him that there will be moments when one or the other will grow tired of the yoke, will be repelled by any contacts with the other. The discussion ends with some salty repartee and a burst of laughter. Marc thought as he left: "If only Assia were like that!" that is, "like her".

Conversely, Assia has a strongly maternal feeling in her conjugal love, and Annette never experienced true conjugal love. Assia regarded Marc as her child (pp. 997, 998). Annette, indeed, tells Assia that Marc is the child of both. "He is a child", she said, "he is your child. The man who loves us is our child. He must be cradled, given the breast, and if the puppy bites, it is because he is teething" (p. 1022). In Assia's heart, he was her child more than her husband, and the best of her love was devoted to the child (pp. 1060, 1138, 1157).

Our surmise that Marc is suffering from an oedipal fixation is supported by Rolland's analysis of an incident in *Mère et fils*. While Annette was teaching in a provincial 'collège', Marc stayed in Paris as a boarding student in a lycée. His mother occupied his thoughts frequently, whether he regretted her absence or was trying to tear himself away from her. He sought to outrage her in his memory; he thought about the free life that she had led and that she was forbidding him to live. He also saw in fantasies other women who did not resemble his mother but whom he identified with her, and thus he satisfied upon her, in the dark regions of the subconscious, his repressed emotions — the hydra with a hundred heads (p. 492).

Two dreams of Annette's further reveal the confusion of maternal and conjugal love that appears in Rolland's works. The first occurs when Annette, on the way to the Swiss border to help in Franz's escape, dreams that Marc, surprising Franz and her together, believes that the German is her lover. He is enraged by jealousy, and Annette, to prevent his betrayal of Franz to French authorities, attempts to stab her son. Annette's own ambivalent feelings are revealed here, as well as Marc's, who is jealous of his mother's sexual life. The second dream is also about Marc, who appears under various names, and whom she must save from some unknown danger — obviously a death wish. She is unable to arise in order to save him, until the moment she awakens as the train arrives at the station where she is to meet Franz. She seems to have identified Franz with Marc in her confusion of feelings. Annette herself becomes partially aware of the nature of her love when Germain and Franz are reunited. The love that she thought was purely maternal (why should it be maternal, when she is little older than Franz?) is rather *amour-passion* — but she does not understand this, nor the rôle that maternal love plays in it, nor the identification of Franz with Marc.

Fear of women predominates in Marc, but the reverse of the medal, a strongly sensual nature, is also important. The conflict between the two gives rise to sharp tensions in the young man. During the wild 1918 armistice celebration Marc violently kisses a young girl. Swept along by inner forces and by mob hysteria he is no longer master of himself. He cannot understand himself, nor the nature of his conflict, which is a struggle between his intelligence, his emotions, and his sensuality (almost a conflict of goodness against cruelty, of idealism and reality), a conflict not unknown to his creator. Although the cause of his conflict in this case would seem to be a trifle, ambivalent feelings were strong within him; his fear of sex was sufficient to cause one kiss, however taken, to arouse his tensions to an intolerable pitch. Later in his life he tastes somewhat of the world of pleasure, but finds it generally not to his liking. Following one part of his temperament he determines to live chastely. Rolland says that Marc has the choice only between two extremes, no women or all women. This may well be true, and the reason may lie in his peculiar fixation. The same attitude reappears when Sylvie tries to arrange a match between Marc and her protégée Bernadette. The only woman, besides his mother and Sylvie, whom Marc feels close to during this period of his life is his fellow student Ruche, and his relations with her — partly it is true because of her attitude — are strictly platonic, and a bit mawkish on Rolland's part.

The relationship of Marc and his mother — which seems to be a thinly veiled transposition of the author's — reaches an unusual stage during their walk in the Swiss mountains. Here they become equals, no longer mother and son separated by age and attitude, but brother and sister. They are in complete harmony and communion; Marc feels his heart beat as fast for his mother as for his wife.

In *Annette et Sylvie* we meet Annette shortly after the death of her father. Through her memories and Rolland's narrative, we learn about Raoul Rivière, and in the account of his character and of his death we find another key to Rolland's philosophy. Rivière, a very successful and stylish Parisian architect, elegant, witty, essentially amoral, was more of a bon-vivant than an intensely ethical man like most of Rolland's creations. His main concern was with an easy, successful, brilliant life and career. He was an egotist, disillusioned but not blasé. He had always lived for himself and he revolted against death; his agony was rebellious and violent in contrast to the almost eager acceptance of death by various of Rolland's characters, who live wholly in the service of others or of some cause far greater than the individual. Christophe, Annette, and St.-Louis are examples, and we remember the eager quest for death, the suicides of Aërt and of Professor Berthier. Marc is one of the few in Rolland's works who die a sudden and unexpected death by violence. He had not wholly renounced some forms of egotism, although he had devoted himself to a cause.

Shortly after the episode in the mountains Marc is killed by the Black Shirts in Florence. His rôle in life had been fulfilled; he was then resorbed into the womb of the earth. His own destiny, shaped by his mother, drew him back into that from which he had come, and now Annette, the Mother who bore him, formed, dominated, and led him along the path to self-sacrifice, has brought him irrevocably to live only in her mind and memory — for Assia marries again and has another child, and Sylvie is part of herself — where she shares him with almost no one. Annette, having given the world part of herself, has taken it back, although at a heavy cost. Now that she has paid the ransom she is free to act and to appear before the world in a powerful position.

The last loss that occurs in Annette's life is the death of Sylvie. After that death, which represents the disappearance of more than forty years of her life, she is completely free; the last veil of illusion has fallen and she stands within the threshold of universal life. She lives in a state of hyperesthesia of sight, in a condition of continuing consciousness, a state of continual and intimate contact with the world and the life forces. The past, present, and future become as one to her, and all the universe is in her as she is in it. The umbilical cord has not been cut (says Rolland), which fastens the world to her; whoever touches the child touches the mother. To Annette it seems that she had given birth to the world; again she is the Mother.

Less perfect as a work of art than *Jean-Christophe* (which has its flaws), *L'Ame enchantée* is perhaps more revealing of the personality of the author than is the earlier novel. It is an extremely significant work in this respect, especially in view of Sigmund Freud's reaction to it. Rolland met Freud in the spring of 1924 in Vienna, and later wrote to J.-R. Bloch (June 15, 1924) that Freud, who had read the first volumes, approved unreservedly *L'Ame enchantée*. His scientific experiments, said Rolland, confirmed completely Rolland's own experiences. He attached great value to Freud's approval of the novel.[10]

The last volumes of *L'Ame enchantée* appeared in 1933. The first volumes had appeared ten years previously. The third volume (*Mère et fils*, 1927), appeared a year before the first volume of the *Beethoven. Les Grandes époques créatrices. I. De l'Héroïque à l'Appassionata* (1928). The same years were marked by the publication of *Mahatma Gandhi, Le Jeu de l'amour et de la mort, Pâques fleuries, Les Léonides*. In 1929 and 1930 there were published the three volumes of his *Essai sur la mystique de l'Inde vivante. I. La Vie de Ramakrishna. II. La Vie de Vivekananda et l'Evangile universel* (2 volumes). In the thirties the remaining volumes of the Beethoven exegesis were completed and published. The works are of course only the principal markers that appear from time to time throughout his life. The milestones between, — public protests and appeals for mercy, justice, and help; prefaces; articles concerning political events, are equally important in understanding all aspects of his life and thinking.

The twenties and thirties were also marked by his keen interest in two large and somewhat mysterious countries, India (and the Orient), and Soviet Russia — especially the new society he believed was being built there. The same period saw his growing hostility and opposition to the rightist dictatorships springing up in Europe, especially Italian Fascism and German Naziism.

---

[10]   About Freud, Rolland wrote: "Il lit énormément; et j'ai attaché un grand prix à son approbation, sans réserves, de mon *Ame enchantée*. Son expérience scientifique confirme entièrement la mienne" (Letter to J.-R. Bloch, June 15, 19 24).

XIII

EAST AND WEST: ROLLAND AND THE ORIENT

Rolland's war-time activities and political pamphleteering continued to influence his readers and the public at large, and thereby
sometimes to falsify his position as a thinker and writer. His
reputation abroad was already greater than at home. John Galsworthy invited him to be an honorary member of the English
section of the P.E.N. Club (letters to Mme Cruppi, Dec. 30, 1921,
and to Stefan Zweig, Dec. 31, 1921). Two years later Rolland and
his sister went to London (May 1923) for the first meeting, where
be made the acquaintance of Shaw, Wells, Galsworthy, and
E. D. Morel; he also visited Thomas Hardy and Israel Zangwill.[1]

But his attention was perhaps most strongly attracted to the
Orient, especially India. Interest in that part of the world, it is true,
went back to his days at the Ecole normale, when he had read
Burnouf's histories of the Orient and of oriental philosophies
(letter to Christian Sénéchal, Sept. 3, 1932).[2] During the war of
1914, while in Switzerland, he had become acquainted with the
orientalists Neville and Moutet (*Journal des années de guerre*
[Paris, 1952], Index; letter to Madeleine Rolland, May 3, 1917).
His innate idealism had early found a congenial climate in the
religious thought of the Orient. There, especially in Japan, he had

---

[1] Letter to Rabindranath Tagore (June 11, 1923), published in *Rolland and
Tagore,* ed. Aronson and Kripalani (Calcutta, 1945), pp. 40-41. For Rolland's
relations with these writers see Starr, "Romain Rolland and H. G. Wells",
French Review (January, 1957), 195-200; Starr, "Romain Rolland and Thomas
Hardy", *Modern Language Quarterly* (June, 1956) 99-103; and Starr, "Romain
Rolland and G. B. Shaw", *The Shaw Bulletin* (September, 1957), 1-6.
[2] For echoes of this interest, see *Jean-Christophe* (Paris, 1950), pp. 1004,
1071-1072.

found an atmosphere in which the vital force that religion represented for him was strong (letter to Mme Bertolini, Feb. 7, 1906; *Chère Sofia. Choix de Lettre de Romain Rolland à Sofia Bertolini Guerrieri-Gonzaga*, I [Paris, 1959], pp. 251-253). To Mme Marchand he had expressed an idea that appears in *Jean-Christophe*: Europe, consumed by flames of violence and inhuman materialism, was rushing headlong towards an abyss. But what must be will be; we can only observe and try to understand, he had said. But the earth, happily, will not cease to flower, nor the heavens to shine. And he saw other lights arising, especially in the Orient (letter to Mme E. Marchand, May 8, 1907).

In the early months of the war, he had expressed the opinion that Europe was committing suicide and that Asia would soon snatch from it its living heritage. His feelings about this possibility were mixed. To Georg Brandes, who feared war and the resultant threat from the yellow races, Rolland replied that the yellow races seemed to him no worse than the white, no more stupid nor wicked than Occidentals; and white or yellow, the human spirit would continue to advance. Greco-Latin wisdom would be enriched by Far Eastern culture (letter to Alphonse de Châteaubriant, Dec. 18, 1912).

By 1915 he feared the military might of Japan, which he called the Prussia of the Far East (*Journal de guerre,* p. 354; May, 1915); force was not what he hoped for from any nation or race. The fact that Japan did not then begin its program of westward expansion in no way changed his opinion as to the possibility of its overrunning Europe. We know almost nothing, he wrote to an interned French soldier (May 2, 1918, *Journal de guerre,* pp. 1480-82), about mysterious and ancient Asia, which within fifty years will have enveloped us in its tentacles. What he feared from the Orient was the invasion of Europe by Mongols. He feared the Russians particularly because of this aspect of their character.

In the period of disillusionment after the treaties of 1919, as he became better acquainted with Orientals and certain Oriental religions and philosophies, the prospect of Asian domination seemed less dismaying. Rolland wrote to René Schickelé, November 19, 1921, that he feared nothing from the victory of Asia.

In the first place all the Asiatics he had known seemed very close
to him in their thinking. They had contributed new elements for
the enrichment of his own mind and thinking (letter, published
by Pierre Grappin, in *Les Annales de l'Université de Paris,* 1950,
pp. 434-444). Soon he frankly stated that he was one of a small
number who no longer found the civilization of Europe sufficient,
and who therefore looked towards Asia, believing that the
civilization of India and China might have the answer for this age
of chaotic confusion ("Introduction", *La Danse de Civa* by
Ananda Coomaraswamy [Paris, 1922; New York, 1924]). In 1924,
facing the possibility of U.S. domination of the world, he was
repelled by the capitalism of this country no less than by its
puritan idealism, and in the great clash which he foresaw between
Anglo-Saxon America and Asia, he was inclined to believe that
he would fight on the side of the spirit of Japan and India, although
he urged that every effort be made to prevent this enormous
conflict.[3]

Closer contacts between Rolland and Orientals began during
the latter years of the First World War. He regarded these contacts
not only as enriching for himself, but also — and more important —
as a means of contributing to the work of bringing about the
union of these two great rivers of humanity (*Journal de guerre,*
p. 370; date of entry, 1915). In February, 1915, the Hindu writer
Ananda K. Coomaraswamy sent Rolland a copy of his article,
dedicated to Rolland, on a world policy for India (*The New Age,*
Dec. 24, 1914) and began a correspondence which was to last

[3] "Je m'épouvante parfois de l'idée que les États-Unis pourraient, un jour,
dominer le monde. Et je ne crains pas moins l'idéalisme américain que son
capitalisme. Qui sait si je ne crains pas encore plus l'idéalisme puritain? —
Car il ne comprend rien, rien au reste du monde; et il est si tranquillement
convaincu qu'il n'est d'autre idéal que le sien — que les autres, il les extermine.
— Je prévois le grand choc, fatal, entre l'Amérique anglo-saxonne et l'Asie —
probablement aussi et l'Amérique latine. Et le problème angoissant est pour
moi de quel côté l'Europe sera-t-elle? — Certes, il faut tout faire pour empêcher ce conflit, auprès duquel celui de 1914-1918 aura été un jeu d'enfants.
— Mais, je ne le cache pas, s'il devait avoir lieu, mon esprit combattrait avec
l'esprit de l'Inde et du Japon, — voire avec ces précurseurs que j'ai appris à
estimer dans l'Amérique ibéro-latine, particulièrement au Mexique" (Letter
to Maxim Gorki, August 1, 1924).

for some time. Coomaraswamy later sent him an edition of the *Baghavad Gita,* and his own book *The Arts and Crafts of India and Ceylon.* After reading them, Rolland expressed the wish to lead the thinking of his own race onto these high plateaux undreamed of by his countrymen (*Inde, Journal 1915-1943* [Paris Lausanne Bâle, 1951], p. 11). Rabindranath Tagore's speech at the Imperial University of Tokyo warning the East against Occidental civilization made a strong impression on Rolland (see his: "Aux peuples assassinés", *La Vie ouvrière,* Oct. 29, 1919, p. 3; and *Inde,* pp. 11-12). He noted in his diary, April, 1917 (*Inde,* pp. 13-14), that Tagore had expressed ideas about the unity of mankind very similar to his own. All the people of the world aspire to unity and are impelled in that direction unbeknownst to themselves. The present is simply the negative side of a great movement, the darkling dawn, from which eventually will come peace and light. From the crisis in a materialistic civilization was to arise an era of unprecedented spiritual and moral development. He expected the American countries — particularly Mexico and the South American nations — to harmonize the various differences in races and peoples. The great mistake of most Europeans in this respect is impatience; the calm, slow movement of Oriental philosophy is more realistic, for such great changes can come only slowly.

Tagore came to Paris, April 19, 1921, and visited Rolland at frequent intervals. The first mention in Rolland's works of non-resistance or of non-violent resistance occurs in his account of their conversations, which were carried on in English and French with the help of Madeleine Rolland (*Inde,* pp. 17-22). The next visit of the Hindu was in 1926, June 21, at Villeneuve. Four years later, Rolland and Madeleine went to Geneva to meet him (July, 1930). In July and August, 1920, a young Hindu from Bengal had come to visit Rolland. Their conversations were largely about music (see Dilip Kumar Roy, *Among the Great* [Bombay, 1945], pp. 5-63). Rolland noted relationships between the Hindu songs Roy sang and the Gregorian melodies, even greater relationships with the Greek hymns which are the source of the Gregorian plain song. The popular or folk songs that he sang could be, Rolland said, folk songs from France.

Other visitors from India were numerous; but besides Tagore, the one whose visit was most important in Rolland's life was Gandhi. In 1920 he knew almost nothing of the Hindu leader. He asked Mme Cruppi if she had heard of this astonishing man, who could arouse all India if he wished, but who imposed upon it the doctrine of non-resistance (letter dated August 25, 1920). However, when the publisher Ganesan of Madras asked him to write an introduction to the collection of Gandhi's articles, *Young India,* he refused. Although he had high esteem for Gandhi, he differed from him on some points, and he preferred to write about him with more freedom than such an introduction would permit (*Inde,* pp. 28-30; August, 1922). Their first meeting was in 1931; when Gandhi went through Europe in September on his way to the Round Table Conference in London, Rolland was unable to meet him at Marseilles because of poor health. The visit finally took place in December; Gandhi arrived in Territet (Switzerland), returning from London, on December 6; there Madeleine Rolland met the group. With her help Rolland was able to enjoy several long and profitable conversations with the Mahatma. His account (in *Inde*) is detailed and interesting; we hear the two men discussing the problems that concerned both, many of which have become almost ineradicably associated with Rolland. We can see the slight figure of the Indian leader, his gestures, appearance, and attitude, in a series of vivid and entertaining flashes from Rolland's pen.

He wished very much to visit his new acquaintances in their own lands (letter to R. Tagore, July 11, 1923), especially Tagore: "I have so much to learn from you! And I believe that I shall have a mission to fulfill there, a predetermined duty till the end of my life. The union of Europe and Asia must be, in the coming centuries, the most noble task of mankind", he wrote.[4] In 1921 he had done all he could in favor of Tagore's appeal for the

---

[4] Letter quoted by D. K. Roy, *Among the Great* (Bombay, 1945), pp. xiii-xiv, from an article by K. R. Kripalani ("The Greatest European since Tolstoy", *The Hindusthan* [January-March, 1945], 4), who first reproduced Rolland's letter. In 1930-1931, in the epic duel between Gandhi and the British Empire, Rolland saw not the combat between Asia and Europe but the marriage of the two halves of humanity. The two great rivers of the Human Spirit are at last

free university he was organizing. At that time Rolland had been deterred from the trip by a feeling of inadequacy because of his ignorance of English (cf. his letter to Tagore, April 22, 1921, reproduced in facsimile in *Rolland and Tagore,* ed. Aronson and Kripalani [Calcutta, 1945], facing p. 29).

As part of his contribution to the task of effecting a harmonious union of the two halves of humanity, Rolland wanted to bring the best of Asiatic thought to European readers. To this end he had been trying since 1919 to start at Paris an international review, free of political bias, which would devote generous space to the thought of the Orient. The project was delayed, principally by financial difficulties, but he hoped that the first number might appear in October, 1922.[5]

If Rolland felt an immediate kinship with the Orient, especially with India and its thought, it was, he believed, because there was some family affinity between an Aryan of the Occident and an Aryan of the Orient.

Now I am a Frenchman of France born in the heart of France, in a family which has been nurtured on the soil for centuries. When I was barely twenty I had no knowledge of the religions and philosophy of India. — I believe therefore that there is some direct family affinity between an Aryan of the Occident and an Aryan of the Orient. — And I am convinced... that it was I who descended... the slopes of the Himalayas along with those victorious Aryans. I have their blue blood flowing in my veins (from a letter to D. K. Roy, published in Alexander Aronson, *Europe looks at India* [Bombay, 1946], p. 181).

If he recognizes this previous life later in reading, it is because it slumbers within him, he felt. And he affirmed that, from early childhood on he had felt the breath of this life.[6] The Indian

---

joining, he wrote in "Préface à l'Autobiographie de Gandhi", *Europe* (1931), 465-490.

[5] Letters to J.-R. Bloch (Aug. 16, 1919) and to Tagore (May 7, 1922), in *Rolland and Tagore,* p. 30. This was a long-cherished desire of Rolland's. It was at least partially satisfied with the founding of the monthly review *Europe,* the first number of which appeared in February, 1923.

[6] It may be objected that he is reading his later experiences into these childhood memories. We do not deny this possibility, but he anticipated the objection. In *Le Seuil, précédé du Royaume du T* (Geneva, 1946), pp. 25-28, he outlines two principal causes of error in the quest for one's true self among

thought that he came to know during these post-war years enriched and strengthened his own thinking; it helped him to see more clearly the depths of his own thought. It was not chance that led him to India; he found a familiar ring in Hindu writings. By an unforeseen route, Indian thought led him back to certain currents of thought of an older France, currents he had failed to recognize before (he is presumably referring to the French mystics).[7] Rolland was of course also following a deep current of interest in the Orient which began early in the nineteenth century, when many writers and thinkers were eagerly studying Oriental mysticism and philosophy. Rolland had, as we have seen, read the works of some of these men, — Burnouf for example. Thus again he reveals himself as a man primarily of the nineteenth century, just as he had in *Jean-Christophe* and *L'Ame enchantée*; in spite of the dates of their publication and setting, they are nineteenth-century novels.

Another reason for his affinity with India was his dualistic conception of the world (see his *Empédocle d'Agrigente et l'âge de la haine* [Geneva, 1918]), his belief that from all the numerous differences will come reconciliation, that out of the dissonances

---

one's memories. The first is the ready-made thinking that is imposed upon us at the cradle. The second is the secret dishonesty of the mind. This is the dishonesty involved in following one of the two paths to self-knowledge. The two roads are cognition and desire. But the path of Desire includes Hope. If to this be added Will, the mind says "I believe", and then assumes this belief to be cognition — but it is desire, not cognition. If, however, we follow Desire frankly and lucidly, knowing that it is the path, it will reveal much, for Desire is the voice of the instincts inscribed in one's being before cognition; it is the blind groping expression of a Reality which precedes (and perhaps exceeds) all knowledge. This is the path he chose and followed in the pages of *Le Seuil*.

[7] "Le hasard (— qui se préparait: il n'y a jamais de hasards dans une vie puissante, comme la vôtre ou la mienne — une vie écrite, avant que nous eussions pris la plume) le hasard qui m'a, depuis quelques années, mis en contact intime avec l'Inde, m'a simplement aidé à voir plus clair au fond de ma propre pensée. Car *mon* Inde n'a rien d'exotique; l'exotisme, loin de m'attirer, me repousse. Ce que d'autres retrouvent dans l'Evangile ou dans la Bible, ou dans les Grecs et les Méditerranéens, (dont j'ai grapillé quelques treilles), je l'ai reconnu dans la pensée des Himalayas: et, par un détour imprévu, elle m'a ramené à certaine pensée de France, très ancienne, encore très vivante, que je méconnaissais. Elle ne m'a pas révélé la mienne, elle l'a enrichie et assurée" (letter to J.-R. Bloch, Easter, 1929).

comes ultimate harmony, that what we take to be bad or unjust may merely appear so because we cannot dominate the whole intricate structure of the universe with our mind; all these beliefs found a congenial atmosphere in Hindu philosophy and religion. In his preface to the *Dance of Civa* Rolland insisted that the vast soul of India proclaims throughout its crowded but well-ordered edifice the domination of a supreme and sovereign synthesis. Everything has its place and its function in the divine concert. On the contrary, in the West, he said, cold, hard logic isolates the unusual. India is ever mindful of natural differences in souls and philosophies, but endeavors to blend them in order to recreate the total unity in its greatest perfection. Rolland strove always towards a comprehensive view of the world that would include all the varieties and dissonances. He preferred, he said, the Brahmin philosophy because it seemed to contain all the other schools of Asiatic thought. It was even capable of adjusting itself to the vast new hypotheses of modern science. The cosmogony of Einstein, he continued, of stellar space, nebular spirals, boundless creations in space-time, is not strange to him — in it he hears Brahmin thought.

In this period he wrote his lives of Gandhi, Ramakrishna, and Vivekananda. In volume two of the *Vie de Vivekananda,* he foresees a new age of synthesis in which the united efforts of the Orient and the Occident will create a new order of thought, freer and more universal. As he had already pointed out, he refused to admit two divisions of humanity based on geographical factors. Rather he saw two kinds of souls: those who rise and those who fall. On one side, the patient, ardent, tenacious, and intrepid ascent of man towards light, science, beauty, love, progress. On the other side, obscurity, ignorance, apathy, fanatic prejudices, and brutality. Those on the first side are his allies and brothers; their fatherland is free humanity, of which the great nations and peoples are but provinces.[8] The essential condition for such spiritual development as he sees slowly forming here is Liberty. He found

[8]   Article dated April, 1925, published in Chinese translation in the *Short Stories Magazine* (Shanghai), January 10, 1926, and in French in *Les Lettres françaises,* April 21, 1949.

the same belief in Liberty in Vivekananda, and commented that Europe, which had been able to bring about this condition in the realm of politics much more effectively than India, had fallen far short of attaining it to the same extent as India in the field of the spirit (*Vie de Vivekananda* [Paris, 1929], II, p. 18). Again, he hoped for the fruitful cooperation of the East and the West.

This belief presupposes the essential unity of human thought and spiritual life. Here again he found, in the emergence of similar modes of thinking in such widely separated places as India and the Americas, another proof of the unity of all that exists. A predisposition to Vedantism existed in the United States, he said, long before the arrival there of Vivekananda. This disposition is not linked to a corpus of doctrines in a single country — here he disagreed with the Indian Vedantists — but is a universal disposition of the human soul at all times and in all places. But chance favors or retards this disposition during the evolution of different races and civilizations. The spirit is latent in all, but is especially strong in those who bear within them some spark of creation (*Vie de Vivekananda*, I, pp. 72-75).

In Vivekananda he found a congenial conception of the idea of human progress in the spiritual sense. Rolland was also interested by the Hindu's attempt to synthesize Hindu faith and modern science, the ideals of the *Vedanta* and the social attainments of today, pure Spirit and the numberless gods who are lesser ideas of pure Spirit. All religions are true, inasmuch as they are phenomena of consciousness, of various stages in the development of the human spirit which climbs blunderingly towards the peaks of its being (*Vie de Vivekananda,* I, p. 25). But, although the human spirit is universal, it is not always at the same point, and Rolland compared it to a symphonic unity composed of many distinct voices (*Mahatma Gandhi* [Paris, 1926], p. 49).

Rolland was reasonably critical, and at first he was dubious about the mystical experiences of Ramakrishna. He later came to believe that the path followed by Ramakrishna was similar to the one he had himself travelled in developing his own philosophy (*Vie de Ramakrishna* [Paris, 1929], p. 50, n. 3), but the tendency towards the sole contemplation of the eternal displeased him.

Our task, he said, is to bring about the equilibrium of Occidental action and Oriental intuition (*Le Seuil, précédé du Royaume de T* [Geneva, 1947], p. 108; text of 1926).

Rolland's *Mahatma Gandhi* appeared in 1924; the postface, "L'Inde depuis la libération de Gandhi", is dated March, 1924. Like the *Beethoven* of twenty-one years before, *Mahatma Gandhi* found a wide and responsive audience. It ran through a number of editions (1926, 1929, 1930, and 1946). The biography stood for more than a mere literary work in Rolland's life. It was part of his mission to spread abroad this admirable system of thought, the most beneficial and efficacious one of its times, opposed to violence of all sorts, as well as to verbal and ineffective pacifism.[9] The biography is also a eulogy and a defense of non-violent resistance. Rolland found at the basis of Gandhi's faith in non-violent but active resistance an intangible love 'amour-amor caritas', not abstract and sentimental, but specific and active, which finds one of its sublimest expressions in *ahimsa,* the doctrine of non-injury to any form of life. These are conceptions which were present to some degree in Rolland's own thinking even before he had heard of Gandhi. He did not find everything desirable in the Mahatma's thinking, and he did not hesitate to criticize many of his more purely political and social ideals which ignored modern phases of the struggle in a financial and industrial society.

Rolland's study of Hindu philosophies and religions and his interest in the Orient corresponded to certain needs in his own soul, certain traits of his own character. In the Oriental religions and philosophies he found a climate of ideas and ideals similar to his own. Within the framework of his development, this period 1920 to 1930 is very important as one of transition, as he swung

[9] "Avec plaisir je vous enverrai mon Essai sur *Mahatma Gandhi.* Ne vous occupez pas des conditions. Il n'y a point de conditions! Je considère comme une faveur et une mission sainte de répandre cette admirable pensée. Elle est non seulement la plus bienfaisante, mais la plus efficace à l'heure actuelle. Elle s'oppose à la fois à toutes les violences et au pacifisme verbal, veule, invertébré. Ne croyez pas qu'il y ait le moindre rapport entre l'*action* intense, héroïque d'un Gandhi, sans violence matérielle, mais d'une immense maîtrise de soi, avec la *non*-action, la *non*-résistance, la passivité des paysans russes..." (Letter to Maxim Gorki, February 20, 1923); Gorki had expressed an interest in translating the biography into Russian.

rather rapidly to a socially critical frame of mind. The first clear, public step along this road was his life of Mahatma Gandhi, which is, of course, mainly concerned with the prophet and preacher of non-violent resistance, non-violent social action. The period closed with the three volumes of the lives of Rama-krishna and Vivekananda. These biographies, as their sub-title indicates, attempt to bring to the European reader some under-standing of the mysticism of India (*Essai sur la mystique et l'action de l'Inde vivante*).

In the next decade he devoted himself more and more to po-litical action and social causes. Pamphlets, protests, and signatures flowed from the Villa Olga between 1930 and 1940. He was the honorary chairman of special committees or of organizations which worked for peace or against Naziism and Fascism, or stood for the defense of Soviet Russia. The change is clearly reflected in his novel *L'Ame enchantée,* the first volumes of which appeared in the twenties. The last volumes, *La Mort d'un monde,* 1933, and *L'Enfantement,* 1933, are the novel of social and po-litical action in contemporary Europe, the Europe of the period between the two World Wars. The death of a world is the decay and death of bourgeois capitalist European society. The birth is that of a socialized, if not socialist, proletarian society in the world, especially in Europe.

XIV

ROLLAND'S RELIGION

Rolland's interest in the Orient and his reactions to Oriental philosophies and religions cannot be completely understood without more knowledge of his religion and his beliefs. We know that he had lost his orthodox Catholic faith when still a very young man; we also know that he was a religious man, unorthodox though his beliefs may be. The prime necessity, the very keystone of a harmonious and complete life was, he believed, the religious sentiment, but "Libre religion, cela va sans dire" (letter to Mme Bertolini, Feb. 2, 1911; *Chère Sofia. Choix de lettres de Romain Rolland à Sofia Bertolini Guerrieri-Gonzaga*, II [Paris, 1960], p. 92). 'Libre religion'; this is the key to his complex personality; he was throughout his life an essentially religious — but at times anti-clerical — Frenchman, who needed above all freedom to speak the truth. Frequently accused of anti-intellectualism, there was in him a deep strain of mysticism. He was highly intellectual, but he distinguished between the broad intuitive and imaginative use of the intelligence and a rather narrow and sterile intellectualism. In his *Journal des années de guerre* (Paris, 1952), p. 35 — entry for August 5-7, 1914 — he wrote that his true personality was essentially religious, and God is the God Maëlstrom who drinks in all lives, by death, love, and sacrifice. Late in his life he would call 'oceanic' this vague, limitless aspiration towards union with the hidden forces of the universe (letter to Raymond Pichard, May 10, 1936; and compare the final pages of *L'Ame enchantée*).

In an entry dated July, 1889 (*Le Cloître de la rue d'Ulm* [Paris, 1952], p. 310), he had said that he believed in God, and that all living beings express His power. He believed that God was inherent in himself and in every creature but at the same time distinct, since, beyond himself, God embraces all other beings. Death is the confluence of the individual soul and the Infinite River. He wrote to Malwida von Meysenbug, July, 1895 (*Choix de lettres de Romain Rolland à Malwida von Meysenbug* [Paris, 1948]) that he had no doubts about this God and the soul of the world, the light of Life of which we are but moments. No form of life disappears — God may change but He will always exist, and for the best. Rolland noted that all faiths and all beliefs find their resolution and harmony in this Being. He was convinced that he believed in all faiths; all antinomies are fused in the one Being, who is the same for all but to whom our anthropomorphism lends our own form. The important thing is to awaken this force in each of us. Rolland did not understand why we attach so much importance to the name we give to Him. The name is merely a stage setting — which he too enjoys — but which may change. Only the Eternal does not change.[1]

By a religious sentiment he meant also the feeling of an excess of life, of limitless faith in life. The fullness of life is not limited to those who claim a religious nature. The artist who creates, the savant who seeks and finds, are filled with it. It is found in action, in love, and in maternity. "And you may be very certain that each of these forms of happiness, when it is attained, is perfect and complete in itself" (letter to Mme Cruppi, June 18, 1910). This is the sentiment of God, felt by the adolescent Christophe during a mystic ecstasy. He perceived God; he *was* God. God made the limits of his being burst, and filled the universe (*Jean-Christophe* [Paris, 1950], p. 264). This God was manifested to him in all the life surrounding him, from the smallest to the largest of living things (*Ibid.*, p. 266). Divinity is all that exists; it is the

[1] "Au moins faudrait-il être bien convaincu qu'en défendant toutes les fois, je ne doute d'aucune d'elles, mais que je crois à toutes... toutes les antinomies se fondent en un Etre qui est le même pour tous, mais auquel notre anthropomorphisme donne notre forme à chacun, catholique, panthéiste, sceptique ou même nihiliste; — toujours Dieu, toujours l'éternelle force... L'important est de réveiller cette force en chacun de nous..." (Letter to Alphonse de Châteaubriant, March 15, 1930).

central fire, eternal and immediate, at the core of life. This eternal quality constitutes man's true and essential self, which is independent of the body and of the mind.[2] The conception or description of the divinity as the 'central fire' seems to have come from his studies in the Heraclitan philosophy. For two schools of thought were very important in the formation of Rolland's early philosophy, and through that, of his religious attitudes and beliefs. The first was Spinoza; the second, the pre-Socratic philosophers, Heraclitus and Empedocles among others. In his *Empédocle d'Agrigente suivi de l'Eclair de Spinoza* (Paris, 1931), he tells of the sudden illumination produced in his mind and soul while reading Spinoza's *Ethic*, an illumination in which the infinity and the unity of Being, or Substance, or God, was revealed to him (1882-1884) (See also *Le Voyage intérieur* [Paris, 1959], pp. 31-41). It was not the entire philosophy of Spinoza that appealed to him, but rather the complete sense of freedom that he gained from it. It was not the master in the geometrical demonstration who conquered him, but the realist. Writing about it in 1924, forty years later, Rolland uses lyrical and poetic terms to describe his experience: 'vertige', 'vin de feu', 'horizons inouïs', 'l'Océan de l'Etre'. And all became Peace for him, he said; he enjoyed the fulness and harmony; he participated in a spasm of beatitude which he related to Schiller's "Ode to Joy".

The convincing nature of the intuitive knowledge of Spinoza attracted Rolland more than the philosophy itself. He took especially Spinoza's basic principle of the infinite unity of Nature, with which God is identified (*Deus sive natura*). With the help of the definitions and axioms, Spinoza in his *Ethic* had proved the absolute unity and the infinity of the Substance, and conceived of Thought and Extension as attributes of the Substance, the sole

---

[2] "Je sens très fortement le divin; qui est, comme le feu central, au cœur de toute vie. De cette éternité (ou de cette permanence), j'ai une certitude immédiate et directe... Que le moi persiste, (comme je le crois), ce n'est pas encore à dire qu'il persistera sous la forme qu'il a revêtue, pendant notre vie. Je sens très bien que mon moi est indépendent, non seulement de mon corps, mais de mes pensées. Je sens la puissance de la vie et la force divine qui gonfle l'univers. Je m'assimile à elle, autant qu'il m'est possible; autant qu'il m'est possible, je tâche d'en prendre conscience, d'enjouir et d'en faire jouir ceux que j'aime" (Letter to Mme Cruppi, September 19, 1912).

Reality. His teaching of the Unity and sole existence of Nature, which contains within it the multiplicity of the individual, appealed to Rolland. He took the 'Scientia intuitiva', from the second part of the *Ethic*, as the highest means of knowing, for by it the adequate essence of things (that is, truth) can be seized.

At the age of twenty-two, Rolland, in his "Credo quia verum", had formulated a statement of his philosophy (See *Le Cloître de la rue d'Ulm,* pp. 351-379). In a draft of a letter to Suarès, Easter, 1887, Rolland wrote that he no longer imagined the Substance (in Spinoza's sense) as an IDEA of Reason. He conceived of Being by means of sensation, not reason. I FEEL, he stated, the Being in and by itself; I FEEL the Being in which everything exists, and by which everything exists. He defined Being as that which is All — total sensation, the sensation of being All, complete and free (*Le Cloître,* pp. 77-78; Easter, 1887). He started from the clear, simple, universal notion, "I feel, therefore It exists..."; It is the impersonal Being (i.e., Spinoza's substance). In other notes from the same period, concerning one of his fellow-students he wrote (*Le Cloître,* p. 88), "Thus, both of us believe in the existence of the Ego... Mine is pantheistic, and my individual person is only a tiny part of it."

In his Credo he affirms that only the present situation is absolutely real. Only the Being, by and in itself, is certain; this is the Being, he said, of which Spinoza had an intuition in the first pages of his *Ethic*; it is a need of our spirit, a necessity of our reason. The present and passing Sensation discloses the Being. The Being, however, is not the ephemeral sensation, which cannot be fixed. In every sensation limitless Existence is affirmed. Rolland anticipated the criticism that it was intuition which reveals absolute Being to him, by asking the question: What is intuition? His answer was that intuition is the present (hence REAL) but profound sensation, eternal (therefore CERTAIN), of the One. Thus he proved to his own satisfaction the infinite Unity which contains the Universe. God is everywhere and is all things. God is entirely sensation and the ensemble of all sensations.

As for the question of Liberty, he said that the problem is badly stated. There is no liberty except in the Absolute Being.

Within Him are joined Liberty and Necessity. As a man, Rolland had two means of being free: the first, the way everybody can follow, is to be what he is without worrying about anything else. The second way, the resource of those who think, is to elevate himself to the veritable Being. This divine love becomes an individual in each of us and in those who are close to us; it is clothed in their limbs and their eyes. But we do not realize that this Being which we now embrace is not an individual; it is the universe. Or rather, it is the universe which is embraced within both of the individuals. Thus, he concluded, the exterior world does not exist. But its illusion exists and is imposed on us. There exists nothing but God in his numberless forms. And man is an ephemeral incarnation of God. But man refuses to live as Spinoza wished, by Reason, in Reason. For through Reason he would have only a vague perception of Eternal Life, and he would sacrifice to this vague perception the direct vision of his own existence.

Rolland started from the identity philosophy of Spinoza, but the concept of the unity of the Substance left him unsatisfied. Being seemed to him to be or to consist of two basic principles or drives. He found this in Empedocles and in the Manichean doctrines, as well as in Christianity. But he sought a third principle in which these two could be harmonized. He found it in the divine harmony, which arises from the rhythm of the struggle. Thus all dualistic contrasts, — body and soul, love and hate, object and subject, — would find harmony in an ultimate synthesis.

The dualism which he thus attempted to harmonize came to him from the Pre-Socratic philosophers. When he publicly explained his philosophy in a letter to Ellen Key (*La Revue,* 1914, pp. 171-181), he said that he did not then separate the human spirit from the divine spirit, but that he did not believe that the divine spirit fills the universe; it only attempts to fill the cosmos. The struggle between two principles is clear to him, he wrote, from the long course of history. It is a question of knowing if there is a third principle in which the other two are included or harmonized. The Empedoclean conception of the alternate victory of Love over Hate, and then of Hate over Love had long been familiar to him.

In a letter to Alphonse de Châteaubriant, Feb. 2, 1915, he said
that he was not discouraged nor desperate; never having believed
in progress, he was not astonished by the recurrence of barbarism.
When one is accustomed to the firmament of Spinoza's thought
with its divine mechanism, and able to hear the rhythm of
Empedocles' pendulum: "Eros... Ares... Eros... Ares" (Love...
Strife...), one preserves the peace of intelligence and understanding.

Rolland believed that his ego would persist after death — but
in a changed form. Conscious immortality of the individual
depends upon the universal consciousness of God, in which is
reflected all that has been, that is, and that will be. The more we
participate in this divine life, the more we can hope for conscious
immortality. The immortality he is sure of is less life after death
than consciousness of participation in the deep life forces; he
becomes especially aware of these forces during the act of creation.
At such times he distinctly feels the very core of his being, 'le moi
profond', which is perhaps, he repeated, the core of all life.
And he feels it when he loves and when he is intensely moved.
This is the self whose immortality he is sure of.[3]

All evil is egotism and disappears when our body dies; he
believed that only the divine part of our soul survives, that part
which loves and is heroic, virtuous, and idealistic. In many people
this part does not exist, and they die completely, like animals,
without the possibility of an after-life. Religious practices, prayers,
and masses have nothing to do with this religion and this resurrection. Resurrection and Life consist in the perception of
eternal God. Since He is the Good, the Beautiful, and the True,
all those who love Art with all their soul, who consecrate their
lives to the pursuit of Truth and Beauty, who are charitable and

---

[3] "Pour moi, j'envisage la disparition de tout ce qui constitue ma personalité
aux yeux des autres, sans que cela porte atteinte à mon être véritable. Jamais
je n'ai assimilé celui-ci à mon enveloppe de chair, pas plus qu'à son mécanisme
mental. Quand je crée — (quand je crée vraiment, non pas quand je travaille
après coup sur ma création, d'une manière raisonnée et logique) — je sens
distinctement le moi profond, qui est le noyau de ma vie, — peut-être le noyau
commun de la vie. Et je le sens aussi quand j'aime et quand je sens avec inten-
sité. Voilà le moi auquel je tiens. L'autre, je joue avec. Il arrive qu'il m'ennuie;
alors, je joue avec d'autres" (Letter to Mme Cruppi, August 21, 1910).

who devote themselves to their fellowmen, all these live in God and are immortal. He did not believe in the popular idea of personal immortality (*Journal des années de guerre,* p. 786). What worse condemnation of the individual than to be chained throughout eternity to such an imperfect world?

The immortal life he thus affirms is not the physical, or spiritual, individual life of the body, but the force that pervades all the manifestations of the universe. After several years of self-observation and of reading the Christian and Hindu mystics, he was strongly inclined to feel the universality of his soul in the world-soul, and the permanence of both (see his *Vie de Rama-krishna* [Paris, 1929], and *La Vie de Vivekananda et l'Evangile universel* [Paris, 1930], for his readings in Indian mysticism). HE, the essence of him — call it soul, or the daemonic, whatever it was that was Rolland — existed before his birth, as presumably it will exist after his material death. In *Le Seuil, précédé du Royaume du T* (Geneva, 1946), pp. 93-94 (text of 1926), he declares his belief in existence before birth; the non-physical part of man is sure of survival because it can neither be born nor destroyed. It exists, and has always existed. And this part of man, eternally existing, is the force that he calls life.[4]

This is his religion, his faith, built not on blind acceptance, but solidly constituted of Love and Reason. Faith, he thought, is not solely mysticism, irrational and emotional; it is also the result of lucid reason and of conscious Will. Faith is not the result of revelation alone, but of an inner certainty attained through an intellectual and rational intuition. Inner revelation alone is not sufficient, for it is pure sentiment, incommunicable, not susceptible of proof. To believe means to believe that one knows, and thus belief depends upon will and an authoritarian certainty. Nor should one believe merely because one wishes to

---

[4] "Je n'ai jamais cru à l'anéantissement de l'esprit. Je ne crois pas que l'esprit naisse ni meure. Et ce n'est point par une duperie secrète de mes craintes ou de mes désirs. Car je m'accomoderais, pour moi, du grand repos. Mais mon esprit ne croît pas que le grand repos nous attende. Du moins, pas encore. Je sens partout la vie. Et nos chers disparus ne sont pas les moins vivants" (Letter to Mme Landowski [Mme Louise Cruppi's daughter], February 8, 1925, written after the death of Mme Cruppi).

believe; he must believe because it is the truth. Truth is the ultimate touchstone. The cowardice of refusing to see a troublesome truth is too great a price to pay for the happiness and security of a faith (letter to Mme Bertolini, July 30, 1912; *Chère Sofia,* II, p. 159). Rolland respected beliefs, but he could and did distrust them; if they claimed to be a substitute for reason, he considered them as enemies (letter to Mme Bertolini, Nov. 14, 1913; *Chère Sofia,* II, pp. 188-189).

Rolland's religion, like his art, was strongly conditioned by his sense of responsibility towards mankind. The truly religious person must wish for the happiness of all men, each in his own way. This is what Rolland calls 'foi-amour'; anyone inspired and animated by this loving faith will love men for themselves, not for his own sake or for God's glory. One is selfless; any other faith is egotistical — and hence closely related to evil (letter to Mme Bertolini, June 23, 1912; *Chère Sofia,* II, p. 153).

The essential characteristic of all his thinking is his conception of becoming. His God is perpetual rebirth, ever-changing creation. In his studies on the Indian mystics he said that he did not believe in a personal God, especially not in a God of sadness and pain. He believed rather that there is no God except that which, in man and in the universe, is a perpetual rebirth. Creation is renewed each minute. Religion is never a completed work. It is the act and the will to act, ceaselessly and without repose. It is the surge of the spring, never the pool (*Vie de Ramakrishna,* pp. 15-16).

This conception of religion leaves man completely free; in fact, man develops this divine essence in himself; it exists to the extent that man creates it. Like the existentialist, man is a free agent in the universe; nothing is determined in advance, not even God, not even the victory over error of the Being whom we call God. Error, Evil, and Injustice exist in the world. Man struggles for Good, Beauty, and Light. God struggles in man for the same goals (letter to Louis Gillet, July 13, 1903; *Correspondance entre Louis Gillet et Romain Rolland* [Paris, 1949], p. 218). But the victory is not assured. The tragic and divine element in the universal Being is freedom. For this reason the triumph of one principle over the other cannot be assured in advance. A victory imposed by destiny would be defeat, and the triumph of fate over the divine (see Rolland's letter to Gustinus Ambrosi, March 5, 1923, published by J.B. Barrère, "L'Ame religieuse de Romain Rolland", *Mercure de France* [March 1, 1950], pp. 414-433).

In Rolland we have the spectacle of an intensely religious man who was not a believer in the Church. His reasons for refusing the Church were many and complex. To Louis Gillet he had written that he was not a Christian, and could not again become one. I have only to hear you define Christianity, he said, as a doctrine which is reconciled with everything, to feel loathing for it (letter of March 3, 1900; *Correspondance*, p. 68). Rolland's broad tolerance must not be confused with lack of principles. In fact, he was severe in his demand that the principles one believes in should be the guide of one's life. He set this standard for himself rather than for others. Others may have different beliefs, but they should follow some set of principles. He did not find in the Church this broad and strict requirement.

Another reason was his revolt against and disbelief in the doctrine of original sin, which places the fault of one on the heads of all (*Journal de guerre*, July 2, 1915; pp. 420-421). During the First World War he noted in his journal that the sanctification of suffering was repugnant to him, and that this was what had separated him from religion (*Journal de guerre*, Oct., 1916; p. 935). Such an unjust doctrine, which denies man's responsibility, undoubtedly aroused his opposition when he was very young. Throughout his life, in all his works he insisted that man is a free and responsible agent, and that the individual must be judged by his works and actions, not by his words, appearances, or surroundings. There is perhaps another reason for his rejecting, emotionally as well as rationally, the doctrine of original sin. This was his profound, irrational conception of his soul as something intensely pure and loving. How could he reconcile original sin with his emotional convictions? Organized religion seemed to him to speculate too much on the weaknesses of the individual. As a man he is a free agent; as an individual he is determined to remain faithful to his quest for truth, regardless of comfort and security. Happiness is to be found in truth, not truth in happiness (letter to Mme Bertolini, Oct. 6, 1913; *Chère Sofia,* II, p. 186). Man's attempt to palliate his own weaknesses, to seek refuge in the Church or in some vague cult, was not his conception of religion.

Another cause for his break was the monotheism which was incompatible with his feeling of the all-pervading forces of creation. The monotheistic and monolithic God of the Scriptures, in whose cult he had been reared, repelled him. (*Le Seuil,* pp. 37-38; text of 1926). This God was completely separated from all nature, whereas Rolland felt God in nature; he did not see nature as a mere manifestation of God's power of creation. He had had to accept this religion when a child, because it was a force superior to his parents. It was presented to him as the strongest, and this force implied in the presentation repelled him. He had come very early to feel that force was one of the principal attributes — at least in the minds of His faithful — of this God. And even as a child, he rebelled against this 'monarque étranger' (*Le Seuil,* pp. 40-45).

Besides the acquiescence to force implicit in such a religion, another aspect of the individual's attitude toward religion and of the Church's attitude toward men repelled him. This was the personal self-interest of the members of a church. This reproach he addressed not only to the Catholic Church but to the Christian religion in general, and indeed, to most other organized religions (letter to Louis Gillet, May 2, 1902; *Correspondance,* p. 194). Formalism and ritual were equally foreign to his temperament. During Gandhi's visit in 1931, he wrote in his notes that he found Gandhi's evening prayers beautiful and even impressive, but that he himself felt nothing but indifference towards them (*Inde, Journal 1915-1945* [Paris Lausanne Bâle, 1951], p. 254).

In letters to Raymond Pichard, late in his life, Rolland summarized his position towards the Catholic Church. He did not have an orthodox faith; he admired and respected the Catholic metaphysics, but his respect and veneration were not faith. His intelligence had been given to him in order to recognize the limits of faith; but intelligence is not faith. Only intuition and love, not intelligence, can penetrate to the heart of religion.

But intelligence and doubt are also part of God. Indeed, any manifestation of the mind or spirit is part of the divinity, and cannot be disregarded.[5] He had no intellectual quarrel with Christianity, nothing against the Christian faith — except that it was not his. He saw in it only one form — one of the highest — of human hope. He felt that one must fulfill one's life, with or without hope. Man must be independent of hope.[6]

His admiration and respect for the Catholic dogma were deep, but were not faith. The distance that separated him from true faith was slight but profound. He hoped, in 1943, that he would be enabled to cross that abyss, but the crossing would not be caused by fear or hope. Truth alone could provide the bridge. But truth is also one of the attributes of God, just as is doubt or any other form of the intelligence. And again we arrive at the greatest barrier between Rolland and the Church, namely his demand for absolute freedom of thought and of inquiry (see his letter to Father Raymond Pichard, May 24, 1943).

The essentially combative attitude of Rolland can be perceived in his religious temperament and beliefs. His interest in Empedocles is especially revealing. The struggle between two opposites, and the alternating victories of each over the other left a deep im-

[5] "La grande métaphysique chrétienne catholique est une magnifique cathédrale de l'esprit. Je l'admire, à l'égal de ces autres cathédrales de pierre, qui en sont la robe auguste. — Mais mon respect et mon amour pour cette foi ne sont pourtant pas la foi. L'intelligence m'a été donnée, pour reconnaître loyalement ses limites. Je ne les franchis que par 'la petite espérance,' dont parle Péguy, le rêve du poète, et l'amour. Mais cette intelligence reste au seuil. Elle serait près de prétendre que la consigne qu'elle a reçue de Dieu, est de garder le seuil. Le doute aussi est de Dieu" (Letter to Father Raymond Pichard, October 18, 1941).

[6] "Mais je n'ai rien contre eux [Christians]... Je respecte leur foi, qui fut celle de mon amie la plus chère — ma mère — et j'aime en eux tout ce qu'elle a de beau, de bon, de bienfaisant et d'exaltant... Il n'a pas tenu qu'à moi que je ne l'eusse point. — Mais je ne l'ai point. Je n'y vois qu'une forme (une des plus hautes) de l'espoir humain. J'aime l'espoir... Sans estimer que l'on *doive* se passer d'espoir — (j'en suis bien loin! je l'ai soufflé, autant que j'ai pu) — j'estime que l'on doit *pouvoir* se passer d'espoir, être tout ce qu'on est et doit être, accomplir, sans plier, toute sa destinée, avec ou sans l'espoir, — parce qu'c'est notre raison de vivre et c'est la loi, parce que c'est là seulement être un homme. Un homme ne dépend pas de l'espoir, mais de plus haut que l'espoir..." (Letter to Father Raymond Pichard, October 4, 1939).

pression in him because it struck a responsive chord. Related to this is his belief that not only man is free, but also God — and destiny itself. In fact, God must defend himself and his believers must defend Him in the struggle of conflicting forces in the universe. God's triumph is not certain; if it were, He would not be free but in the grip of a superior destiny. In this area man too is a free and responsible agent; he must struggle also for his development, because nothing is static; everything is in a state of flux, in a continual process of becoming.

The life of a society or a nation is also in a state of continuing change. Any living society or nation is a living organism, dynamic, never static. Rolland's belief in the necessity and duty for the citizen to participate in political action derives from his belief in the continuing process of evolution — but without any pre-ordained direction — to which all living organisms are subject.

Physical death is another stage in this never-ending flux. For those who are truly living, the creative acts — physical, spiritual, intellectual, artistic — live on. Thus Marc is continued by his mother, Annette, after his death, and their combined work is continued by the still younger generation, who build on a foundation consisting of the victories and defeats of their elders. The action of these characters is largely if not entirely political and social. Their spiritual, intellectual, and physical energies, are, as were Rolland's, caught up in an intense effort to solve the main problems of the period between the two World Wars, such questions as pacifism, non-violent resistance, Naziism, Fascism, Communism, Capitalism, social justice.

XV

ROLLAND AND RUSSIA (1917-1937)

If the twenties may be called Rolland's 'oriental period', the thirties may be described as his 'Russian period', if one understands that the label describes his main, but not his sole interest, and that such interests do not have a single origin and do not originate at a specific moment. He had been interested in Russia since the abortive revolutionary action of 1905, which he called one of the greatest deeds of history. He believed that in ten years the revolution would be completed in Europe (letter to Mme Bertolini, Dec. 29, 1905; *Chère Sofia. Choix de lettres de Romain Rolland à Sofia Bertolini Guerrieri-Gonzaga*. II [Paris, 1960], p. 248). His biography of Tolstoy had brought him the acquaintanceship of relatives of the Tolstoy family. Closer contacts with Russia began during the First World War.[1] His relationship with Maxim Gorki was an important factor in his interest in Russia.[2] He wrote to Gorki, May 22, 1922, that he would like to meet him at the international reunion of intellectuals at Varese. In their correspondence they discussed questions concerning Russia and her new society. Rolland spoke commiseratingly of the disillusionment

---

[1] Starr: *Romain Rolland's Internationalism* (University of Oregon Thesis Series, Eugene, Ore., 1939). Starr: *Romain Rolland and a World at War* (Evanston, Ill., 1956). Starr: *A Critical Bibliography of the Published Works of Romain Rolland* (Evanston, Ill., 1951). Cf. especially the introduction.

[2] "Avez-vous lu les articles que publie Gorki? Il en est qui me rappellent les pamphlets de Camille Desmoulins. Une verve comique, mordante, de petites scènes burlesques qui sont de petits chefs-d'œuvre. Mais je vous réponds qu'en France il n'aurait pu en publier la dixième partie. Ah! il ne respecte pas le peuple! Il persifle le progrès en vrai aristocrate. C'est curieux, chez un artiste aussi populaire. — Mais jusqu'à quel point l'est-il, populaire?..." (Letter to Mme Cruppi, August 19, 1918).

with the Russian Revolution that the preceding years had brought
to Gorki. Humanity is still very near the animal level, he said, and
very little is necessary to arouse the taste for cruelty in Occidental
peoples.[3] When Gorki accused the Russian people of cruelty in
their opposition to the intellectuals, Rolland wrote (October 20,
1922) to Alphonse de Châteaubriant that he was not uneasy about
this innate conservatism of the Russian people. He saw in it a
salutary brake on a civilization burning itself up. If scientific
progress, being essentially destructive, were unchecked there would
soon be no more humanity.[4] Russia, he continued, suffers from the
age-difference handicap, just as Germany had suffered from the
retarding effects of the Thirty Years War.[5] He analyzed the
Russian soul (letter to Gorki, Oct. 30, 1923), which he found full
of vitality, above average in intelligence, moved by curiosity, low
in morale, and without any 'moralité' (moral common sense, in
Rolland's mind). The Occident had had an abundance of
administrators to enforce society's rules. The efforts of superior
men in European countries were to rebel against the rules, to

[3] "Il ne faudrait pas grande chose pour que se réveillât dans nos peuples
d'Occident le goût de la cruauté froide, que vous dénoncez avec horreur chez
les paysans russes. L'humanité est encore si près de la bestialité primitive!
Il ne faut qu'un rien pour qu'à tout instant elle y retombe. Et son cerveau —
(cette géniale maladie!) — se combinant avec ses fauves instincts, j'ajoute le
sadisme. On ne peut s'étonner: nous venons de très bas et nous sommes allés
trop vite" (Letter to Maxim Gorki, October 12, 1922; copied in Rolland's
'Journal intime' [May 1, 1922, to December 31, 1923], unpublished).
[4] This does not mean that he was an enemy of science or of the scientific
spirit. His interest in the various branches of science and his desire to study
mathematics have been commented on elsewhere in this biography. At this
time, he continued to regard true science as an invigorating tonic. "Je ne puis
assez applaudir à l'initiative qui a fait introduire dans la Revue *Europe* la
science vivante, avec l'article magistral d'Edouard Monod-Herzen.—C'est un
puissant tonique. Il revigore les revues littéraires, — sans lui toujours un
peu fades. Je ne saurais plus m'en passer" (Letter to J.-R. Bloch, July 2, 1924).
[5] "Au lieu que l'Angleterre et la France ont avancé, jour par jour, étape par
étape, l'Allemagne a brûlé les étapes, et elle est arrivée, haletante, convulsée,
les yeux lui sortant de la tête, au *salto mortale* de 1914; elle aura beau se relever,
elle sera toujours, maintenant, le pays des grands bonds et des chutes au fond;
de l'un à l'autre extrême: tyran ou asservie [*sic*]. — Eh bien, votre Russie
me paraît souffrir de ce qu'elle n'est pas venue 'à l'heure', dans la civilisation
d'Europe" (Letter to Maxim Gorki, October 4, 1923, copied in the unpublished
'Journal intime' [May, 1922 — December, 1923]).

break through them when they become unyielding social chains (class, caste, or nation). This is the law of vital equilibrium. However the opposite condition obtains in Russia. There, nothing checks the people. Russia, he thought, needed an iron discipline; but, he cautioned, for discipline to become part of the Russian way of living and thinking, a great deal of time will be necessary. Discipline however is not violence; he never condoned the violence that he saw in various acts of the Russian government or people. In fact, he felt that the human spirit in this respect had retrogressed; war and violence are poisons infecting revolutionaries and conservatives alike. There are differences of ideas, but not of methods, between fascists and bolsheviki (letter to Mme Bertolini, Dec. 31, 1922; *Chère Sofia*, II, pp. 290-291).

His conception of revolution was very broad. He did not hold up either the French or the Russian revolution as models worthy of imitation or admiration. He wrote to Georg Brandes that he did not have 'la religion de la Révolution française'. It had excited his enthusiasm from an esthetic point of view as an exaltation of human vitality, but he had not intended to idealize it in his plays (letter dated Feb. 25, 1922; *Correspondance de Georg Brandes* [Copenhagen, 1952], I, 432-434). In a letter to the Russian State Academy of Arts and Sciences, October 20, 1925, he defined very clearly his conception of Revolution. It is less a course of action than a spirit which never admits the petrification of forms of life or of society, which tolerates no social falsehood, which is incessantly at war with prejudices, and which ceaselessly reconstructs human society. Again his deeply rooted feeling and intuition of the continual flux of all existence, the idea of never-ending change, is the basis of this definition. In this view, each social and political form marks only one hour on the dial of Life. No form is eternal; everything that exists is in constant change. When the discrepancy between the fixed forms of the past and the new conditions of the present are great, the result is a sharp change. If resistance is too great, violence will result; otherwise, changes may be accomplished without violence.[6] It is true

6 The letter as it appeared in *Quinze ans de combat* (Paris, 1935), varies somewhat from the form in which he wrote to Kamenev, October 20, 1925. We

that this spirit need not be one of violent revolution. But this does not mean that Rolland condemned or condoned revolutionary violence. Revolution is a part of evolution. "I do not condemn revolution", he wrote to E. R. Relgis, July 24, 1928, in reply to the statement made by the latter that "We condemn revolution because we are against all violence."[7] "I believe that revolution, like evolution, is a necessary and inevitable part and form of human development; it is the 'sudden variation' of De Vries, a law, not yet defined, but august in its cruel brutality. The change can be an explosion of enthusiasm and love, as was the French Revolution in its beginnings. Revolution is an almost inevitable rhythm in the symphony of history." History had shown, he wrote, the inevitable succession of causes and effects, of the past and the future; however, that view is incomplete, for the total comprises more than the sum of its elements; the links are not discernable ahead of time. Periodically, in the course of evolution, there is a sudden mutation. It is as if a new being were born, in which are embodied all the expressions of the spirit and of social life, a new form of the human conscience ("Introduction" to Henry Prunières: *Une nouvelle histoire de la musique* [Paris, 1934]).

---

reproduce here the principal paragraph, exactly as Rolland recorded it in his diary:

"L'Esprit vraiment révolutionnaire est celui qui n'admet jamais que se figent les formes de la vie, et, sous ces formes, que s'arrête le torrent. L'esprit vraiment révolutionnaire est celui qui ne tolère aucun mensonge social, et — ce qui est bien autrement important encore et bien plus difficile à combattre — aucun mensonge avec soi-même. L'esprit vraiment révolutionnaire est incessamment en guerre avec tous les préjugés qu'incessamment reconstruit la société humaine, sur les ruines de ceux qu'elle a détruits" (Letter to O. Kamenev, President of the Société de l'Union pour les rapports culturels avec l'étranger, and to P. Kogan, president of the Comité de l'exposition de l'art révolutionnaire de l'Occident [October 20, 1925]; copy in Rolland's 'Journal'). And see his "Panorama" in *Quinze ans de combat* (Paris, 1935), p. xxxvii. This is essentially the same idea that he had already expressed in "Les Idoles", *Journal de Genève* (December 10, 1914) (later in *Au-dessus de la mêlée* [Paris, 1915]). See also his letter to *Le Bonnet rouge* in its number of November 17, 1916. Here he attacked the tendency of man to allow a social or artistic form to become an ideal that holds tyrannical sway over the present. See my *Romain Rolland and a World at War* (Evanston, 1956), pp. 42-43, 129.

[7] Relgis published the letter in hi *Romain Rolland* (Montevideo, 1950), pp. 77-78.

Evolution is not an end in itself, but a stage in man's progress (*Europe* [July 15, 1939], 289-302). It comes about because the intelligence matures in a natural process. Man escapes blind necessity or fate as he penetrates and understands the laws of this evolution. In this sense revolution is more than a political struggle, and the Revolution of '89 more than the political overthrow of the Ancien Régime and the victory of one class over another. It was the rupture with the preceding epochs of the enslavement of man to destiny. It was accomplished by reason, which was the incomparable strength of the great revolutionaries. In this respect, '89 is superior to the present, when revolution (at least the Russian Revolution) surrounds reason with such close guard that it seems less like a protégé than a prisoner.

What is important is the building of a more just and humane society. During the years of the bitterest anti-Russian propaganda and coalitions, Rolland vigorously defended the new society he believed was being created in the U.S.S.R. Notwithstanding his belief in the attainments of the Soviets, he firmly refused to join the Communist Party. In Henri Barbusse's *Monde* (March 9, 1929, pp. 2, 15), Jean Tousseul quoted Rolland, who had assured him that he was not a Communist and did not share the theories of Moscow, but that he felt it his duty to form a solid front with the Soviet revolution against its enemies, no matter what the errors of the Soviet governments, if the forward march of humanity is to be ensured.[8] Two years after this statement he was even more emphatic about his independent position in respect to the Communist Party — and his equally firm resolve to defend the U.S.S.R. He had never been and never would be a communist, he wrote, but it was his duty to protect the Russian people and their revolution

---

[8] "Je ne suis point communiste et je ne partage point les théories de Moscou. Mais je défendrai toujours, de toute mon énergie, la Révolution russe et ses conquêtes... Quelles qu'aient été les erreurs politiques des gouvernements soviétiques (et certes elles ne sont pas plus graves que ne le furent jadis celles de notre Révolution française), notre devoir est de faire front avec la Révolution Soviétique contre ses ennemis, si nous voulons assurer la marche en avant de l'humanité" (Rolland, in *L'Appel des Soviets* [November, 1928]; quoted by Jean Tousseul).

against counterrevolution.[9] Whatever authority Rolland had in this struggle was because of his absolute independence, his refusal to enroll in any party, and his sincere attempts at impartial judgments and criticisms.[10]

There were many aspects of the new Russia that aroused Rolland's admiration and affection, not the least of which was its young people. He felt that he knew Soviet youth through the letters that he continually received from young Russians — and through those he met during his trip to Russia. What interested him most was their admirable vitality, their great zeal for life, and their interest in the reconstruction of their country, in the construction of a new society and a new world. He praised their freedom from race prejudices, their freedom from race consciousness, their joy and optimism, their sincerity, and their eagerness to eradicate the flaws they found in themselves.[11]

Rolland had long wished to visit this vast and rather mysterious country. In 1931, Kalatov, director of the state publishing company, invited him to spend the summer there. Rolland however felt obliged to decline the invitation, in part because of the advanced age of his father (ninety-five), but more because of his own poor health. He believed that it would be difficult to replace him in the

[9]   "Beaucoup d'entre nous (et celui qui écrit ces lignes) n'ont jamais été, ne seront jamais des communistes. Je mourrai libre individualiste, comme j'ai vécu. Et parmi les communistes d'Occident, combien rejettent la direction politique de Moscou! Mais aujourd'hui, trêve à toutes les directions! Contre l'ennemi commun nous nous groupons. Individualistes ou communistes, ou socialistes ou syndicalistes… nous ne tolérerons pas que, sous le couvert menteur de la religion et de la justice, et de la civilisation et de l'humanité, les plus immondes réactions, celle de l'argent, celle du sabre, celle de la trique, celle de la tiare, asservissent notre Occident et prétendent lancer nos peuples contre les grands peuples frères de la Révolution russe et contre leur effort héroïque" ("Avec le grand peuple russe. Deux voix lancent l'appel contre les forces de réaction. Romain Rolland. Theodore Dreiser", *Monde* [April 19, 1930], 3). See also Rolland's reply to the Poll: "Quelle sera votre attitude en cas d'agression contre l'Union soviétique?" His statement was published in *L'Humanité* (July 9, 1930), 4. *L'Humanité*, originally a socialist paper, has been a Communist Party newspaper since 1920.

[10]   See his letter to Gorki (Jan. 8, 1931), published in *La Nouvelle critique*, special number (Summer, 1950), 36-40. The letter is an extract from the projected book by René Plaud: *La Vie et l'Œuvre de Gorki,* with a preface by Rolland.

[11]   Rolland, "XIXe anniversaire de la révolution", *Regards* (Nov. 11, 1936).

ranks of the defenders of Soviet Russia, should he disappear.[12]
He finally made the trip in 1935, after his second marriage. In a
letter to Maxim Gorki, May 12, 1935, Rolland discussed at length
the arrangements for the trip. He left Villeneuve on June 17,
and spent three weeks in Russia at Moscow and at Gorki's nearby
country home.[13] His enthusiasm for what he saw in Moscow
was great. In his farewell letter to Stalin, with whom he had
conversed at length (*L'Humanité,* July 22, 1935, p. 1), he expressed
his pleasure at having come into such stimulating contact with a
people busy creating a new world in a surge of heroic but regulated
enthusiasm. What he saw and felt confirmed him in what he had
intuitively known concerning Russia before his visit.[14] The dominant impression he received was of the powerful afflux of vitality —
young people, bursting with the consciousness of strength and
vigor. He felt this strength in his personal contacts, in the display
and parade he witnessed in the Red Square, in the sentiments
expressed unanimously by the delegations of workers, and especially in the numerous letters he received from all parts of Russia.
They partook of a collective movement — of joy, faith, and certainty in the truth and victory of their cause. He admitted that
there was only one head: the Communist Party; but of its leaders
he wrote glowingly that the basis of their nature and their action
is an unshakeable faith in a doctrine which embraces the totality
of human problems and which concentrates on social action.
The essence of their doctrine is a dialectic; it continually adapts
itself to the ceaseless movements of eternally evolving nature.
Thus it has the character of a great scientific hypothesis in the

[12] Romain Rolland écrit que cela [the trip to Moscow] ne lui sera sans doute
pas possible. "Ma santé... est très chancelante, surtout après la pneumonie
dont j'ai été atteint l'an passé... ma vie (à laquelle personnellement je ne tiens
pas beaucoup) vaut d'être prolongée de quelques années encore, car je me rends
bien compte que, dans les rangs des défenseurs de l'U.R.S.S., il serait très difficile
de me remplacer en Occident." "Notes et réflexions", *La Métropole* (Antwerp,
Aug. 9, 1931).
[13] Letter to Alphonse de Châteaubriant (June 16, 1935). J.-B. Barrère,
Romain Rolland par lui-méme (Paris, 1955), p. 185, gives the dates of the trip
as June 23 to July 21; these are probably the dates of his arrival at and departure
from Moscow.
[14] See his "Retour de Moscou", *Commune* (Oct., 1935), 129-133.

period of its development, when the system built upon it corresponds triumphantly to all the data of experimentation and thus opens new paths of investigation.

The characteristic of the leaders, he believed, was this faith in their cause, and their will to devote themselves to its service -- with the certainty that it will triumph, with or without them. This passionate disinterestedness distinguished them from the Italian Fascist leaders and constituted their great superiority. Such men as Stalin breathed optimism and certainty, without illusions but also without fear — because they were working for the finer, better, more just future for all humanity.[15]

These men of faith and this materialistic dynamism on which their universe rests, or turns, move toward an ideal of social justice and pan-humanism, which is the most idealistic of man's dreams. Rolland was attracted by this idealism. He had stated in his *Vie de Ramakrishna* (Paris, 1929), that there is more religious faith in the Russian people than in many a religious man of Western Europe (pp. 14-15). They call themselves 'realists' because they endeavor to bring their ideals into reality. But they are animated by a flame of idealism at times sentimental and utopian.

His trip to Soviet Russia was greeted in Europe with silence, although there were some attacks and carping articles, especially in the periodical press. Distorted accounts caused Rolland to feel impelled to defend the U.S.S.R., international peace, the League of Nations Pact, and himself, in *L'Humanité* ("Aux calomniateurs", Sept. 9, 1935). After the appearance of André Gide's *Retour de l'U.R.S.S.* (Paris, 1936), Rolland wrote a biting article (*L'Humanité,* Jan. 17, 1937).

His defense of the U.S.S.R., however, if unflagging, was not uncritical. He had written in 1924 that he was very suspicious of Moscow. The battle, a gigantic one, between Washington and Moscow had started. It would have the entire world for battlefield. He insisted on his admiration (for different reasons) for the energy and boldness of the two colossal saurians who would

---

[15] "Retour de Moscou", *Commune* (Oct. 1935), 129-133. He called Fascism a Bolshevism in reverse. See his letter to Eugen Relgis, in Barrère, *Romain Rolland par lui-même,* p. 165.

confront each other, — and especially for Moscow, which, with a very sure eye had been able to see the revolt latent in all the races of the world and was working to bind them all together around herself. But he was not, he assured Mme Cruppi, the sort to be used as a tool for these designs.[16] In *L'Ame enchantée* (*L'Enfantement,* 1933, I, p. 58), Rolland called the Russian dictatorship an ideological, social, economic, and police-state dictatorship, established with an iron hand over the immense Union of Soviet Socialist Republics; they would like, he said, to establish it over the rest of the world.

On the other hand, Rolland praised the cooperative and collective operations carried on by the Soviet Union, the cooperation of science and labor in their conquest of nature. These attempts seemed to point the way for fruitful cooperation all over the world (letter to Mrs. Dwight I. Chapman, May 18, 1935). After his return from Moscow, he wrote Gorki a long and highly enthusiastic letter about his impressions of Russia (*La Nouvelle critique,* special number, [Summer, 1950], 36-40). As the world crisis provoked by fascism became more and more acute, Rolland's defense of the Soviet Union became more and more unquestioning. In his New Year's Message for the U.S.S.R., which appeared in *L'Humanité* on January 5, 1937, he stated flatly that at that time he wanted to express his confidence and faith in the Soviet Union, its immense people, and its leaders. Adverse criticisms from his pen at this time were very few, and very general and vague; for example, in a text of 1940, considering the errors of socialism in extirpating all traces of religious sentiment, he stated that no dialectical materialism, no matter how intelligent, could substitute for religion. The goals of Russia and of socialism are very important and very difficult, and all the energies of man, his mysticism and

---

[16] "Je me méfie beaucoup de Moscou. J'entends n'être pas son instrument. — La lutte (une lutte gigantesque) est engagée entre Washington et Moscou. Elle aura pour champ de bataille le monde entier... J'admire l'énergie et l'audace des deux sauriens colossaux qui vont s'affronter, — et surtout de celui de Moscou, qui, d'un coup d'œil très sûr, a maintenant su lire au fond de la révolte de toutes les races du monde, et travaille à les nouer en tresse autour de sa tête de Méduse. Mais je ne suis pas fait pour servir ses desseins" (Letter to Mme Cruppi, Sept. 17, 1924).

his ethics are needed. It was because the Soviet Union forgot this fact that it had sometimes committed almost mortal errors (*Souvenirs de jeunesse* [Lausanne, 1947], p. 185).

Rolland's interest was deeper than a mere sympathy with a promising social experiment. He believed that the Russian people represented a stage of human development that he himself had long been working for. He had made some efforts towards developing a people's art in the theater at a time when it was impossible because there was no true people conscious of its roots, common interests, and needs for collective action and thinking. Such a condition existed now in Russia. The people (le peuple) which he had been seeking in Western Europe he now found in Russia (see "A Gorki. Lettre de Romain Rolland au *Gazette littéraire...*", *Les Nouvelles soviétiques* [July, 1931]). Proof of this affinity appeared to him in the wide influence his own *Théâtre du peuple* was having in Russia.[17]

Rolland insisted at the same time on his right to criticize. In his polemic with Henri Barbusse he had insisted that the application of Marxism was too rigid and mechanical for human society, which is infinitely complex and varied.[18] But his adverse criticisms of Russia's government, like those of France in *La Foire sur la place* (*Jean-Christophe*), and in *Au-dessus de la mêlée*, were made for guidance and improvement. His criticisms did not imply condemnation of the U.S.S.R. On the contrary, the very brutality of Moscow in the service of exploited classes — Rolland, after the war, was convinced of the fact and the necessity of class struggle — was like a fresh wind, purifying and stimulating in comparison to unorganized, spineless, and hypocritical liberalism of the Occident. This kind of liberalism plays into the hands of the worst exploiters of men.[19]

[17]   Nina Gourfinkel, *Le Théâtre russe contemporain* (Paris, 1931). See also Rolland's letter to J.-R. Bloch (May 2, 1931): "Indépendamment de cette satisfaction personnelle, que je ne crains pas d'avouer, (car c'était là un de mes vœux cachés), j'ai jubilé en assistant à cette extraordinaire floraison. Ah! quel malheur de n'être point né là-bas!"

[18]   See Starr, *Romain Rolland's Internationalism,* and Starr, "Romain Rolland and Russia", *Romanic Review* (April, 1949), 106-113, for discussions of this point.

[19]   Rolland's sempiternal fight for energetic action, strength, faith, courage,

Consciousness of the class struggle implies the responsibility of the writer. Rolland wrote to Henry Chabral, June 4, 1931, that the individual soul can find salvation by faith, love, or free reason. But if it does not wish this salvation to be an escape from the mass in which its body has its roots and in which it sows its seed, the soul must face the terrible problems of the exploited classes and masses on which is built the heavy structure of our civilization (letter published by Pierre Grappin, *Annales de l'Université de Paris* [Oct.-Dec., 1950], 434-444). The class he identified himself with was the great mass of people who must work for their living and who are largely responsible for all the products necessary for man's physical needs and comforts, and even for man's spiritual needs. In 1934 he wrote to Maurice Thorez for the testimonial celebration offered to one of the early fighters for the French workers, Marcel Cachin, hailing the faithful servant of the proletariat (which was, he said, a fine title) who had not ceased giving himself generously to the cause of reason, justice, and man's happiness (*L'Humanité,* Sept. 12, 1934).

All the events of the late thirties seemed to him to be leading in the direction of the elimination of all but this one conflict. The Spanish Civil War was the beginning of the process. All parties were international now; there were the internationalisms of the peoples of the world, of financial powers which had placed everything under the yoke of the State, and of nationalisms themselves. When the field was swept clean of ruins only two armies would be left: the army of the reaction and the army of the revolution. And as soon as the problem has reached that stage, he continued, its solution will be imminent. The immense mass of the people of all countries, workers, farmers, free intellectuals, and the new proletariat formed from the middle classes, will become masters of their house — the world.[20]

In France the party that was leading in this fight was the Parti Communiste Français; Rolland wrote the Party a letter of

positive will, and lucid thinking followed by action — a fight he waged since before 1900 — can readily be discerned here. "Mieux vaut le mal entier que le bien émasculé", *Mahatma Gandhi* (Paris, 72nd ed.), p. 186.

[20] Rolland, "Le Duel", *Regards* (July 14, 1937). Text dated June 25, 1937.

appreciation for the address devoted to him during its eighth convention. In the letter (*L'Humanité,* Jan. 27, 1936) he called its members his comrades, and expressed his joy at having found, after almost a lifetime of seeking, the broad highway leading to victory over the ruins of the past. The peoples who go up this road are establishing a rational order of justice and humanity. The movement was triumphant in Russia, and the Parti Communiste Français was aiding in its universal development. He again addressed enthusiastic letters to the Party in January and December, 1937 (*L'Humanité,* Jan. 25, Dec. 25, 1937). He declared that the Party had become, by the logic of the historical process and its own wisdom, the true representative of the French people and their national and international policies; it was the strongest and most logical representative of social justice.

His defense of the new Russia was accompanied by his fight against Fascism. In 1923 Fascism had seemed to him to be a transition movement of peculiarly Italian character, but he then really knew little about it.[21] By September, 1925, he had begun to perceive the danger of the rising movement (letter to J.-R. Bloch, Sept. 5, 1925). He had just received a first-hand account, and was ashamed of the French intellectuals who were doing nothing and of the French government, which was supporting the regimes of Primo de Rivera and Mussolini. Ten years later he was completely clear as to the nature of Fascism, and he defined it very broadly. In *L'Humanité* (July 25, 1935, p. 1) and in *Quinze ans de combat* (Paris, 1935, pp. 207-210), he called it a nationalist statism which had dozens of deceptive masks, military or clerical, capitalist or democratic, even socialist. The characteristic is that it subordinates everything to the state. Its essence, he assured the readers of *L'Humanité,* September 11, 1936, is the delirious ideology of the supremacy of one race, people, or nation over all others. In this respect it differs from the old imperialism, which tended to conquer new territories for the enrichment of the metropolitan state, and

---

[21] Letter to Alberto de Angelis, Nov. 23, 1923; published by de Angelis, "Ricordo di Romain Rolland", *Nuova Antologia* (Sept.-Dec., 1945), 387-395.

incidentally or accidentally did some good. Fascisms on the other hand live on war and on war alone.[22]

By 1927 Rolland had become so convinced of the prime necessity of action against Fascism that he accepted with Albert Einstein and Henri Barbusse, the honorary chairmanship of the first great antifascist meeting, at the Salle Bullier in Paris, February 23, 1927, under the chairmanship of Professor Paul Langevin.[23] In April, 1927, the 'Comité de défense des victimes de la terreur blanche', sent a telegram signed by Barbusse, Rolland, and Einstein to President Coolidge in protest against the persecution of Sacco and Vanzetti (see Le Populaire, April 12, 1927). The following year, in a letter to the Sonntagsberg Convention in Austria, Rolland called for the creation of an 'Internationale de la Paix', a federalization of all the opponents of war.[24] In 1929, the 'Union des écrivains démocrates', whose purpose was the defense of peace, had founded a section especially for writers desirous of participating in a pacifist movement. The section, which was not a political action body, counted among its adherents Herriot, Rolland, Barbusse, Einstein, Emil Ludwig, and Upton Sinclair (see La Revue du centre [Nevers, March, 1931]).

In the spring and summer of 1932 he was busy with preparations for the World Congress against War and Fascism, which was to meet at Amsterdam in August, and of which Barbusse was the principal organizer (letter to Eugen Relgis, Aug. 26, 1932, in Relgis, Romain Rolland [Montevideo, 1951], pp. 158-160; see also Rolland, "Peoples and Wars", The Nation [Sept. 21, 1932], 251-252). He insisted on the necessity of a Congress of all parties; unfortunately however, the only energy then at work was in the extreme left-wing parties. The bourgeois intellectuals were too egoistic to act, or wished to wait and see what would happen

[22] The same, or a very similar article appeared in English: Rolland, "The Brussels Peace Conference. A Message to the Congress", Labour Monthly (Oct., 1936), 625-628.

[23] See Madeleine Brunelle, "Le vrai Romain Rolland", La Pensée (Jan.-Feb., 1952), 41-50.

[24] Letter dated July 24, 1928; see Eugen Relgis, Romain Rolland (Montevideo, 1951), pp. 78-79.

before committing themselves (letter to Stefan Zweig, May 31, 1932).[25]

In June, 1933, Rolland was named honorary chairman of the 'Comité Antifasciste International', which held its first meeting in the Salle Pleyel under the direction of J.-R. Bloch, Henri Barbusse, and Paul Vaillant-Couturier (see Madeleine Brunelle, in La Pensée [Jan.-Feb., 1952], 41-50). Rolland was also honorary chairman, along with Barbusse, Langevin, and Margueritte, of a 'Comité d'Amnistie et de défense des Indochinois et peuples colonisés', formed in 1933-1934 after the mutiny of Yen-Bay, and the trials at Hanoi and Saigon (1930-1933). In June, 1936, he inspired the organization of the 'Comité mondial contre la guerre et le fascisme', with Langevin, Norman Angell, and Francis Jourdain, the artist and sculptor (See Brunelle, in La Pensée [Jan.-Febr., 1952], 41-50). In September of the same year, he addressed a message to the 'Congrès de la Paix', parts of which were published in L'Humanité [September 6, 1936].

After the savage attacks in Spain by nationalist-led Moorish troops, — the bombardments of open cities, hospitals, and populous city quarters, — Rolland, intensely indignant, appealed to all nations for help for the victims of the war (L'Humanité, Nov. 22, 1936, and in Europe [Sept.-Dec., 1936], 565-566). He predicted the eventual bombing of Rome, Berlin, London, and Paris. Republican Spain, the Spain of the Frente popular government, he called the Chevalier de l'Humanité (France-Espagne, Nov. 11, 1936).

As early as 1933 he had outlined a policy for dealing with Hitler, and he adhered to this line of thought until the Peace of Munich in 1938. In an article "La Paix est mortelle pour l'hitlé-

[25] See Annette Vidal, "Henri Barbusse et Romain Rolland", Les Lettres françaises (Sept. 14, 1950), p. 8; also his message read at the first meeting of the convention, and his account of the meeting and the opposition to it, in Europe (Sept. 15, 1932), 149-151, 249-255; both the latter were published later in his Par la Révolution, la paix, pp. 45-49. The translation of his message appeared in The Nation as "Peoples and Wars" (Sept. 21, 1932), 251-252. See also his greeting to the Congress, read by Guy Jerram, and published in L'Humanité (Sept. 3, 1932). For further details about his part in the organization of the meetings, see his correspondence with Stefan Zweig, especially letters of July 20, 25, 27, 1932.

risme" (*Monde,* March 24, 1933), he repeated that peace alone is mortal to dictators and that war is the last resort of bankrupt states. Two years later he called for an alliance between France, Russia, and Great Britain to maintain peace and thus throttle Hitler (see his article in *Monde,* March 29, 1935; also in *Par la révolution, la paix* [Paris, 1935], pp. 169-171). The only way to stop the impending war, he said, was to form the compact wall of Britain, France and Russia (*L'Humanité,* March 7, 1936). Nations must be strong, determined, and allied against any infraction of European security in order effectively to apply sanctions. True security is the welfare of all, and the pact must be open to all nations. Such a pact should not be for the purpose of maintaining the *status quo.* Unjust treaties, such as the Versailles Treaties, must be revised, but in such a way as to show strength, not compromise or weakness. The opponents of Hitler must show no weakness.

If Fascism seemed more immediately menacing to him than colonialism, his indignation against the latter can be seen in his increasingly sweeping condemnations of contemporary Western European society. Such odious manifestations of imperialism as the war the French carried on in Morocco in 1924-1925 had aroused his opposition. In reply to Barbusse's one-sided poll concerning the Riff War (*Clarté,* July 15, 1925, p. 272), Rolland had said that he joined enthusiastically in the protest against the war. In the first place it was ruinous for France, and an error even from a narrowly national point of view. As he had warned of the long-range evil results of colonial policies during the First World War, he warned in 1925 of the danger of loosing upon Europe the gigantic insurrection of Asian and African races against the brutal and greedy imperialism of European nations. He included the Communists in his warning. They saw only the overthrow of imperialism in this arousal of Oriental peoples; but the forces thus aroused would not distinguish between European imperialism and European communism; Moscow's bolshevism might some day perish under the Asian steam roller. The iron net in which the Christian civilizations of Europe were caught was imperialism. France had done some good things in Algeria, but its Empire there was founded on crime, force, and injustice, and only evil could result. Britain and India were in the same dilemma. He hoped that the United States would profit by the mistakes of other nations and reverse the policies that were building up future storms in the Pacific and South America. In this imbroglio, the only chance for world salvation was to put the brakes on the machinery of imperialism — armies and money — and call a real States General Council to seek an honest *modus vivendi*. The peoples of the world must take part, for theirs was the only true will for peace. The League of Nations — which he termed ludicrous — was of no avail, for it represented the governments, not the peoples.[26]

He criticized modern Democracies for their duplicity, especially when they claim to spread civilization by colonialism. Europe had profited materially form this oppression of other races. He also warned against Pan-Europeanism which was being organized by the very states recently at swords' points. Pan-Europeanism was merely a means for them to exploit and pillage other parts of the world (*L'Humanité,* May 20, 1931).

As the Japanese and Chinese war lords grew bolder, Rolland appealed to his readers to aid in the establishment of true peace, impossible in these two countries as long as they bowed under the yoke of the generals (*L'Humanité,* Nov. 4, 1931). European and American coalitions of capitalists and imperialists must be eliminated from Asia in order to bring about true peace. Such action would of course lead to revolutionary social changes. He hoped that the Chinese and Japanese would overthrow these groups; and he hoped that such changes would be brought about also in Europe and America. He called on the peoples of the world to combat the fascist, plutocratic, imperialist conspiracy of the Japanese invasion of China. The governments of Europe and America — and the French government first and foremost — were utilizing Japanese imperialism as a headsman's axe to decapitate the revolution in China ("Nous en appelons...", *Europe* [Jan.-April, 1932], 472).

The Abyssinian war represented another grave threat to the

[26]   Rolland, "The Iron Net", *Survey Graphic* (Aug. 1, 1926), 495-496.

peace of the world. It was especially dangerous, he thought, because the Third Reich hoped to profit by it. He called on the intellectuals of the world to assume their proper place in the battle against war and Fascism. But the peace he was working for was not merely a 'front' for imperialism, old or new, but one based on justice, freedom, and equality. At that moment the walls of the Kremlin were the master pillar of the whole edifice of peace — as far as it had been constructed.[27]

These questions all have to do with the principal line of action that Rolland had been following since 1918: the attainment and preservation of peace. The peace he meant he had defined clearly in 1928. There is the peace of force, as embodied in the Versailles Treaties, almost the only kind now known in the world. But even this peace was no longer possible for extended periods of time. A new idea was arising that made it archaic. The new ideal was the fatherland of all humanity, world-wide. The old ideal of the national fatherland was moribund. A true peace, for which people must have the will to work, would be the fraternal peace of the workers of the world ('La Volonté de paix', in *La Volonté de paix* [Oct.-Dec., 1928]; published later in *Par la révolution, la paix,* pp. 100-104). A peace based on the political, social, and economic status quo of Europe would be impossible; it was an illusion and a non-sense, he said, and quoted from Senator Borah to prove his point (*Par la révolution, la paix,* pp. 108-109). The causes of war he found in the industrial and financial groups which profit from it. However, since these in their turn were merely outgrowths of imperialistic, capitalistic society, the entire social order would have to be changed if they were to be changed. Thus he concluded that revolution was necessary ("Appel à la ligue des combattants de la paix", *Par la révolution, la paix,* pp. 31-36).

In considering how such changes are to be accomplished, there arises immediately the question of violence. Rolland's pacifism was an active force, a positive attack against evil, against all that produces war. It was not the path of least resistance or of weakness.

---

[27] Rolland, "Le plus grand danger. Pour la Conférence plénière du Mouvement Mondial contre la guerre et le fascisme, réunie à Paris le 23-24 novembre 1935", in *Comment empêcher la guerre* (Paris, 1936), pp. 7-11.

He did not, for instance, agree with Bertrand Russell that anything is better than war. On the contrary, "Le pire des maux est l'avilissement, le reniement d'un homme ou d'un peuple (the greatest of evils is the degradation and denial of a man or of a people)", he wrote to Georges Pioch, April 13, 1933 (*Comment empêcher la guerre* [Paris, 1936], pp. 20 ff). His pacifism was resistance and courageous action. He was subsequently accused of renouncing his pacifism and of having recourse to violence. In a letter of 1931 to Jean Guéhenno, he protested that he did not and never would approve of violence; but there are many things in the universe that must be accepted without approval — life and its mutual destruction, as it has been imposed on us, for example. The problem of today's action would be to bring about the union of non-violence and revolution. He had just finished reading Gandhi's autobiography (*The Story of My Experiments With Truth*), which he called a marvellous breviary of reason and action, and he was convinced that the union of the two is possible and fecund under certain conditions.[28]

However, four years later conditions in Western Europe seemed to him not only unfavorable but actually contrary to the effectiveness of non-violence, as he assured Subhas Chandras Bose in a letter dated April 27, 1935; he had come to the conclusion that it could not be the pivot of all social action. It was only one of many possible forms of action, and still in an experimental stage. All means must be used against the old social order, which is a criminal order and does not hesitate to attack its enemies by any and all means. His task was, he repeated, to endeavor to unite the forces of non-violence and revolutionary action, violent if necessary (*Inde,* pp. 384-385). To those who, like Gandhi, proposed passive resistance, Rolland in 1936 opposed the difference between Western Europe and India. In his article "L'Indivisible paix", he pointed out that Gandhi had not succeeded in this movement in a country of 300 millions of people accustomed for centuries to the teaching of 'ahimsa'. What could Europeans do, who had

[28] Letter to Charles Baudouin (March 14, 1931); published in *Hommages à Romain Rolland* (Geneva, 1945), pp. 152-158.

a different history and had been deprived of their leaders, of their élite of workers and intellectuals? And thus non-violent resistance became a remote ideal for him, attainment of which lay in the future.

XVI

LAST YEARS OF A NON-CONFORMIST (1934-1944)

The course of action and thinking which we have tried to outline in some detail as well as in its broad lineaments, had not developed without difficulty. The First World War years had been a period of great change, and in the rapidly shifting atmosphere of the post-war period, all of Rolland's strength and powers of concentration had been strained. The years 1930 and 1931 were particularly grave for him. His farewell to many previously held ideas, ideals, and beliefs, was expressed in his "Adieu au passé", in 1931 (*Quinze ans de combat* [Paris, 1935]). Concerning this account of his break with the past, he wrote — for publication — to Feodor Nikolaevitch Petrov that this article was only a symbol, and that he had actually reached that point as early as 1917.[1] But to Stefan Zweig he wrote (June 10, 1931) that the years 1930-1931 were a more tragic period for him than 1914 had been, and that the change had been great.[2]

In the spring of 1934, he celebrated his second marriage, with Mme Marie Koudachova. The union had its origin in a corre-

---

[1] The letter appeared in German translation in *Das Neue Russland* (May-June, 1931), p. 33; and in *La Revue des indépendants* (Nov. 1, 1931). See my *Critical Bibliography of the Published Writings of Romain Rolland* (Evanston, 1951), no. 445.

[2] "Je m'arrête, je ne devrais pas me fatiguer, ces jours de cure, avec toutes ces pensées qui me brûlent et que j'ai, depuis des mois, des ans, amassées dans mon silence. Il faut, pour l'instant, me laisser refaire mes forces, que je n'ai pas économisées depuis ma maladie. (Ces deux années 1930-1931 ont été pour moi un tournant plus tragique que celui de 1914). Vous ne savez pas quel grand combat s'est livré en moi. Vous en verrez plus tard — si je vis — les effets. L'article du 15 juin n'est qu'une amorce" (Letter to Stefan Zweig, June 10, 1931). The article of June 15 to which he refers is his "Adieu au passé".

spondence begun during the twenties. Some years before 1928-1929, he had written to Mme Koudachova, the widow of a member of the Russian nobility who had been killed during the Revolution. Mme Koudachova was half French, her mother having been born in Sedan. In 1928, Rolland wrote to Maxim Gorki (April 5) that he had read some charming French verse which she had sent to him from Moscow. A year later, July 28, 1929, in order to deal directly with the Leningrad publishing house "Vremia", which was undertaking an edition of his complete works, he wrote to Gorki that he wanted the services of Mme Koudachova, whom he referred to as a personal friend.

Mme Koudachova had long been an admirer of *Jean-Christophe* and its author. Her first acquaintance with the novel had been made in 1923. She had been so moved by it that she wrote to the author. Although their correspondence revealed similar tastes, mutual esteem and respect, it lasted only the year. Mme Koudachova ceased to write when Rolland reproached her for certain incidents in her private life. She put him out of her mind until 1928, when, while secretary to Professor Kogan, director of the foreign language section of the State Editions, she read proof of the Russian translation of *Jean-Christophe*. At this time she again wrote to Rolland, and their attachment began to assume a more personal character. Their first meeting took place in August, 1929. In 1930 Rolland asked her to come to Switzerland with the idea of making her permanent residence there, and in 1931 she came. They began by believing that a free union was possible, but the arrangement soon became too difficult. In the face of a threatening international situation they decided to legalize their union, and were married in the spring of 1934.[3] As early as her installation in 1931 in the Villa Olga, Mme Koudachova had

---

[3] "Vous aurez appris par les journaux... mon mariage prochain avec Madame Marie Koudachef, Elle est mon amie et mon aide dans mes travaux, depuis plusieurs années. Française par sa mère, veuve du prince Serge Koudachef qui mourut en 1920, dans la guerre civile, au Caucase, mère d'un garçon de dix-sept ans qui travaille avec intelligence et ardeur, à Moscou, dans une école d'ingénieurs, elle a traversé les rudes années avec vaillance. Nous avons décidé d'assurer légalement nos liens, pour les défendre contre les dangers de la tourmente qui vient..." (Letter to J.-R. Bloch, April 15, 1934).

become an indispensable aid to Rolland in his various activities. She served as an extremely intelligent and faithful secretary (see a letter of August 22, 1931 to Hermann Hesse, in *Hesse und Rolland. Briefe* [Zurich, 1954], p. 83), and was particularly helpful as a translator of Russian (letter to Maxim Gorki, March 6, 1932).

After his trip to Russia in 1935, he took one other trip during the summer, a trip which was to play an important part in the last years of his life. This was a visit to his native 'pays', the Nivernais country — Clamecy, neighboring Vézelay, Avallon, and Auxerre. His trip put him in mind of returning to his place of origin, especially when certain laws and attitudes in Switzerland made that country less attractive as a place of residence (letter to Stefan Zweig, Nov. 4, 1936).

His seventieth birthday was the occasion of various celebrations in his honor. On January 16, 1936, his voice was recorded in a short speech for Radio-Bâle and Radio-Lausanne. The record also contained a German translation of his speech, a talk by Wilhelm Herzog, a German admirer of Rolland, and the third act of *Danton* (see Rolland's 'Journal inédit'). On January 25, 1936, he made a recording of a speech for Radio-Moscow. The last day of January of the same year, two days after his seventieth birthday, a testimonial meeting was organized for him in Paris by representatives of various great international organizations and French cultural associations. The meeting was attended by delegations from more than thirty organizations in the Paris area. J.-R. Bloch was the organizer, André Gide presided, and Paul Langevin was among the speakers (Marcel Cachin, "Romain Rolland", *L'Humanité* [Jan. 30, 1936]). At a meeting organized by the Thaelmann committee on January 19, 1936, a motion of praise for Rolland, the honorary chairman, was voted unanimously for his work in behalf of peace and international solidarity (*L'Humanité,* Jan. 20, 1936). *L'Humanité* for January 26, 1936, also carried tributes to Rolland from men of varying political persuasions.

Writing to Maxim Gorki (February 11, 1936) about the presentation and enthusiastic testimonial meeting of January 31, Rolland allowed a note of triumph to appear in his remarks. At last he was harvesting all the hope that he had sown in the people of Paris, to whom he had dedicated *Le quatorze juillet* thirty years previously. He would now like to write certain works which had long lain in his consciousness, but it was difficult to find the time (letter in *La Nouvelle critique,* summer, 1950, pp. 36-40).

In June, Gorki's death brought Rolland the sharpest grief he had experienced in several years. Not even his father's death had evoked such a moving expression of sorrow.[4] During the first week in August, 1936, he returned to Paris, the first visit in almost ten years, for the presentation of *Le quatorze juillet* at the Alhambra Theater ("Romain Rolland à Paris", *L'Humanité* [Aug. 9, 1936]). Jean Zay, Minister of Education, paid tribute to Rolland, who was heartily greeted by the audience; he himself spoke briefly but with emotion.[5]

The same year saw a gradual diminution of the liberty he had so prized in Switzerland. The Federal Council had promulgated a law forbidding the entry into Switzerland of all printed matter of Communist origin or inspiration, or expressing views favorable to anarchy and anti-militarism, or containing anti-religious sentiments (letter to Zweig, Nov. 4, 1936). Such a reduction of sources of information would hamper his work, and he began to think seriously of returning to France. After his August trip to the Nivernais, he considered permanent residence there. A year later he took the decisive step, and by the fall of 1937 was ready to sign the contract for purchasing the property at Vézelay, although he did not intend to move for a year (letter to Zweig, Sept. 26, 1937). The more oppressive atmosphere of Switzerland was not the only reason, cogent though it was. Literal ruin was approaching; his editors were holding out against the 'Front populaire' government and its supporters, and his royalties had declined sharply; they were being paid in the devaluated francs of 1937-1939. He

[4] *Europe* (July 15, 1936), 289-290; *L'Humanité* (June 2, 1936); *Regards* (June 25, 1936).
[5] See the account in *Regards* (Aug. 3, 1936). See also the photos of Cachin and Rolland, in Barrère, *Romain Rolland par lui-même,* p. 157. Rolland's contacts with leftist leaders were numerous. Barrère also publishes photos of Maurice Thorez, Benoît Frachon, Louis Aragon, and Elsa Triolet with Rolland at Villeneuve, in 1934 and 1936 (*Ibid.,* pp. 166, 176).

urged Zweig to see if he could arouse interest in Hollywood for a film based on *Jean-Cristophe* (letters to Zweig, Nov. 12, 1938, and March 17, 1939). Early in 1938 the move to Vézelay was made, and by June 12 they were installed there, although Rolland and Madeleine intended to spend the winter months in Villeneuve (letters to Zweig, June 24, Aug. 25, 1938).

When the German Chancellor effected the Anschluss with Austria in March, 1938, and proved the accuracy of Rolland's previous warnings, the latter supported the intellectuals of France in their appeal for unity in their ranks as an example to the rest of the nation. The appeal was attacked by pacifists and rightists, and Rolland answered by publishing a similar appeal in *L'Ordre* (also in *L'Humanité,* March 31, 1938). Such a union, he declared, was more imperious than at any other time; it was no longer merely the fate of one nation which was in the balance, but that of civilization itself. For in spite of his optimism of a few years before, he feared that Fascism threatened all the culture of the world in its most precious conquests, in its heroic efforts towards progress, dignity, and liberty. France had the fearful honor of being the last continental bastion of liberty in its most vital forms for all human order and progress: political, social, intellectual, and religious.[6] Early in September, 1938, Rolland, Paul Langevin, and Francis Jourdain sent a telegram to Daladier and Chamberlain, urging an immediate pact among the Democratic powers to prevent Hitler's occupation of Czechoslovakia.[7] Shortly before the signing of the Munich pact, September 29-30, Rolland signed a petition against war, addressed to Daladier, which had been drawn up by the 'Comité de vigilance des intellectuels' (Alain and Jean Giono, among others). The appeal supported the Munich policy, demanded continued negotiations by the French government to solve the crisis, and repudiated absolutely any use of military force (text in Giono, *Précisions* [Paris, 1939], pp. 8-9). Anti-leftist groups seized this opportunity to make Rolland one of their own followers. He protested against this wilfully erroneous inter-

[6] See the account also in *Commune* (April, 1938), 1004-05.
[7] See the text in Jean Giono, *Précisions,* Vivre libre, Cahier II (Paris, 1939), pp. 8-9.

pretation (*L'Humanité,* Oct. 14, 1938), and insisted that his name
had been exploited by the adversaries of the Confédération Générale du Travail and the Parti Communiste Français. He assured
his readers of his fidelity to both organizations, which had always
fought valiantly against war. But, he added, the peace of Munich
is a degrading capitulation which will furnish new arms against
France and the Free World. He revealed the reasons for his
signature in a letter to J.-R. Bloch, October 2, 1938. At the height
of the tension during the Munich talks, the declaration against
war came in the mail. It was unfortunate that it had been prepared
by Alain, Giono, and others of similar persuasion, for the public
at large cannot distinguish between a declaration against war
formulated by this group and one by Langevin and Jourdain,
which would have expressed Rolland's stand more exactly.
But Langevin and Jourdain had not drawn up such a declaration.
Because of his situation in Vézelay — he had already had some
unpleasant experiences with the populace — he had signed the
appeal, despite his disagreement with some of its tenets.[8]

In reply to a letter from a Jewish group, Rolland published one
of his most eloquent condemnations of Hitler's Germany (*Revue
juive de Genève,* Dec., 1938, p. 144). He expressed his horror and
pain at the outrageous violation of human rights in Germany,
Spain, and China. Those in Germany who were humiliated and
revolted by the anti-Semitic outrages would see this Empire fall
into the dust, as others had crumbled in the past. The invasion of
Czechoslovakia brought his outcry: "Deuil sur l'Europe",
Europe (April 15, 1939) 433-434. Prague weeps today, but Germany
will weep tomorrow; the violation of a sovereign nation will be a
terrible blot in the history of Germany. "You will be", he said,
"again subjected to the pitiless law of the conquerors." The
familiar idea of 'le vanqueur vaincu', so frequently expressed by
Rolland, was to find its confirmation within a very few years.

The Berlin-Moscow pact, signed August 23, 1939, apparently
caused no word of censure or approval from Rolland. He had,
it is true, condemned the degrading Munich agreement of 1938,

[8] See Bloch's account, taken from Rolland's correspondence, in *Commune*
(Dec., 1938), 1841-43.

but whatever his feelings about the German-Soviet pact of 1939, he gave no expression to them, as far as we have been able to determine from an examination — as yet incomplete — of his papers.

After the outbreak of the war, September, 1939, Rolland did what he could in the struggle against Hitler's armies. In his seventy-third year, his body weakened by the tuberculosis that constantly threatened him and confined him to the 'sacred hill' of Vézelay, the fighter of 1914-1919 was unable to participate frequently. Among his rare expressions is a letter to Daladier, the prime minister (*Le Temps,* Sept. 19, 1939). In it he asked that, in those critical days when the French Republic was arising to bar the road to Hitler tyranny sweeping over Europe, an old fighter for peace who had always denounced the perfidy and frantic ambition of the Third Reich be permitted to express his entire devotion to the cause of the Democracies, of France, and of the world of today, now in such danger. The pain and grandeur of such a combat was that there was no hatred for the unfortunate German people, whom an atrocious despotism had enslaved and debased. September would soon bring the anniversary of the battle of Valmy, at which time Goethe had written on his map at the frontier of France: "Here begins the land of freedom." It has remained the land of freedom. Liberty is the most precious treasure of all humanity; and it is for humanity that we defend it; let humanity, he concluded, help us to save it.

But there was no doubt in his mind about the necessity of defeating Nazi-Fascism. In a letter to J.-R. Bloch, November 20, 1939, he insisted that, as he had constantly maintained, the first necessity is the crushing of German Hitlerism. Discussions can be held afterwards, but first the monster must be crushed; it was a question of life and death.[9]

[9] "En ce qui concerne les événements généraux, j'ai la simplicité de croire que la ligne de conduite est très claire, — et que tous les efforts de tous les Français, en ce moment, devraient converger vers ce but premier — sinon unique: l'élimination totale de l'Hitlérisme allemand. '*Delenda est...*' — après on discutera. Mais d'abord, écraser le monstre. C'est une question de vie ou de mort. Je n'ai jamais varié là-dessus" (Letter to J.-R. Bloch, November 20, 1939).

His health was poor, and in February, 1940, he returned to Switzerland to consult the doctors who knew him best and to liquidate the lease of the Villa Olga. He returned to Vézelay shortly before the invasion of France (letters to Stefan Zweig and to Madeleine Rolland, February 20, April 7, and March 17, 1940; see also René Arcos, *Romain Rolland* [Paris, 1950], pp. 112 ff, and *La Pensée* [July-Sept., 1945], 29-39). Rolland was deeply affected by the dangers of the war to friends and acquaintances. He worried about Georges Duhamel (letters to Arcos, July 30, Aug. 6, 1940), and on October 12 he wrote to his friend that they had just had the visit — rather distressing — of Alphonse de Châteaubriant, who was then writing in the collaborationist periodical *La Gerbe*. He himself was able to get about only with difficulty. Several trips to Paris were made necessary by the need for medical care. His eyesight had begun to fail during these years, and there was no possibility of medical services in Vézelay (see the *Correspondance entre Louis Gillet et Romain Rolland* [Paris, 1949], pp. 321-322, 328).

After twenty-seven years of separation, Rolland and Louis Gillet renewed their friendship under the cloud of foreign occupation. The next year, June 22, 1943, Rolland went to visit Gillet, who was ill at the time. Rolland himself was recovering from a minor nasal operation which had necessitated the trip to Paris. He visited his old friend with a great deal of pleasure and emotion.

Vézelay too was occupied by the Germans. The approach of the armies, preceded by lines of fleeing refugees, caused words of intense feeling to flow from his pen (Rolland, *Le Périple* [Paris, 1946], pp. 160-161), and to echo in the last volume of the *Beethoven* series. His own home was among those in which enemy soldiers were billeted. Rolland was never molested by the occupation authorities. According to Mme Marie Romain Rolland, the attitude of the Germans was very correct. In a moment of panic, Rolland and his wife began to burn papers and letters (addressed to Rolland) that might compromise their writers. Indirectly and unofficially the Kommandantur caused word to be sent that the continued presence of burnt paper and paper ash would make interference obligatory, otherwise no action inimical to Rolland would be taken. The burning stopped, and the paper and letters remained untouched and unconsulted in Rolland's files, until Mme Marie Romain Rolland began generously to make them available to scholars after the war.

Rolland was busy during this time with the last volume of *Beethoven. Les Grandes époques créatrices,* and also with a new project, the life of his first editor and partial associate, Charles Péguy; this biography appeared in the bookstores early in 1945, after his death. At the same time, he was, as he said, renewing his contacts with the great soul of the past as he watched the catastrophes of the present sweep around the base of the hill of Vézelay. It was Beethoven who provided him with the courage and calm that he regularly displayed in the presence of others.[10] His wife was reading Meister Eckhart to him, while he himself was reading 'notre vieux Péguy' (*Correspondance L. Gillet et R. Rolland,* pp. 321-322). He had also turned to Aeschylus, whose 'bronze words' apply to present scourges and men, to those possessed by hybris now as well as in former times (letter to Mme E. Marchand, Jan. 29, 1942). Besides Aeschylus, he was reading Sophocles and the Gospels. He was also fascinated by modern scientific thought, and was reading de Broglie, Max Planck, Einstein, Lorenz, and Paul Langevin (letter to Mme Marchand, July 23, 1941).

On September 8, 1940, writing additional pages of introductory and valedictory nature for *Le Périple* — which he had written in 1924 — he expressed his faith, his invincible belief, and his indestructible confidence in man and life, a faith, a confidence, and a belief which had arisen within him again, from the depths of defeat itself. As he said in this text, he had known defeat of old, and its bitter, but tonic flavor. Furthermore he had reached the firm conviction that every event in the world advances man along the road towards unity; this belief he had expressed during the First World War in the essay "La Route en lacets qui monte". In *Le Périple* (p. 159) he said that he had transposed the old proverb: "Aide-toi! Le ciel t'aidera", to "Aide le ciel, en ayant foi." If one can rise sufficiently above everyday routine to under-

[10] *Beethoven. Les Grandes époques créatrices. La cathédrale interrompue.* III. *Finita Comoedia.* VI (Paris, 1945), p. 130.

stand the destiny which leads blinded peoples, one can understand that destiny works for man. This he understood, he said, in the worst days of the defeat of 1940, when he saw the enemy armies hastening along the dusty summer roads. The people who flee and the armies who pursue are the instruments of a *Führer* [sic] much more powerful than the one leading the German nation in war.[11]

After the fall of Paris to the Allies four years later, and the consequent expulsion of the Germans, Rolland's name again appeared before the public in a moving message to the 'Comité national des écrivains'. Charles Vildrac had succeeded in sending Rolland the first number of the clandestine paper *Les Lettres françaises,* containing an appeal by the writers' committee, to which Rolland subscribed wholeheartedly. Yes, he answered, we — the world and we — have become more aware of the value of France, since her very existence had been jeopardized. Whoever says France, says Liberty and Humanity. It is her mission to defend them. Much more than that, it is the essence of the true France (*Les Lettres françaises,* Sept. 16, 1944).

On December 9, 1944, a message from Rolland, in commemoration of France and of the families of the intellectuals who had fallen victims to the Nazi barbarism, was read in the Sorbonne. It was first published in *Les Nouvelles littéraires* (it must be noted that left-wing publications had no monopoly on Rolland) on April 5, 1945, on the first page. The twenty years of disillusionment in France, following the war of 1914 and its immense sacrifices, twenty years of exploitation by politicans and of an egotistic atmosphere of pleasure and indifference had so weakened France, in the midst of a Europe in which new or renewed nations were deliriously proud and avid, that her collapse, he wrote, was certain. The haunting question was that of the reaction within the French soul. The miracle occurred; from the depths of the abyss

---

[11] "Je n'ai pas cessé de croire, comme vous, à la marche aveugle, sanglante, douloureuse, des peuples vers l'Unité, — quoi qu'ils veuillent: ils sont menés par la main de fer des Lois profondes. Même ceux qui croient aller contre sont les instruments de l'Ordre nécessaire, travaillent pour lui. Mais ni le temps, ni la peine ne sont économisés. La Force invisible, qui en dispense, agit en grand seigneur, qui prodigue ses biens — nos vies — à pleines mains" (Letter to Raymond Pichard, October 12, 1940).

there burst forth the ray of faith and the sacred flame of indestructible hope; from all classes and parties there arose the willingness to sacrifice self at the moment of arriving at the threshold of an independent career. These were the most beautiful and stirring acts that had come to his attention. Their letters of farewell would preserve their fame in an eternal France. Believers or non-believers, they all believed in the great and eternal forces and participated in their ascent (Rolland, "France et Liberté", Les Nouvelles littéraires [April 5, 1945]).

And our country, he said, has the mission of embodying and defending liberty in a world which continually tends to relapse into passivity. Each of these young victims affirmed the life and victory of France and of Liberty. Rolland proposed that a monument bearing their names be added to the facing of the Arc de Triomphe de l'Etoile.

These were the last words Rolland was to write for the public. Soon afterwards, on December 29, 1944, he succumbed to his old enemy tuberculosis, at the age of seventy-eight.

Thus ended the long struggle of the one against the many. It was a struggle of a man against himself, as well as against others. His defiance of the world is reflected in his own inability to cooperate closely with others — even for a musical performance — and in his desire to live by his pen, independently of others. It is also reflected in his characters, many of whom are equally — or more — defiant of the world — especially Christophe, Marc Rivière, Aërt, and in the very subjects of many of his scholarly studies: Beethoven, Michael Angelo, Tolstoy, Berlioz, Hugo Wolff, and Wagner.

Unorthodox, even heterodox in relation to organized religions, he was deeply religious, if not mystical. Stubbornly clinging to an ideal of absolute freedom, he both accepted and rejected revolution and Communism. Unable to accept society as it existed, he was equally unable to convince militant Communists or Marxists of his approval and support of their ideals. The bourgeoisie, on the other hand, regarded him as a fiery advocate of Communism. He was completely opposed to all fascisms, and he was able to convince Fascists and anti-Fascists of his attitude in this respect. During the First World War he was regarded by the French as unpatriotic and pro-German, while the Germans considered him a French chauvinist; many neutrals thought he had taken a stand that was, to say the least, questionable. He had perhaps laid himself open to such accusations by his failure to return to Paris after the outbreak of the war, by his decision to remain in Switzerland.

It is true that he stubbornly attempted to remain, not 'above the fight', but above the mad and unjustifiable passions of the time; however, the result was that he appeared to be unable or unwilling to take a stand. As a matter of record, he had refused to take a stand at least once before the First World War; at the time of the Dreyfus case he had refused to express a judgment, saying that the evidence was too confused — a reason that sounds somewhat specious in the mouth of a man trained in the methods of historical research. Perhaps this was part of his struggle against himself — an innate reluctance to take a stand, and an intellectual belief that it was necessary to declare oneself.

His record in personal relationships tends to bear out this supposition. He was unable to give himself completely in personal relationships, save in a very few instances; but he felt that true friendship was a rare, wonderful, and desirable thing. He also felt that love, '*amour-passion*', was necessary for a complete and full life. Nevertheless, he was unable generally to achieve that relationship. In fact, his most successful efforts were his vicarious loves in his creations, especially Christophe, Olivier, Annette, and Marc, not to forget Aërt and Colas Breugnon.

His struggle against himself is symbolized or even embodied in pairs of opposites, in what might be called the duality or the polarity of his creations. Christophe and Olivier are opposites, although complementary to each other. As we have seen they represent the man that he was and the man that he would have liked to be, as well as the man who could bring help and courage to his readers. In *L'Ame enchantée,* this duality is still more pronounced. There are conflicting personalities, many of which are opposites but complementary: Annette and Roger Brissot, and Annette and Sylvie. There are also accompanying conflicts of individualist and collectivist, of thought and action, of heart and mind, of intuition and intellect, of two succeeding generations.

His own life was an attempt to synthesize such opposites as those which appear in his creative writings; but he seems to have met with less success personally than artistically. However, with the passage of time, it is likely that he will increasingly appear as a typical figure, embodying all the varying and intricate problems and questions of a trying and complex period. He is perhaps still too near to us to be adequately judged; time alone will reveal in him the eternal aspects of what is good and what is ephemeral. For, in his own words, what is lasting is good, and evil is only egotism and shortsighted lack of life and understanding.

CHRONOLOGY OF ROLLAND'S LIFE

1866, January 29	Birth of Romain Edme-Emile Rolland.
1873-1880	Student at the 'Collège de Clamecy'.
1880	Rolland family's move to Paris to permit the son to begin advanced studies.
1880-1883	Student at the Lycée Saint-Louis and the Lycée Louis-le-Grand.
1882, September	Visit to the Dauphiné and the first contact with the Swiss Alps.
1883-1886	Preparation for the competitive entrance examination to the Ecole Normale supérieure; two failures, in 1884 and 1885. In July, 1886, the examination was successfully passed.
1886-1889	Student at the Ecole Normale supérieure.
1889, August	Received eighth in the competitive examination for the 'agrégation' in History; appointed to the Ecole française de Rome.
1889-1891	Fellow at the Ecole française de Rome.
1892, October	Marriage with Clotilde Bréal, daughter of philologist Michel Bréal.
1892-1893	Official mission in Italy for the Ecole des Beaux Arts. Sojourn in Rome. Research for doctoral thesis.
1895, June	Received the doctorat ès lettres after the successful defense of his thesis; appointed to teach courses at the Ecole Normale supérieure and the Ecole J.-B. Say.
1901, February	Divorce.

1903-1911	Courses on the History of Music at the Ecole des Hautes Etudes Sociales.
1903-1912	Composition of *Jean-Christophe*.
1910, October 28	Severe injuries in a motor car accident on the Avenue des Champs-Elysées.
1912, July	Resignation from the Sorbonne, after two years of leave.
1914, June	Arrival in Switzerland, where he spent the war years.
1919, May 19	Death of his mother.
1921-1933	Writing and publication of *L'Ame enchantée*.
1922	Installation at the Villa Olga (Villeneuve).
1924-1931	First contacts with the Orient.
1927-1937	Studies on Beethoven.
1931	Gandhi's visit.
1931-1940	Anti-fascist activities.
1934, April 28	Marriage with Mme Marie Koudachova.
1935, June-July	Trip to Moscow.
1937, September	Purchase of house at Vézelay.
1938, May 1	Moves from Villeneuve to Vézelay.
1940-1944	Maintains apartment at 89, boulevard Montparnasse in Paris, while continuing to live in Vézelay.
1944, December 29	Death of Romain Rolland, at Vézelay.

INDEX